TRANSNATIONAL LAWMAKING COALITIONS FOR HUMAN RIGHTS

Transnational Lawmaking Coalitions is the first comprehensive analysis of the role and impact of informal collaborations in the UN human rights treaty bodies. Issues as central to international human rights as the right to water, abortion, torture, and hate speech are often only clarified through the instrument of treaty interpretations. This book dives beneath the surface of the formal access, procedures, and actors of the UN treaty body system to reveal how the experts and external collaborators play a key role in the development of human rights. Nina Reiners introduces the concept of "Transnational Lawmaking Coalitions" within a novel theoretical framework and draws on a number of detailed case studies and original data. This study makes a significant contribution to the scholarship on human rights, transnational actors, and international organizations, and contributes to broader debates in international relations and international law.

Nina Reiners is a postdoctoral researcher in International Relations at the University of Potsdam. She is associated with the Berlin-Potsdam research group "International Rule of Law," and the Global Governance Centre at the Graduate Institute, Geneva.

Transnational Lawmaking Coalitions for Human Rights

NINA REINERS
University of Potsdam

CAMBRIDGE
UNIVERSITY PRESS

CAMBRIDGE
UNIVERSITY PRESS

University Printing House, Cambridge CB2 8BS, United Kingdom

One Liberty Plaza, 20th Floor, New York, NY 10006, USA

477 Williamstown Road, Port Melbourne, VIC 3207, Australia

314–321, 3rd Floor, Plot 3, Splendor Forum, Jasola District Centre, New Delhi – 110025, India

103 Penang Road, #05–06/07, Visioncrest Commercial, Singapore 238467

Cambridge University Press is part of the University of Cambridge.

It furthers the University's mission by disseminating knowledge in the pursuit of education, learning, and research at the highest international levels of excellence.

www.cambridge.org
Information on this title: www.cambridge.org/9781108845540
DOI: 10.1017/9781108976763

First published 2022

A catalogue record for this publication is available from the British Library.

Library of Congress Cataloging-in-Publication Data
NAMES: Reiners, Nina, 1984– author.
TITLE: Transnational lawmaking coalitions for human rights / Nina Reiners, University of Potsdam.
DESCRIPTION: Cambridge, United Kingdom ; New York, NY : Cambridge University Press, 2021. | Based on author's thesis (doctoral – Universität Potsdam, 2017). | Includes bibliographical references and index.
IDENTIFIERS: LCCN 2021024120 (print) | LCCN 2021024121 (ebook) | ISBN 9781108845540 (hardback) | ISBN 9781108976763 (ebook)
SUBJECTS: LCSH: International law and human rights. | Treaty-making power.
CLASSIFICATION: LCC KZ1266 .R445 2021 (print) | LCC KZ1266 (ebook) | DDC 341.4/8–dc23
LC record available at https://lccn.loc.gov/2021024120
LC ebook record available at https://lccn.loc.gov/2021024121

ISBN 978-1-108-84554-0 Hardback

Transnational Lawmaking Coalitions for Human Rights

NINA REINERS
University of Potsdam

CAMBRIDGE
UNIVERSITY PRESS

CAMBRIDGE
UNIVERSITY PRESS

University Printing House, Cambridge CB2 8BS, United Kingdom

One Liberty Plaza, 20th Floor, New York, NY 10006, USA

477 Williamstown Road, Port Melbourne, VIC 3207, Australia

314–321, 3rd Floor, Plot 3, Splendor Forum, Jasola District Centre, New Delhi – 110025, India

103 Penang Road, #05–06/07, Visioncrest Commercial, Singapore 238467

Cambridge University Press is part of the University of Cambridge.

It furthers the University's mission by disseminating knowledge in the pursuit of education, learning, and research at the highest international levels of excellence.

www.cambridge.org
Information on this title: www.cambridge.org/9781108845540
DOI: 10.1017/9781108976763

First published 2022

A catalogue record for this publication is available from the British Library.

Library of Congress Cataloging-in-Publication Data
NAMES: Reiners, Nina, 1984– author.
TITLE: Transnational lawmaking coalitions for human rights / Nina Reiners, University of Potsdam.
DESCRIPTION: Cambridge, United Kingdom ; New York, NY : Cambridge University Press, 2021. | Based on author's thesis (doctoral – Universität Potsdam, 2017). | Includes bibliographical references and index.
IDENTIFIERS: LCCN 2021024120 (print) | LCCN 2021024121 (ebook) | ISBN 9781108845540 (hardback) | ISBN 9781108976763 (ebook)
SUBJECTS: LCSH: International law and human rights. | Treaty-making power.
CLASSIFICATION: LCC KZ1266 .R445 2021 (print) | LCC KZ1266 (ebook) | DDC 341.4/8–dc23
LC record available at https://lccn.loc.gov/2021024120
LC ebook record available at https://lccn.loc.gov/2021024121

ISBN 978-1-108-84554-0 Hardback

To Heinz Litgen

Contents

Figures

Tables

Acknowledgments

This book started as a PhD dissertation, developed into a two-year postdoctoral project, and was rigorously discussed and reflected upon in a variety of settings before it finally became this book. Despite all the changes made, new cases included, and theory expanded, and although multiple alternatives were pitched, the title of this book now brings this project back full circle, back to where it started – to the dissertation. "Transnational Lawmaking Coalitions for Human Rights" received support from many people and institutions. Some were crucial at an early stage, some provided decisive input without probably being aware of it, and others were a constant flow of support. I follow here with an essential, but by no means exhaustive, list of people and institutions I wish to recognize for their support.

Andrea Liese is my expert authority on international institutions and has been encouraging ever since I walked into her office in Potsdam. I will never take her truly exceptional mentorship for granted. I benefited immensely from the patience and advice of Harald Fuhr. My PhD time in Potsdam's Karl-Marx-Strasse and on Campus Griebnitzsee was truly a team experience which I was lucky to share with other curious minds at the Faculty of Social Sciences and Economics. Rather than name all fellow PhD students, postdocs, students and research assistants, professors and colleagues in the university, and faculty administration who made this time so special for me, I would like to single out Per-Olof Busch, Marion Dräger, and Thomas Hickmann for their support.

Particularly formative for this book's journey was my time at the University of San Diego in 2016. Hans Peter Schmitz, who generously shared his knowledge about international human rights and advocacy, asked the right questions and became an exceptional advisor and mentor. The research group (KFG) "International Rule of Law" proved to be an excellent environment in which I could sharpen my arguments and understand international law – and

lawyers – much better. Heike Krieger, in giving particularly discerning attention to my project, added valuable contributions to my thinking about human rights law. The Graduate Institute in Geneva became my second academic home during the book's journey. I thank Nico Krisch for his enduring support and for the decisive time as a visiting scholar with his "PATHS of International Law" team. Stephanie Hofmann gave me a forum to discuss a first proposal of this book, and I thank her dearly for her encouragement. I also thank everyone who participated for their input.

I further extend my gratitude to the following people who read proposals and chapters of this book at various draft stages and provided helpful comments at conferences, workshops, or during the final writing stages: Hannah Birkenkötter, Thomas Dörfler, Benjamin Faude, Sassan Gholiagha, Heidi Haddad, Tine Hanrieder, Jana Herold, Anna Holzscheiter Andrew Hurrell, Anja Jetschke, Max Lesch, Lydia Malmedie, Anthea Roberts, Andrea Schapper, Andreas von Staden, Jonas Tallberg, Ezgi Yildiz, and Fuad Zarbiyev. I also thank the organizers and participants in colloquia and research seminars at the University of Stirling, the Graduate Institute Geneva, the ECPR Standing Group on Law and Courts, and the University of Stockholm for inviting me to discuss this book project. I hope you can see many of our discussions reflected in the final manuscript.

The following institutions were crucial for the success of this book project: I thank the Fritz Thyssen Foundation for the generous funding of a two-year postdoctoral grant and the opportunity to participate in the intellectually stimulating environment of their "Human Rights in the 20th Century" study group. I thank the Academic Council on the United Nations System (ACUNS) and the United Nations Association of Germany (DGVN) for providing opportunities to interact with UN scholars and practitioners. Furthermore, I thank the Potsdam Graduate School, the German Academic Exchange Service (DAAD), and the Office for Equal Opportunities in Potsdam for financial support that made many conferences and research stays possible.

Without the individuals in and around the UN in Geneva who gave me their time, provided access to their networks, sat down with me for a coffee or lunch, and helped me better understand their work, this book would indeed not have been possible. I particularly thank the staff of Office of the High Commissioner for Human Rights and in the UN archives in Geneva, who reacted to all my requests despite their workload and would even notify me two years later about potentially relevant documents discovered. Claire Mahon and Ana Maria Suárez Franco deserve special recognition for helping me to navigate the Geneva human rights world.

At every stage of this project, Cambridge University Press has been supportive and encouraging. I am truly grateful for making my first book-publishing experience one I could get used to. Three reviewers generously provided helpful comments on my manuscript. I thank Alex M. Smith for his magical edits and for staying so excited about my not-too-exciting academic writing. I also thank Christina Schneider for thoroughly checking references and improving figures and tables.

Thanks to family, friends, and colleagues in Fischeln, Berlin, Frankfurt, Geneva, Madrid, London, Rome, Stockholm, Gothenburg, San Diego, Jakarta, and beyond and between, who allowed me to stay focused and distracted me when needed.

Abbreviations

AAAS	American Association for the Advancement of Science
APT	Association for the Prevention of Torture
CAT	Convention against Torture and Other Cruel, Inhuman or Degrading Treatment or Punishment
CAT Committee	Committee against Torture
CCPR	Human Rights Committee
CED	Committee on Enforced Disappearances
CEDAW	Convention on the Elimination of All Forms of Discrimination against Women
CEDAW Committee	Committee on the Elimination of Discrimination against Women
CEDAW-OP	Optional Protocol to the Convention on the Elimination of All Forms of Discrimination against Women
CERD	Committee on the Elimination of Racial Discrimination
CESCR	Committee on Economic, Social and Cultural Rights
CICC	Coalition for the International Criminal Court
CMW	Committee on Migrant Workers
COHRE	Centre on Housing Rights and Evictions
CRC	Convention on the Rights of the Child
CRC Committee	Committee on the Rights of the Child
CRC-OPAC	Optional Protocol to the Convention on the Rights of the Child on the involvement of children in armed conflict

CRC-OPIC	Optional Protocol to the Convention on the Rights of the Child on a communications procedure
CRC-OPSC	Optional Protocol to the Convention on the Rights of the Child on the sale of children, child prostitution and child pornography
CRPD	Convention on the Rights of Persons with Disabilities
CRPD Committee	Committee on the Rights of Persons with Disabilities
CRPD-OP	Optional Protocol to the Convention on the Rights of Persons with Disabilities
ECOSOC	Economic and Social Council
FAO	Food and Agriculture Organization of the United Nations
FIAN	FoodFirst Informations and Action Network
GATS	General Agreement on Trade in Services
GC	general comment
GR	general recommendation
HRC	Human Rights Council
ICBL	International Campaign to Ban Landmines
ICC	International Criminal Court
ICCPR	International Covenant on Civil and Political Rights
ICCPR-OP1	First Optional Protocol to the International Covenant on Civil and Political Rights
ICCPR-OP2	Second Optional Protocol to the International Covenant on Civil and Political Rights
ICED	International Convention for the Protection of All Persons from Enforced Disappearance
ICERD	International Convention on the Elimination of All Forms of Racial Discrimination
ICESCR	International Covenant on Economic, Social and Cultural Rights
ICESCR-OP	Optional Protocol to the Covenant on Economic, Social and Cultural Rights
ICJ	International Commission of Jurists
ICRC	International Committee of the Red Cross
ICtJ	International Court of Justice
ILA	International Law Association
ILC	International Law Commission

ILO	International Labour Organization
IMF	International Monetary Fund
INGO	international non-governmental organization
IO	international organization
IPA	international public administration
IPCC	Intergovernmental Panel on Climate Change
IR	international relations
IRENA	International Renewable Energy Agency
NATO	North Atlantic Treaty Organization
NGO	nongovernmental organization
NHRI	National Human Rights Institution
OEWG	open-ended working group
OHCHR	Office of the High Commissioner for Human Rights
OMCT	World Organisation Against Torture
OP-CAT	Optional Protocol to the Convention against Torture
PPP	public–private partnership
SPT	Subcommittee on Prevention of Torture
TAN	transnational advocacy network
TLC	transnational lawmaking coalition
UDHR	Universal Declaration of Human Rights
UN	United Nations
UNESCO	United Nations Educational, Scientific and Cultural Organization
UNGA	United Nations General Assembly
UPR	Universal Periodic Review
WHO	World Health Organization
WTO	World Trade Organization

1

Introduction

On November 8, 2013, an experienced advocate for economic and social rights sits down with me in Palais Wilson, the home of the Office of the High Commissioner for Human Rights (OHCHR) and meeting venue for the human rights treaty bodies. We chose the empty childcare room over the crowded cafeteria. I asked her for this interview to learn more about how the work of one such treaty body, the Committee on Economic, Social and Cultural Rights (CESCR), facilitates the work of non-governmental organizations (NGOs) at the domestic level. Why do human rights organizations like hers prepare parallel reports and statements on states, often requiring resource-intensive collaboration with other actors, or travel to Geneva without being allowed to speak during the constructive dialogue between treaty body and state delegation? Even the intergovernmental Human Rights Council (HRC) grants its observers more visible participation opportunities in their procedures.

She explains her organization's advocacy as a result of many NGOs' conviction that treaty bodies provide a meaningful channel through which "to influence lawmaking,"[1] which materializes particularly, she says, in their work to draft and adopt General Comments (GCs).[2] To explicate further, she cites an earlier-morning dialogue between a treaty body member and a government official, in which strong disagreement ensued regarding this particular state party's obligations under Article 7 of the International

[1] Interview with an NGO Officer.

[2] I use the term *general comments* to refer to the interpretations of the human rights treaty bodies. Two treaties, the International Convention on the Elimination of All Forms of Racial Discrimination (ICERD) and the Convention on the Elimination of All Forms of Discrimination Against Women (CEDAW), use the term *general recommendations*. When not pointing to specific General Comments or General Recommendations, this book subsumes the two treaties' general recommendations within the term *general comments*.

Covenant on Economic, Social and Cultural Rights (ICESCR) in the aftermath of the 2007–2008 global financial and economic crisis.[3] Pressed on the austerity measures the government imposed as a response, which clawed back domestic advances in the protection of just and favorable conditions of work and "raised important concerns regarding the principles of non-retrogression, progressive realization, non-discrimination and minimum core obligations" (OHCHR 2012: 8), the official defended them as a move of necessity to restore economic stability.

Notably in their pushback, this government was no rogue dissenter but rather one of many state parties arguing, whether directly or by inference, that they hold latitude to decide on exceptions from human rights obligations in the event of such crises. Probing the governments' lines of argument, I ask my interview partner if states shouldn't here know better on the subject of their obligations, given that CESCR concluding observations and International Labor Organization (ILO) conventions provide additional clarification on this exact topic. The advocate for economic and social rights looks at me, shakes her head, and expresses sympathy for the government's position. In her view, the obligations as set out in the Covenant itself and, particularly, Article 7 are vague and thus in need of more direct and comprehensive clarification than that provided by concluding observations and ILO conventions. *That* kind of clarification, she says – *authoritative* clarification – comes by way of general comments.

She follows this vignette by recounting a general comment drafting process she initiated with a treaty body member – a longtime NGO colleague of hers – years earlier, in which she facilitated consultation with civil society and trade unions on state obligations under Article 7. With reference to the only recently adopted Optional Protocol allowing for individual complaints, she described her role and that of the other involved actors, all of whom had a professional interest in the justiciability of the ICESCR, as part of a global strategy of strengthening economic, social, and cultural rights. In 2016, three years after our interview, the Committee on Economic Social and Cultural Rights adopted General Comment No. 23[4] on the right to just and favorable conditions of work as set out in Article 7. It laid out states' obligations in times of

3 The financial crisis posed serious threats to the progress made in the development of ESC rights (Nolan 2014; Ratjen and Satija 2014). For the context of the debate in the UN, see OHCHR 2012.

4 UN Committee on Economic, Social and Cultural Rights (CESCR), General comment No. 23 (2016) on the right to just and favourable conditions of work (article 7 of the International Covenant on Economic, Social and Cultural Rights), April 7, 2016, E/C.12/GC/23, www.refworld.org/docid/5550a0b14.html [accessed February 24, 2021].

economic, fiscal, and political crises and austerity measures and also included new categories of work and workers that evolved since the Covenant's drafting.

This episode from my first research stay at the UN in Geneva exemplifies the very direct access that human rights professionals like her have to the UN treaty bodies. As representatives of specific human rights organizations, they come to the premises of Palais Wilson to make proposals for agendas, share information on treaty implementation at site events, present parallel reports to support the monitoring of state reports, and make written and oral statements on the treaty bodies' days of general discussion. While their interest to "influence lawmaking"[5] in the treaty bodies is not surprising, the seemingly very direct and natural opportunities granted to do so are. I had never put much thought into the processes that lead to the adoption of a general comment; like many other human rights scholars, I looked at them only as one of the instruments available to fulfill the expert committee's mandate as *monitoring* bodies. Closer examination, however, appeared to paint the picture of an instrument whose impacts were much more productive than prescriptive – indeed this NGO professional was but one among many individuals who came to the treaty bodies' sessions to above all influence not monitoring but *lawmaking*.

This lawmaking became the core focus of an empirical inquiry into the treaty bodies' work to produce general comments, whose findings are what this book bears. This inquiry was guided less by legal questions than by an interest to determine how exactly general comments, which lack formal status in international human rights law and require no formal consent by states, are elaborated and adopted - and more particularly, how this happens within a treaty body system presently mired in stakeholder contestation, a decade-long reform process, and resource burdens. Because what surprised me most about this emphatic notion of the general comments' seeming efficacy to influence law was that they were managing to do so, with such stresses notwithstanding.

So how *do* the treaty bodies, against this pessimistic backdrop and a lack of formalized procedure, draft and adopt their interpretations – and how does this answer bear on our understandings of international organizations, transnational actors, and international law? Derived from the research of this aforementioned inquiry, which dives beneath the surface of formal access

5 Lawmaking is quoted here from the interview in the opening vignette. This book discusses and analyzes several examples of general comments that influenced the development of international human rights law, and as such, I use the term *lawmaking* to specify an activity that produces outputs that can be argued for as (soft) law (Lagoutte, Gammeltoft-Hansen, and Cerone 2016).

rules, procedures, and actors of the UN treaty body system, this book's answer is that they do so through their members' close collaboration with non-state actors in an informal, short-lived process of liaising I conceive as a *Transnational Lawmaking Coalition* (TLC) for human rights. Through the instrument of treaty interpretations, these coalitions press for clarification of state obligations in response to global challenges, crises, and/or state inaction, and consequently contribute to the development of international human rights law. Specifically comprising at least one UN treaty body member alongside human rights professionals, these coalitions maneuver outside the above stresses, or rather fill in the space they leave behind, as an actor strategically using treaty interpretations to account for better protection of human rights.

1.1 INTERPRETING HUMAN RIGHTS: THE POWER AND PRACTICE OF TREATY BODIES

This book's focus on who makes human rights needs certain clarification regarding its embeddedness in broader debates about the history, origins, and nature of human rights. My account on human rights in international law and politics does not deny that the institutionalization, including the "legalization" of human rights in global governance,[6] has not always been driven by actors with the best interests for all in mind. Some actors might have been more purposeful, and other actors well-meaning but damage-doing in their endeavor to respect, protect, and fulfill human rights for all. Some governments, and increasingly so it seems, have either lost or never had a genuine interest in protecting human rights. In this regard, I agree with scholars who have repeatedly highlighted the hostage-taking of human rights by states, international institutions, and non-state actors (Hopgood 2013; Moyn 2018; Mutua 2007). Yet, not complying with or violating human rights is often justified with the weaknesses of human rights law,[7] and only to a lesser extent

[6] For legalization, see the IO special issue 2000 (Abbott et al. 2000 or Abbott and Snidal 2012), and also: Aalberts and Gammeltoft-Hansen 2018; Finnemore and Toope 2001. For human rights in other institutions than the UN Geneva bodies, see for example Walling 2015, 2020; Zvobgo and Graham 2020.

[7] In this book, human rights are understood as law when they are codified in one of the core treaties or their optional protocols. As such, I draw a distinction between human rights as law and as norms (Finnemore and Sikkink 1998; Jurkovich 2020b). Arguments about the meaning and application of laws in-use (Wiener 2009) are thus in-built features of human rights law, providing for the possibility of norm change (Sandholtz 2007). In my view, treaty interpretations of human rights law can serve two functions here: for one, they can further clarify what is needed for this translation of law into practice by highlighting state obligations. For another,

with a general rejection of the value(s) inherent in human rights (Winston 2018). Any scenario of a "twilight of human rights law" (Posner 2014) requires the acknowledgment that the treaties themselves are likely the product of actors who entered their negotiations with different interests. But my approach to the weaknesses of the UN human rights treaty system is not in adding yet another critique of human rights – others have already done so at great length and support for their arguments occurs every day in the news – but in taking an actor-centric perspective and turning to an in-depth analysis of *who* makes human rights law.

Human rights law, and the UN human rights treaties specifically, are far from perfect. Not only those treaties adopted tell us a story about the political forces behind them, but even more telling are those which both remain subject to endless negotiations and open-ended working groups and where support for nonbinding regulations prevails, for example, in business and human rights. My interest in treaty interpretations is grounded, for one, in the (allegedly) less politicized nature of their making, as expert committees decide on their scope and not governments. For another, and this is where this book departs from pessimistic outsets on the state of international human rights, treaty interpretations provide the opportunity to clarify obligations in light of political, economic, and social challenges. In that sense, they can be a tool to *make* rights right – and account for previous shortcomings in human rights law.

This perspective on general comments[8] unsurprisingly does not come from one of formal international lawmaking,[9] but is informed by decades of scholarship on advocacy for human rights. Numerous scholars have already shown how, and under what conditions, human rights matter for people around the globe.[10] Struggles in their name repeatedly tell the story that human rights are, and have always been, contested and that those who claim to speak for them do

they can *make* human rights law, by incorporating norms which have not yet been codified into the treaty. Hence, the focus of this study is the process until norms become validated as law, but that does not mean that human rights are then ready for implementation in all places or immediately achieve acceptable levels of compliance (Chayes and Chayes 1993).

8 General comments carry "significant legal and political weight" (Winkler 2012: 41). While their legal value remains disputed and their impacts vary, these interpretations are "one of the potentially most significant and influential tools available (...) to deepen the understanding and strengthen the influence of international human rights norms" (Alston 2001: 763). Or, to put it differently: the "fact that general comments do not have a formal, binding, legal status does not mean that they lack legal significance" (Oette 2018: 9).

9 For an excellent overview on that matter in international law scholarship, see Brölmann and Radi 2016.

10 Given the immensity of this literature, I include only a selection of scholarship here: Comstock 2021; Creamer and Simmons 2015, 2020; Hillebrecht 2014; Krommendijk 2015;

not always give rise to collective benefits. Their politicization is of key concern for multilateralism and the lives of billions of individuals around the globe. For these individuals, the codification of norms presents a basis on which to articulate demands for justice. International human rights law can matter, yet under the right social and legal conditions. One central condition is that obligations are clear and unambiguous, so that states know what to do for their implementation, human rights advocates at the local level know what to demand, and individuals whose rights were violated have a basis for claiming them and keep leeway for local norm translation to a minimum (e.g. Zimmermann 2017). Human rights, however, count as especially vague, indeterminate, and ambiguous norms in international law. This makes them vulnerable to political, economic, and social challenges, like the financial and economic crisis in the introductory example and explains why they need interpretation through the treaty bodies in the form of general comments.

Unlike courts or intergovernmental institutions, the treaty bodies have largely remained at the sidelines of scholarly attention to the development of human rights. This dismissal has shifted in recent years,[11] with the publishing of research that has demarcated the substantial, tangible ways in which treaty body decisions impact domestic politics and law – that is, how their functions, in practice, go beyond a mere monitoring of the treaties' obligations. Their work has always included a multistakeholder perspective, conceptualizing any success of the treaty bodies as one that goes beyond a dual state-committee relation (De Búrca 2017). While states have established the expert committees as monitoring bodies, general comments have "traditionally been the point at which states articulate opposition to treaty bodies as they often view the practice as going beyond the treaty into the realm of developing new law" (McCall-Smith 2016: 32).

In this book, general comments are to a lesser extent understood as an instrument addressing implementation problems in human rights law than as one reflecting changed normative orientations which have not (yet) been addressed by formal international law. As such, the book follows socio-legal scholarship which assumes that this is succeeded by change in behavior of a wider range of actors to which the law applies (Halliday and Shaffer 2015: 8–11). Helfer, for example, showed how ICESCR's General Comment No. 14 on the right to health became a key document in shaping a right to access to medicine

Merry 2009; Oette 2018; Risse, Ropp, and Sikkink 1999, 2013; Sikkink 2011, 2019; Sikkink and Walling 2007; Simmons 2009.

11 For an overview of scholarship on the treaty bodies, see Bayefsky 2001; Keane and Waughray 2017; Keller and Ulfstein 2012; McCall-Smith 2016.

against intellectual property laws (Helfer 2015). The treaty bodies are thus approached as actors who can shape the development of international law intentionally through treaty interpretations.[12]

The matter of human rights interpretation is "both complex and, to a certain extent, obscure" (Fitzmaurice 2013: 739). TLCs can shed light on this matter by taking an actor-centered approach to the practice of human rights treaty interpretation. The drafting process for interpretations is not further specified in the treaties but left to the discretion of the respective treaty body.[13] This lack of unambiguous secondary rules[14] gives the treaty bodies as collective actors leeway for internal debate about appropriate practices of rule-making (Raymond 2019). In this respect, these bodies differ significantly from international courts, whose decisions strictly contour the detailed procedure of adoption treaties typically define, which only allows for the consideration of certain forms of evidence and substantive law. Treaty bodies, in contrast, have the procedural room to decide themselves which sources of information they consult – and can do so without diluting their interpretations' legal weight; their pronouncements are often cited in the same breath as decisions of international courts and tribunals, considered "key catalysts" of legal developments.[15]

From this perspective, treaty bodies are thus more than mere agents following the orders of their principals, standing today as powerful actors in human rights law and for the improvement of human rights protection around the

12 Similarly, see Diane Desierto, on ICESCR and trade law, who highlighted that "many of the Committee's General Comments anticipated later treaty developments in labor rights protections, education, and access to health care, gaining resonance in international practice much later than when the General Comments were first issued" (Desierto 2017).

13 See Appendix B for an overview of rules of procedures across treaty bodies, for example, Art. 39 (2) ICCPR; Art. 10 (1) CERD; Art. 19 (1) CEDAW; see for example "Rules of Procedure of the Human Rights Committee," January 9, 2019, CCPR/C/3/Rev.11 (Rules of Procedure), which, inter alia, leaves open the criteria according to which the topics for general comments are selected and which sources will be consulted in the drafting process.

14 Within norms research, these rules about norm making have been identified as metagovernance norms (Pantzerhielm, Holzscheiter, and Bahr 2019) or organizing principles (Wiener 2008, 2018).

15 The term was [illegible]ed by CEDAW in *General recommendation No. 35 on gender-based violence agai*[illegible] *pdating general recommendation* No. 19, CEDAW/C/GC/35, July 14, 2017. [illegible] the International Law Commission (2018), Chapter IV, UN Doc. A/73/10 [illegible] quoting of GR No. 35: "the pronouncement may serve as a catalyst for the [illegible] of States parties." From a socio-legal perspective, "they [international and [illegible] instruments] are not binding legal instruments in themselves; rather [illegible] [my emphasis] through these instruments the adoption, recognition, and [illegible]ng, authoritative legal norms in nation-states" (Halliday and Shaffer

globe. Their general comments are tools of choice for the expert committees but also for the many human rights organizations who have traditionally worked with them on alternative monitoring. Rather than assess the treaty bodies' application of formal rules of treaty interpretation in a legal exercise,[16] I am, as I said, primarily interested in how the treaty bodies engage in their interpretations in the face of resource constraints and government backlash against human rights. To be clear, I presume neither that all treaty interpretations are the (sole) outcome of a TLC, nor that all general comments impact the development of international human rights law. But as these instruments, which require no further ratification by states, may sway the future course of human rights protection, then it is important to study how and by whom they are drafted.

1.2 TRANSNATIONAL INFLUENCE ON INTERNATIONAL LAWMAKING

While the book's first contribution is to the scholarship on the UN human rights treaty bodies and their interpretations of human rights law, it speaks to and builds upon a variety of scholarship on IR and specifically on IOs. For one, it seeks to contribute to the rich literature on processes and procedures of international lawmaking. IR scholars have provided excellent contributions to the design of international agreements (Koremenos 2016; Tallberg et al. 2014; Voeten 2019) and the procedures of international lawmaking. This vein of literature has seen substantive contribution by IR scholars regarding, for example, practices of making new rules and norm change (Finnemore and Sikkink 1998; Raymond 2019; Sandholtz 2008), yet most of its scholarship remains focused on negotiations among states, inevitably producing a perspective on lawmaking as a "diplomatic practice riven with power, interest, and values amid sociopolitical hierarchies" (Mantilla 2020: 9). When lawmaking, as in the human rights treaty bodies, is a practice by a committee of independent experts, dynamics are different. As human rights treaty bodies are composed of *independent* experts, this book is also a study on expert committees, connecting scholarship on their role as bodies or entities within IOs with that on experts and the role of legal and other technical or functional expertise (Kennedy 2005; Leander and Aalberts 2013; Littoz-Monnet 2017).

For another, the literature on transnational regulation regimes increasingly challenges conceptions of a state-led order (Shaffer 2012), yet multilateral rule-making remains central to the work of non-state actors (Hickmann 2015, 2017). In the absence or stagnation of such formal rule-making processes (Pauwelyn, Wessel, and Wouters 2014), they remain reliant on international legal

16 For an overview, see Fitzmaurice 2013.

frameworks for norms inherent to their work. As such, this book departs from the observation made by others, that actors increasingly seek alternatives to formal treaty-making in global governance (Benvenisti 2007; Krisch 2014; Pauwelyn, Wessel, and Wouters 2012; Rodiles 2018). It remains focused instead on alternatives given within the formal order: the interpretations of norms of international public law. IL and IR scholarship has recently begun to explore the strategic use of interpretations by states to influence how others interpret international legal obligations and redefine meanings of rules (Daku and Pelc 2017; Krieger 2019; Putnam 2020). A focus on interpretative practices has highlighted the agency of international legal institutions to generate change in international law (Stappert 2019).

Treaty interpretations clarify, and often create, new norms and thus also spur the interest of non-state actors to directly influence their outcome (Squatrito 2012). IO scholarship has demonstrated that this interest is mutual, establishing the "opening up" of IOs to transnational actors as a constant trend over time and across all issue areas (Jönsson and Tallberg 2010; Sommerer, Tallberg, and Squatrito 2015; Tallberg, Sommerer, and Squatrito 2013). The increased participation of transnational actors in international organizations, such as NGOs, advocacy networks, corporations, epistemic communities, and unions, reflects this changing nature of global governance. International organizations no longer saliently represent cooperation forums for states alone, and regularly invite transnational actors to provide expertise or services and publicly communicate their efforts in this regard (Carayannis and Weiss 2021; Ecker-Ehrhardt 2018). Even if they do so simply for means of self-legitimation, any IO today must justify these actors' noninclusion more than their inclusion (Jönsson and Tallberg 2010; Risse 2013; Tallberg, Sommerer, and Squatrito 2013). While access to agenda-setting, implementation, and monitoring is well documented and well explained, opportunities for their involvement are least extensive in the phase of decision-making (Steffek 2013; Tallberg et al. 2014: 770). This phase includes lawmaking, where some studies have well explained how non-state actors can nevertheless be successful in shaping the outcome of interest (Betsill and Corell 2001; Dany 2012; Glasius 2002; Rietig 2016).

Explanations for non-state influence can be briefly distinguished between norm-based models, resource-based models, and those looking at both perspectives to explain varying degrees of impact on different international organizations (Liese 2010). The decision whether and to what extent access is granted to what type of actor is not random, as research on the design of international institutions (Koremenos, Lipson, and Snidal 2001; Tallberg, Sommerer, and Squatrito 2016; Voeten 2019), democratic practices, and legitimacy in international institutions all tells us (Dingwerth, Schmidtke, and

Weise 2020; Dingwerth et al. 2019; Mert 2019; Scholte 2011). International institutions have different functional and normative incentives to include non-state actors (Nasiritousi, Hjerpe, and Bäckstrand 2016); for example, the involvement of civil society actors stands for more transparent decision-making (Scholte 2011), and non-state actors have different strategies to make use of these incentives and with different effects (Dellmuth and Bloodgood 2019; Dellmuth and Tallberg 2017). On an informal cooperation level with the rule-makers, non-state actors can be influential intermediaries (Abbott, Levi-Faur, and Snidal 2017). Organization theories with a focus on organizational culture have, for example, provided explanations as to why not every NGO is equally successful in every international organization, although they support the same norms (Hopgood 2006; Wong 2012). Yet, given the nature of international policy – and lawmaking – these studies focus mainly on intergovernmental settings. This creates an emphasis on *visible* public institutions and processes in international organizations. By contrast, the conditions and circumstances for participation, access, and, ultimately, influence on lawmaking in expert committees are different, and their strategies to engage with independent experts are less visible than when engaging with diplomats or states representatives in international negotiations (Türkelli, Vandenhole, and Vandenbogaerde 2013).

1.3 THE ARGUMENT IN BRIEF: TRANSNATIONAL LAWMAKING COALITIONS

TLCs, to bring the concept back to the fore, both shed light on the particularities of the treaty interpretation process and provide an analytical lens to understanding the key role expert bodies and issue professionals – working informally and sans government-involvement at the boundaries of an IO – play in the development of human rights law. As this book's empirical work will show, TLCs are typically found in situations where state action to tackle global challenges is absent or stuck or social pressure is not (yet) high enough to engage in formal law-making (Mantilla 2020). In that sense, TLCs are no new phenomenon. Efforts by individuals and organizations from civil society, academia, international institutions, and other public and private spheres to advocate for global solutions and lobby for preferred regulations exist in all places where policies are made.[17] Yet, TLCs notably differ in their organizing pursuit: Rather than work toward persuading governments or intergovernmental negotiations, individuals in TLCs deliberately choose international law as

[17] See for example Dellmuth and Tallberg 2017; Hanegraaff, Beyers, and De Bruycker 2016.

a response to the above challenges, and their liaising as a coalition takes place in expert committees. The literature explains IO interactions with other organizations mainly from two perspectives: a more rational one in which the IO grants access in exchange for information or services, and a constructivist explanation based on a normative, often democratic, value of including non-state actors into the IO's work, yet with different intensity across IOs and issue areas and policy phases. This provides for the establishment of both the relevance and the necessity of studying interactions between an IO and other organizations, including the formal and institutionalized access points and more informal processes of exchange often established at an individual, rather than an organizational, level.

On the side of the "other" actors, IO literature, with varying degrees of explicitness, presupposes that an abundant amount of actors – NGOs, social movements, companies, foundations, unions, and so on – *want* to interact. Here, the transnational actor literature, the second main body of scholarship this book addresses, is flush with richly detailed accounts of how they can effectively do so by way of advocacy networks and epistemic communities, which use IOs to make their ideas, knowledge, and demands heard to diplomats and governments. Here is where the UN human rights treaty system offers a fresh perspective on the relationship of IOs and these actors: the development of human rights law, thus the making of law, increasingly happens through treaty interpretations. The decision when such an interpretation is necessary, on which article(s) of the treaty and what aspects should be included, as well as the adoption of the interpretation, is solely left to the discretion of the human rights treaty body. This body is composed of *independent* experts.

TLCs are formed between these experts serving on state-empowered entities, who are authorized to interpret the meaning of international treaties, and individuals from their professional network external to the committee. Compositionally, TLCs consist of a small number of individuals. Actors in a TLC stem mainly from the pool of actor groups in advocacy networks and epistemic communities, for example, international and domestic NGOs, academics and intellectuals, international (and regional) organizations, foundations, or unions. TLCs primarily enact their work through the interpersonal relationships of their individual members. Empirically, this relationship renders within drafting processes from the following bases – either via a former professional relationship outside the IO (e.g., colleagues, supervisors, students) or via previous quality work experience directly with the expert body (e.g., former treaty body member or staff member of international organizations.). The building of their coalition mainly takes place outside or at the boundaries of their organization, as experts are not regular staff of the IO.

Their coalition to draft a potentially law-impacting treaty interpretation is transnational because it is neither international nor domestic. What sounds odd at first reflects the reality that independent experts serving at the international level have acquired their expert status on account of their previous appointments and activities at the domestic or local levels. What is more, they continue in their professions across the duration of their committee service and interact both with actors who may be closer to the international level and with those more connected to their professional community at home. Similarly, the professionals they collaborate with are often found in these contexts sans any connection with the international level in their work.[18]

Through the instrument of treaty interpretations, these coalitions work on the clarification of state obligations in response to global challenges and crises. TLCs as a concept share in the micro-level scrutinizing seen in other actor-centered approaches to international politics by helping to identify which actors engage in which behaviors to deliver specific outcomes. In doing so, TLCs provide an explanation for the promotion of human rights through a variety of actors, like NGOs, TANs, epistemic communities, and international institutions, as all members simultaneously have ties to these organizations and facilitate not only the drafting of the interpretation but also its implementation and application. As such, they are of significance for scholarship on human rights, transnational actors, and IOs and contribute to broader debates as follows:

1.3.1 *TLCs' Significance for Human Rights Research*

Human rights scholarship has always been deeply connected with the study of influential non-state actors (Brysk 2020; Forsythe 2012; Schmitz and Sikkink

[18] As such, members are approached as transnational professionals (Harrington and Seabrooke 2020), allowing for the analysis of their contribution to the coalition based on professional expertise and knowledge, to overcome the state/non-state distinction and organizational focus on all "other" actors. The book will highlight that the "transnational" distinction attached to a multitude of actors is not predetermined for TLC membership. A transnational NGOs, for example, can be identified as "a particular type of transnationally operating non – state actor" (Mitchell, Schmitz, and Bruno-van Vijfeijken 2020: 10) in its accreditation status with an IO. In this book, professionals within a TLC often engage in a border-crossing activity for the first and often only time in their careers. They become transnational *through* the coalition and they "do not necessarily need to campaign for or invent issues," and their "formal institutionalization is not a requirement to be considered relevant" (Henriksen and Seabrooke 2016: 725).

2013) Obviously, this book follows a number of already-forged paths for detecting non-state influence on the making of international human rights law. To set the existing scholarly discourse on this participation: we know a lot about how and under which circumstances non-state actors can set agendas on the international level (Carpenter 2007; Heyse 2011; Joachim 2007), which role they play in the implementation of international policies (Gaer 2003) and enforcement of international law (Eilstrup-Sangiovanni and Phelps Bondaroff 2014), and how their monitoring can impact state practice (Krommendijk 2015). TLCs add further flesh to this picture in providing a framework to understand how and by whom human rights law can be developed through treaty interpretations, potentially impacting the protection of human rights.

1.3.2 *TLCs' Significance for IO Research*

One finding of this book is that international lawmaking is characterized less by top-down or bottom-up narratives[19] than by a (IO) border-crossing and networked structure. While existing scholarship on non-state actors offers many insights on how they influence the drafting of international legal texts (Dany 2012), the majority of these works focus on civil society in organized forms,[20] which tends to privilege their formal roles, organizational structures, and access opportunities. Hence, a broader set of civil society activities and interactions with the treaty bodies are overlooked and remain understudied (De Búrca 2017).[21] This locates the book in the broader research on informal governance (Roger 2020) and on decision-making outside of the "intergovernmental core" (Steffek 2013: 1009) in international organizations by diving deep into the practices of expert committees.

TLCs' contribution here lies in their providing of an explanation for the agency of expert committees in IOs. Delegation of tasks to expert committees, who are allowed the leeway to carry out decision-making processes on treaty interpretations sans the involvement of governments, can be argued as leading to shifts of authority in lawmaking (Broude and Shany 2008). Transnational actors have traditionally contributed to and benefited from such shifts of

19 In contrast to bottom-up approaches to international law (Land 2018; Levit 2007), the top-down perspective approaches the perils of human rights as an international elite-driven project (Hopgood 2013; Moyn 2018).

20 The formal roles of civil society for the treaty body system have been subject to many studies in International Law and International Relations, for example, in Brett 1995; Clark, Friedman, and Hochstetler 1998; Gaer 2003; Martens 2006; Noortmann, Reinisch, and Ryngaert 2015; Price Cohen 1990.

21 Several scholars have highlighted research preferences on formal governance, for example, Biermann and Koops 2017.

authority across all policy fields (Josselin and Wallace 2001; Noortmann, Reinisch, and Ryngaert 2015). TLCs help to explain how actors who are not formally authorized to interpret the treaties can do so anyway.[22] The book sheds light on expert committees in their distinctness from intergovernmental entities and the bureaucracy of an IO. This focus produces empirical insights that support broader arguments to understand IOs from an open-system perspective (Hanrieder 2014; Koch 2015). Members of these expert committees are embedded in professional networks (Seabrooke and Henriksen 2017b) before their election, allowing for their recognition as experts in the first place; and in order to fulfill the various functions expert bodies are equipped with, like monitoring or advising, they do so outside the regular meetings and sessions of the committee.

1.3.3 *TLCs' Significance for Wider Debates in Global Governance*

On a broader note, TLCs matter for IR because they highlight the central importance of the individual as actor in global governance (Bode 2015; Fröhlich 2014; Partzsch 2017; Weiss 2011), who manifests and exerts influence primarily through the personal ties of its members to enable collective action. To be influential in the interpretation of international law, the expertise of the individual and a trustful relationship with the independent expert are decisive.[23] This foci-shift to the micro (i.e., individual) level and their interactions helps explain non-state influence on what usually presents one of the last fortresses of state sovereignty in global governance: the making of international law.

Finally, TLCs contribute to the body of work on "human rights experimentalism" (De Búrca 2017).[24] Although global experimentalist governance theory (De Búrca, Keohane, and Sabel 2014) mainly seeks to explain the interaction

22 The book further shows that formal access to international organizations does not determine their participation. The development of human rights treaty interpretations does not follow externally imposed procedures, which gives spotlight to metagovernance norms (Pantzerhielm, Holzscheiter, and Bahr 2019) and the social practice of rule-making (Raymond 2019). More importantly, neither the process nor the outcome of interpreting human rights treaties requires formal state consent. The process differs from intergovernmental negotiations, where non-state actors indeed have a better chance to be influential when they join forces and push for the same norms.

23 On (changing) functional roles of individual actors, the literature on practice theory provides points for further research (Adler and Pouliot 2011), especially the work on diplomats (Adler-Nissen 2015).

24 They focus "attention beyond the two main official sets of actors which are normally the object of scrutiny – state governments and treaty bodies – and beyond the formal engagement of the state with the expert committee, to include the growing array of local, national, and

between local and international actors for treaty implementation, a point well elaborated upon by way of the spiral model (Risse, Ropp, and Sikkink 1999, 2013), TLCs add to its explanation for how exactly change can happen by taking the implementation experiences of human rights professionals as a source for the treaty bodies' agency to develop human rights through treaty interpretations.[25]

1.4 METHOD AND STRUCTURE OF THE BOOK

From an anthropologist's perspective, human rights treaty bodies are "unpredictable microstructures" (Halme-Tuomisaari 2018: 456). This book aims to facilitate research on these expert committees and their collective decision-making processes and collaborations. To this end, it introduces an analytical framework for the study of transnational actors in international human rights lawmaking, which acknowledges the peculiarities of these microstructures yet applies the benefits of IR methods and tools to identify how macrostructures might reduce the complexity of treaty bodies' behavior and arrive at generalizable findings. My field research[26] in Geneva took place between 2013 and 2019, during which I observed the sessions of various treaty bodies, researched the archives of the UN, held background interviews with many different stakeholders, and gained access to informal briefings. Overall, this book's analysis relies on different primary and secondary sources: official documents (e.g., general comments and session summary records), internal documents (e.g., general comment drafts, material from non-state actors, official correspondence with the treaty bodies, confidential correspondence among drafting group members), interviews and background talks (committee members; civil society; OHCHR staff; stakeholders from other UN agencies, international organizations or academia, see Appendix D), and other sources (e.g., field notes). Based on the collection and analysis of these sources this book is structured as follows:

As the very concept of TLCs rests on this notion of their being a *lawmaking* coalition through treaty interpretations, the general comments, the next chapter introduces the UN human rights treaty bodies and gives data on their

international nongovernmental actors and institutions and the way they inform, implement, and give shape to the regime and the treaty in practice" (De Búrca 2017: 309).

25 In a similar vein, activist theories of human rights (Ackerly 2008; Ackerly 2011) highlight that theoretical reflections about the universality of human rights and corresponding theories of change are reflected in practice where "despite focusing on different kinds of rights and different causes of rights violations across a broad range of contexts, activists have a remarkable consensus on the meaning of rights" (Ackerly 2011: 222).

26 The term "field" is used to describe my research stays at the UN human rights treaty bodies, the UN archives, and NGOs located in Geneva.

decision-making rules, their membership, workload, and, on the instrument of interest for this book, the general comments. This chapter explains what they are, the degree to which the UN treaty bodies use general comments in different functions, and how state parties and scholars understand – and contest – their legal substance. Moving beyond notions of formal authority, the chapter argues for the possibility of general comments' authoritativeness because they serve as necessary reference points to human rights, especially because a broader community (NGOs, domestic courts, specialized agencies) enacts them in the realms of domestic law, politics, and civil society. Ultimately, what this chapter makes eminently apparent is that general comments' authoritativeness depends less on state recognition and more on the multitude of actors breathing life into their interpretations.

The third chapter presents the book's core theoretical contribution of the TLC, a concept that brings fresh insight to the IR and IO literatures. Operating outside the IO borders of the treaty body system, TLCs are informal and temporary coalitions of state-empowered expert bodies and issue professionals that, in pressing for clarification of state obligations through the instrument of treaty interpretations, can contribute to the development of international law without direct government involvement. This chapter distinguishes TLCs from other collective transnational actor-types, introduces the main triggers of a TLC's genesis, explains the logic behind its members' participation in such a coalition, and articulates how TLCs organize their drafting work and under which conditions they are influential.

The fourth chapter forms the book's empirical entry point into the TLC in practice by showing one such coalition as this story's protagonist. More specifically, the chapter draws on novel data sources from interviews, background talks and archival research to reconstruct GC No. 15's drafting process – *telling* the story of how water became a human right – to ultimately unearth the TLC and the various aspects of its lawmaking agency in a specific case. With its November 2002 adoption, GC No. 15 on the Right to Water of the ICESCR provided an authoritative base upon which states could better implement their obligations, and individuals and communities could more effectively advocate for the fulfillment of their right to water – and, in doing so, closed a significant gap in human rights law. Shown with an insular drafting core that both coalesces around a single CESCR member and comprises a select few non-UN technical and legal experts who become involved with great autonomy, the TLC detailed here contours the theoretical expectations advanced in the preceding chapter.

Chapter 5 delves into three additional cases of treaty interpretation by the human rights treaty bodies. The aim of the chapter is to probe the plausibility of the TLC concept across the human rights regime. I use insights and findings gathered from the drafting process of GC No. 15 to articulate a typology that distinguishes the treaty bodies by their likelihood to need external input when drafting general comments. Drawing on a combination of data – documents and existing scholarship, as well as interviews and personal observations – the case studies ultimately demonstrate the TLC concept to be applicable to drafting processes in other treaty bodies, even where their formation is less likely.

Chapter 6 addresses the absence of the state from the procedures described throughout the book with a forward-looking eye on the TLC and the present status of the human rights regime. On the TLC, this chapter advances the argument that such coalitions are in no way to be seen as a mode of international lawmaking without governments, as states, in their status as the treaty body system's ultimate arbiters, have ample opportunities to mold the system to their liking – by way of, for example, elections, ratifications, budget, willingness to participate in the procedures, and compliance with their obligations. Indeed, the Treaty Body Reform 2020 initiative reflects their awareness of autonomy of the treaty bodies themselves. With it likely that states cannot enact this reformation while also maintaining presence in the human rights regime, it will be crucial to see how this conflict plays out in the future.

The concluding chapter summarizes the key insights vis-à-vis the TLC concept – how TLCs form, who they involve, and all other meaningful empirical points about them to know, for example, what makes them legitimate and effective. It discusses how the book's findings contribute to wider debates in global governance, highlights the concept's contribution to different strands of literature in International Relations and International Law, discusses the concept's generalizability beyond the human rights regime, and gives incentives for future research.

2

Human Rights Treaty Interpretation

TLCs for human rights, as the next chapters will demonstrate, form around the common goal to develop international human rights through treaty interpretations. In TLCs, United Nations (UN) human rights treaty body members and other professionals collaborate closely to achieve this goal. While the general motivation and ability of non-state actors to influence the scope and content of international law are well explained[1] in IR, certain questions[2] remain pertaining to the actual substance of a TLC's output, the general comments, that require answers: indeed, *are* general comments authoritative? If so, why?

This book's answer – that, yes, some general comments substantively underscore international law as authoritative legal objects in their own right – is one it provides by connecting explanations of expert authority to experts' recognition by a broader human rights community.[3] As human rights norms depend on a broader actor network for their recognition and implementation (Keck and Sikkink 1998; Risse, Ropp, and Sikkink 1999, 2013), it seems likely that general comments' authority likewise stems from recognition by the broader human rights community – and not only by states. This assumption rests on treaty bodies' high degree of autonomy as bodies composed of independent human rights experts whose interpretations need no further consent by state

1 With the participation of a wider range of actors in global governance, formal international institutions have become increasingly accessible to and shaped by non-state actors (Liese 2010; Squatrito 2012; Tallberg, Sommerer, and Squatrito 2013), including international law (Charnovitz 2006; Noortmann, Reinisch, and Ryngaert 2015).

2 There are other questions that are less salient to this book but are discussed elsewhere; for example, the question of to what extent treaty bodies contribute to soft law (Lagoutte, Gammeltoft-Hansen, and Cerone 2016).

3 This community, as will be shown in the next chapters, includes more members than the "invisible college of lawyers" (Schachter 1977) that usually make up interpretive communities in international law (Johnstone 1990).

2.1 WHAT ARE GENERAL COMMENTS?

It is no surprise that a "right to life" (ICCPR Art. 6) and "a right of everyone to education" (ICESCR Art. 13), as well as "measures to eliminate discrimination against women in the field of health care" (CEDAW Art. 12), are ascribed different meanings by state parties. If a treaty body comes to regard these understandings as out of line with their respective treaty's object and purpose, it is within the body's mandate to make public their interpretation of the right's meaning.[8]

Interpretations from the human rights treaty bodies are rendered in the form of general comments (Alston 2001; McCall-Smith 2016). General comments are "a means by which a UN human rights expert committee distils its considered views on an issue which arises out of the provisions of the treaty whose implementation it supervises" (Alston 2001: 764). Some see them as authoritative decisions, "while others view them as unsystematic and unfounded statements deserving no recognition in the law" (McCall-Smith 2016: 24). In conceiving general comments only as instruments for the implementation of human rights, we might easily reject their significance relative to other instruments. They neither address a state party's violations in ways as targeted as the treaty bodies' concluding observations nor take a rights holder's perspective as in individual complaint procedures; moreover, these comments are less specific on the impact of current events on the realization of human rights as compared to treaty bodies' statements and views. This perspective might underestimate them as probably the vaguest documents issued by a treaty body to determine the obligations in the human rights treaties. A general comment does not even require adoption by state parties, although it applies to them immediately – albeit without any accompanying immediate legal obligations.

As such, general comments are particularly interesting for studying potential transformations of authority in international organizations, given the fluidity and autonomy with which treaty bodies make decisions; they are able to write their own rules of procedure and adopt interpretations with no need for further formal recognition by states, which then constitute the new standard for all future state reports and dialogues. As Table 2.1 depicts,[9] all treaty bodies have established their own rules of procedures (see also Appendix A) and added, where not already included in the treaty, the right to adopt general comments – with only two bodies specifying the process for their

8 When such a necessity arises is less clear, see, for example, Rodley 2013: 632.

9 The table is based on the rules of procedure of the treaty bodies.

TABLE 2.1 *Rules for decision-making*

Treaty body	Members	Quorum	Voting rule
CESCR	18	12	C,[a] M
CCPR	18	12	M
CERD	18	M	M
CEDAW	23	12	C,[a] M
CAT	10	6	M
CRC	18	12	M
CMW	14	8	C,[a] N/A
CED	10	6	C,[a] M
CRPD	18	12	C,[a] N/A

Notes: [a] Other voting rule in case of nondecision
M – Majority
C – Consensus

development. This remarkable autonomy without formal secondary rules adds to their relevance as a subject of scientific inquiry.[10] Treaty bodies aim to make their decisions by consensus, even in cases where only a majority is needed.[11]

Particularly, the bodies' high degree of autonomy (Boyle and Chinkin 2007: 151–157) opens up opportunities for the committees to confront new challenges for human rights. As independent experts with limited resources at hand, the chapter lays ground to the argument of this book that these challenges are confronted through individual action of a single committee member in collaboration with other actors external to the treaty bodies.

International lawmaking comes in different forms, the most obvious of which is treaty-making. Human rights treaties, as with most other international treaties and agreements, are crafted by states and apply to them solely. However, a treaty is not self-explanatory; it needs interpretation, and those interpretative processes constitute another form of making law (Simma 2005). Developing new standards through interpretation is possible (Venzke 2012) but remains disputed as legitimate by expert committees. This debate grapples between two viewpoints: one that sees treaty bodies as overstepping their mandates to "adopt aggressive interpretations and treat those interpretations as dispositive" (Hakimi 2009: 599) and one that finds general comments to "contribute to the formation of customary international law by helping to shape *opinio iuris* and state practice"

10 Rules of procedure legitimate processes to take certain actions (Raymond 2019).

11 One explanation for majority rule stems from the time the treaty bodies were established. During the Cold War, consensus on decisions on state reports was harder to achieve and majority decision-making more likely to be the rule (Rodley 2013: 625–626).

(Mechlem 2009: 930). This latter view itself grapples between different viewpoints: Eckart Klein, for instance, holds that it "is probably through their General Comments [...] that the treaty bodies contribute most to the interpretation, clarification and concretization of legal norms, [...] at least partly a norm creating function" (Klein 2005: 575); Matyas Bodig sees only some general comments as going beyond their norm-filling function interpreting state practice and existing norms to "take on the character of 'norm-creating' soft law" (Bodig 2016: 74); and other scholars yet see general comments as an instrument for treaty bodies to "develop a jurisprudence of the Convention" (Byrnes 1989: 50). But whatever the exact nuance of treaty bodies' shaping of law, increasingly clear is that they indeed shape it through general comments, which, although still referred to by the treaty bodies themselves for their advising character for state reports, "have come to take on an almost exclusively 'lawmaking' function" (Blake 2008: 9; see also Oette 2018: 15).

Figure 2.1 depicts an overview of the number of general comments adopted by the treaty bodies over time.[12] As can be seen, all hurdles regarding the legal

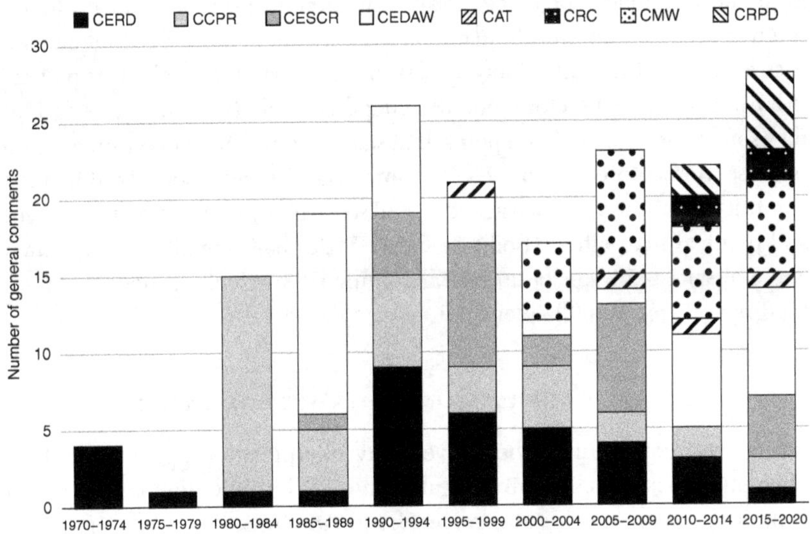

FIGURE 2.1 Adoption of general comments over time (1972–2020)

[12] The general comments of the treaty bodies are available in the United Nations Treaty Body Database. It can be accessed here: https://tbinternet.ohchr.org/_layouts/15/TreatyBodyExternal/TBSearch.aspx
Year of treaty body establishment: CERD (1970), CCPR (1977), CESCR (1985), CEDAW (1981), CAT (1987), CRC (1991), CMW (2004), CRPD (2008). The CED is not included in the figure since it has not adopted any general comments yet.

status of general comments do not preclude treaty bodies from making use of this instrument, who rather employ them frequently, yet at different intensities. In terms of output, CERD, CEDAW, and CCPR have each adopted more than thirty general comments, followed by CESCR and CRC (more than twenty), and then CAT and the younger CMW and CRPD, who have adopted only a few. We find the adoption of general comments to have peaked in the 1990s, coincident with the decade's euphoria for the progression of human rights norms (Jetschke and Liese 2013; Panjabi 1995). Likewise observable is that treaty bodies have made use of this instrument despite an institutional reform process that began in 2009, which became necessary in light of increased workloads without an accompanying expansion of resources (see Chapter 6).

Not all general comments become important reference points in human rights law. Some are received with praise, some are contested, and some are ignored outside the human rights treaty regime. General comments, in contrast to complaint mechanisms or state reports, function as "a means for providing authoritative guidance to a broader group of states": they "benefit from the advantages of being flexible in their timing, open to evolution through revision," and are "fundamentally transcendental, in that they encompass a variety of factual circumstances and are directed at all state parties" (Marsh 2001: 12). Therefore, not all general comments are well received, as they sometimes shed light on points that states are treating indeterminately on purpose. Some observers of the UN human rights treaty bodies hold that the committees follow their own agendas, and some treaty bodies are more activist and political than others (Bodig 2016: 71). States have equally issued written and oral statements on some general comments to reject any degree of their bindingness (see also Chapter 6).

2.2 ARE GENERAL COMMENTS AUTHORITATIVE?

Are general comments authoritative treaty interpretations, given that states often push back against them as legally binding? This question is not without controversy, with scholars and lawyers frequently spreading a view of general comments as "authoritative interpretations" (McCall-Smith 2016: 31) of human rights law. In general, authoritative interpretations in international law are characterized by the source and form of their output. In international law, authority to interpret is primarily derived from a formal treaty. The reliance on formal categories facilitates identifying what is law and what is not law (i.e., soft law). Cast this way, one can claim not all general comments, which the UN treaty bodies regularly adopt, to necessarily serve as authoritative interpretations of human rights law, on the grounds that they do not technically (i.e., formally) bind state parties to the obligations they prescribe. Furthermore, there is indeed empirical merit here, as while some comments are influential for the development of soft law, others are simply ignored. But even so: Recent approaches to authority in international law argue that authority depends less on the formal bindingness of decisions and more on an outcome's *ability* to regulate behavior (Zarbiyev 2018). This ability is determined through neither sanctions nor persuasive means, but rather simply because the decision is made by a certain decision-maker. The International Law Commission's (ILC) interpretations, for example, are not binding but may trigger further regulation by states (Azaria 2020). Deference-based models of authority of international law follow in their argumentation those in IR studies seeking to explain, for example, the authority of bureaucracies in world politics (Barnett and Finnemore 2004; Sending 2015).

This chapter's probing of the question of what makes general comments authoritative approaches them as the derivative of two sources: (1) the blended authority comprising the treaty body's expert authority on human rights paired with its delegated procedural authority to interpret the treaties, and (2) an individual general comment's recognition by a wider audience than just state parties. To frame the outset of this probing – and to provide assumptions for what determines whether a particular general comment will serve as a powerful tool for the development of international human rights law – I submit a good way to start is to distinguish between their functions.

2.2.1 *Function*

Lawmaking on the international level must be distinguished from domestic systems, where the term refers to "the enactment of 'legislation' by highly specialized and routinized political institutions" (Reisman 2005: 15). Although specialized legal institutions, such as courts, do exist at the international level, treaty bodies' lawmaking qualities might be better advised through function rather than setting (Wheatley 2013). Similar to a number of other bodies monitoring international agreements, human rights treaty bodies account for the development of political, social, and economic conditions that determine the implementation of an agreement – and are themselves shaped by broader political, societal, and economic developments. As such, their work can be illustrated with the help of a culinary metaphor that Bruno Simma provided at a conference panel on lawmaking through interpretation. There, he compared the text of a human rights treaty to a deep-frozen pizza: once set in the package, everything one needs for a meal is indeed there, but to make it "ready for consumption," more steps must be taken. In the treaties' case, these steps are "the processes of [their texts'] interpretation and application," which Simma himself regards "as part of the 'making' of international law" (Simma 2005: 581). We may thus conceive human rights treaties as "living instruments" (Keane 2020; Moeckli and White 2016) that take into account new legal, social, and political developments.

To approach the question of general comments' authoritativeness, I suggest distinguishing the instrument between three functions.[13] This step allows one to compare general comments within and across treaty bodies, which – so goes its merit – reveals the varying levels of legality claims made.[14] With that I mean that some general comments clearly aim at facilitating the reporting procedure for the treaty body and the state parties, while others make reference to jurisprudence and employ the language and structure of formal treaty interpretations. While some treaty bodies have been mandated more specifically to do so than others,[15] the rules of procedure (see Appendix B) adopted by each treaty body today all include the opportunity to prepare and adopt general comments for more general purposes. I therefore suggest distinguishing them into the following three categories: (1) those that clarify reporting obligations, (2) those that apply to specific groups, and (3) those that clarify specific rights in the treaties. Figure 2.2 depicts the distribution across treaty bodies.[16]

The first category includes general comments that refer to the clarification of obligations of the state parties in the procedure of reporting. These general comments assist the state parties in preparing their reports efficiently, facilitating the progress of monitoring in turn, while also fostering fruitful discussion between the pertinent treaty body and state delegations. These are usually shorter and include less reference to external developments in law and politics.

[13] This suggestion goes back to Ando 2010. Other scholars only distinguish thematic and specific general comments (Riedel 2005).

[14] Moreover, it allows one to distinguish between general comments clarifying reporting obligations or the application of the treaty to specific groups and instead focus on those general comments that clarify specific rights, which I regard as most likely to become authoritative interpretations of human rights law, given their capacities to advance the understanding of particular treaty norms.

[15] Note, for example, that CAT in Art. 19.3 of the Convention is only allowed to make general comments on a specific state report ("[. . .] may make such general comments on the report as it may consider appropriate"), while, for example, CEDAW in Art. 21.1 can do so based on "the examination of reports and information received from the States Parties."

[16] All general comments were coded for "rights" when they specified the meaning of one or several of the treaty's rights; for "groups" when they specified the application of the treaty's article(s) to specific groups and for "reporting" when the general comment clarified state parties' reporting obligations. The general comments of the treaty bodies are available in the United Nations Treaty Body Database. It can be accessed here: https://tbinternet.ohchr.org/_layouts/15/TreatyBodyExternal/TBSearch.aspx
The CED is not included in the figure since it has not adopted any general comments yet.

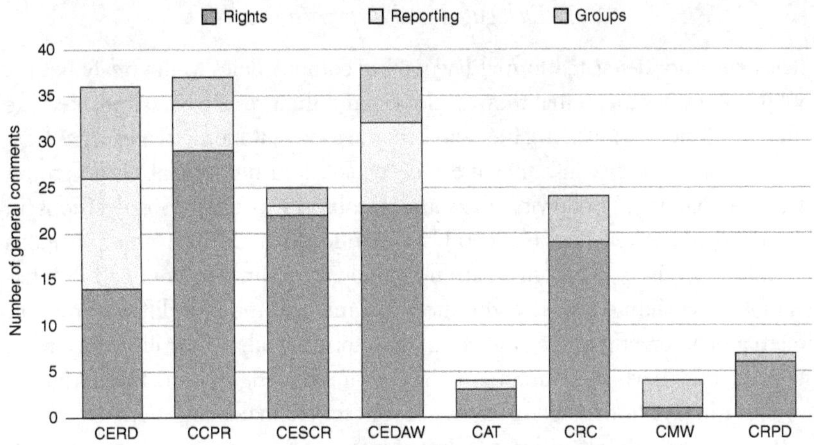

FIGURE 2.2 General comments by function (1972–2020)

The second category, as Figure 2.2 depicts, contains fewer general comments adopted by the treaty bodies that refer to the application of the treaty's norms to specific (vulnerable) groups. For example, CERD adopted General Recommendation No. 27 on the discrimination against Roma, recommending that states adopt several measures "for the benefit of members of [its associated] communities" (A/55/18 Annex V 2000). Here, the committee noted that, although the right to education was implemented by states with all necessary institutions and measures, when they pressed the states on the Roma communities' high dropout and illiteracy rates across their education systems, their answers assigned blame not to their own existing institutions and measures, which they regarded as sufficient, but rather to the Roma's special habits and traditions. Put pointedly, they were unwilling to enact reform. The committee in turn interpreted the provision of the treaty with regard to additional measures that would assist the Roma in safeguarding their traditions while still retaining access to education. General comments can herewith assist states in guaranteeing rights to groups that require additional measures to be able to exercise their rights. Sometimes this recognition by different treaty bodies may even inform the drafting of an entirely new treaty (e.g., CRPD).

The third thematic category of general comments clarifies the content of specific rights and the nature of obligations. This category includes the majority of all general comments adopted thus far. These comments potentially contribute to the normative development of international human rights and are therefore the focus of this study.

2.2.2 *Delegated and Expert Authority*

States have not delegated formal lawmaking competencies to the treaty bodies, but this does not mean that they cannot expand their respective mandates. Like other institutions (Hall 2016), they can become more autonomous and *act* as legal experts, especially because they are *independent* and not official expert groups (Haas 2008a: 109). Following Cox and Jacobson's taxonomy of decisions in international organizations (Cox and Jacobson 1973b: 8–12), treaty interpretations are rule-supervisory decisions in an international organization and part of international lawmaking. Expert committees assume a number of different roles in international organizations, but as a monitoring body of treaties, this book suggests, they have more autonomy in decision-making than analytical frameworks for international organizations account for (Reinalda and Verbeek 2004).

IR's interest in the decision-making of international institutions comes with asking what determines the authority of decisions (Avant, Finnemore, and Sell 2010), distinguishing broadly between political and expert or de jure and de facto authority (Busch et al. 2020; Liese et al. 2021). Expert authority provides key explanatory grounding for nongovernmental authority in global governance. In the case of general comments, we may see governments' delegation of the decision-making authority for treaty interpretations to independent experts as conferring treaty body decisions with expert authority.

This image is not uncontested, as their delegated authority to make interpretations is subject to the condition that states recognize them as acting on their behalf (Hawkins and Jacoby 2008: 1–2). Through progressive general comments, the treaty bodies often experience backlash with regard to their nonpolitical status; moreover, an increasing number of actors seek to influence the decisions of treaty bodies, whose members are well aware of their role, and resistance toward their lawmaking is growing among states and scholars alike. Recently, the progressiveness of treaty bodies has also foregrounded conservative-leaning civil society actors who demand monitoring of the experts themselves.[17] When politicization and resistance take over, expert authority reaches its limits.[18]

[17] These often US-based NGOs take the progressive development of human rights as evidence for a politicization of the treaty bodies: "The activism of UN treaty bodies and the OHCHR on politically sensitive topics outside the scope of human rights treaties, such as LGBT and abortion issues, calls into question the independence and impartiality of treaty bodies and raises the possibility of corruption and self-dealing. Many experts who sit on treaty bodies, moreover, have professional and personal ties to the well-funded organizations and activists who promote these causes. Therefore, a mechanism should be put in place to investigate the background of candidates to the treaty bodies further in order to ensure their independence and impartiality" (C-Fam 2020).

[18] For a different argumentation defending politicization of Special Procedures appointments in human rights, see Domínguez-Redondo 2020.

What determines an institution like the treaty bodies' expert authority? I suggest one main criterion is for its members to possess a certain degree of *autonomy* and *individual resources*, with the scope of their legal expertise the key determinant for general comments' authoritativeness. In general, the UN human rights bodies as state-empowered entities in international law (Sivakumaran 2016) have a high degree of autonomy, tacit in their very status as independent expert bodies (Boyle and Chinkin 2007). Their members, none of whom shall represent state or any other interests, serve as independent experts each acting in their individual capacity, with their main sources of income external to the UN. A range of 10 to 23 such individuals (see Table 2.1 & Figure 2.3) bring expert knowledge from different legal systems and cultural backgrounds to the various treaty bodies. Although elected with regard to regional balance and by state parties (Carraro 2019), they are required to monitor the state reports *independent* from political and regional affiliations.[19] Members must hold citizenship in one of the state parties' countries and be able to travel to committee sessions. Professional requirements for becoming a member are relatively unspecified: one is simply required to have a "recognized competence in human rights" (OHCHR 2017) and a high moral standing.

Figure 2.3 breaks down the composition of the UN treaty bodies from 2008 up until 2020.[20] Since the beginnings of the treaty body system, the majority of members were academics. One explanation for this demographic is that an

[19] The rules of procedures (Appendix B) adopted by the treaty bodies usually include provisions for members' roles in decision-making on their home countries.

[20] The time span refers to the year of election of the committee members, divergent for: CED (members elected between 2011 and 2019), CMW (members elected between 2007 and 2019), CAT Committee (members elected between 2007 and 2019). Included are current professions as stated in official CVs which can be found on the section of the respective treaty body of the OHCHR webpage. Committee members can have more than one profession. In the case of missing information, additional research aside from CVs delivered through the OHCHR was conducted. On coding:

"Academic": Scholars, researchers, higher education lecturers, professors

"Consultant/advisor": consultants to national ministries, independent consultants, special advisors

"Diplomat/government": ambassadors, employees of national ministries, national representatives to IOs and their bodies, public sector employees, employees of government agencies, ministers, foreign secretaries, mayors

"Lawyer": judges, employees of legal training facilities, attorneys, members of permanent courts

"Advocacy": employees of NHRIs, Ombudsmen and -women, employees of NGOs

"Retired/leave": retired or leave of absence

"Other": business sector employees, Special Rapporteurs, OHCHR employees, assistants to UN bodies and specialized agencies

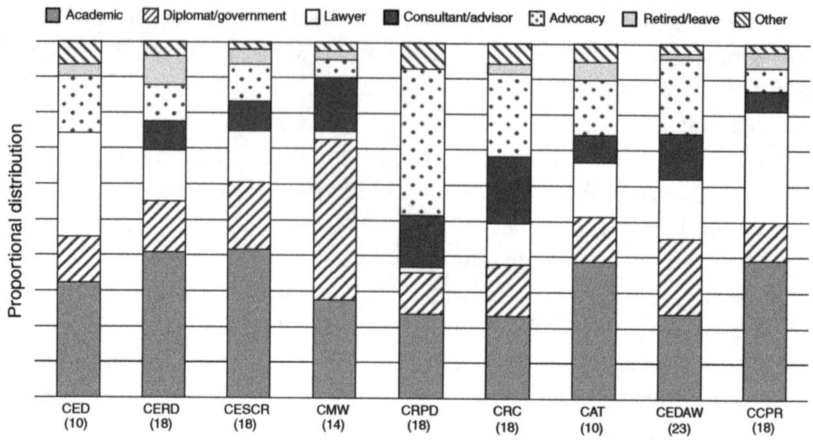

FIGURE 2.3 Professions of treaty body members (2008–2020)

academic represents non-biased, impartial expertise on human rights, making them more apt to be regarded as an *independent* expert than, for example, someone holding public office.[21] As states parties' governments possess the authority to nominate members of treaty bodies that subsequently monitor their human rights performance, it is more likely than not that these nominations include neither the sharpest critics nor those a government does not already hold in high esteem. Election of candidates is often a political process, which some claim to be "haphazard" and shallow, "tak[ing] limited account of qualifications" (Crawford 2000: 9). Additionally, members of the treaty bodies are not permanent staff to the UN and are only paid on a per diem basis for the sessions. An eligible candidate for nomination must assure both their financial security and the flexibility to interrupt their work for the sessions. This latter aspect hinders the candidacies of human rights advocates in smaller NGOs, whose jobs disallow their being absent for three months a year. Compositional differences do feature across the treaty bodies, with CCPR, for instance, showing less openness to non-lawyers and government officials (Rodley 2013: 624). Lawyers are the majority of experts on the treaty bodies, but not the only

[21] As longtime treaty body member Nigel Rodley explains, this does not mean that individuals with government affiliations are unable to make impartial decisions: "[A] member holding a national public official function could find it difficult to treat such countries with the same impartiality as he or she would treat other states. That said, it is this author's experience that some holders of national office have been able to evince more evident and rigorous independence, not to mention genuine expertise, than some of those not formally holding any such office" (Rodley 2013: 624).

ones. The human rights treaty bodies have thus always presented the co-constitution of legal expertise and other (functional) expertise (Leander and Aalberts 2013) in global governance institutions. After all, having a law degree still leaves open various professional paths. On the treaty bodies, we find examples such as public international law professors, human rights NGO advocates, members of the executive branch, or diplomats. So, while lawyers might "dominate the human rights regime" (Onuf 2016: 124), and also the treaty bodies, their expertise neither covers all the law nor do all "litigate human rights cases" (Onuf 2016).

A second important factor that determines the treaty bodies' ability to draft general comments concerns the effects of financial constraints within the UN human rights system and a workload for treaty body members that has increased even from 2015 to 2019 with new members to all treaties and their optional protocols, as Table 2.2 shows,[22] but sans further compensation. While these aspects curtail the autonomy of the treaty bodies, they nonetheless reinforce the very need for treaty interpretation: in order to monitor an ever-increasing number of states reports while fulfilling expectations to give helpful and sound feedback on implementation, a shared understanding of the nature of the treaties' obligations among the states parties is indispensable. Despite significant increases to their workload over the last decades, the size of treaty bodies' staff and allocated resources has remained largely unchanged. The treaty bodies usually meet for two or three sessions every year. These sessions last two to three weeks. Their exact duration depends on the financial budget approved by the General Assembly for the work of the treaty bodies. Although a rising number of states have ratified the human rights treaties, in turn increasing the workload, their spending to support the system has decreased in recent years.[23] These difficulties are both blessing and curse, as one can argue that the system's workload problems are "to a large degree a product of its success in attracting the participation and involvement of States and of other bodies" (Crawford 2000: 3). Nevertheless, the treaty system is under pressure, and the expectations from stakeholders are high.

In a third and final pertinent factor, the treaties authorize the treaty bodies to interpret the treaties (see Appendix B) and include no restrictions on the bodies' processes of interpretation or the forms their interpretations should take. All treaty bodies adopt their own rules of procedure for decision-making, with no further authorization needed. Human rights treaty bodies make decisions on the scope

22 UN Doc. A/74/643 Annex I.

23 For OHCHR funding, see www.ohchr.org/en/aboutus/pages/figures.aspx; for problems arising for the human rights pillar from the lack of funding, see: Pillay 2012.

TABLE 2.2 *Human rights treaty ratifications (2015–2019)*

Treaty	2015	2019	Difference
ICERD	177	182	+5
ICCPR	168	173	+5
ICCPR-OP1	115	116	+1
ICCPR-OP2	81	88	+7
ICESCR	164	170	+6
ICESCR-OP	21	24	+3
CEDAW	189	189	0
CEDAW-OP	106	170	+6
CAT	158	169	+11
OP-CAT	80	90	+10
CRC	196	196	0
CRC-OPAC	162	170	+8
CRC-OPSC	171	176	+5
CRC-OPIC	22	46	+24
ICRMW	48	55	+7
CRPD	160	181	+21
CRPD-OP	88	96	+8
ICPPED	51	62	+11

and applicability of the treaties. Their autonomy for decision-making is high compared to other monitoring bodies (Boyle and Chinkin 2007), but restricted by elections and the limited resources allocated for their increased workload.

2.2.3 *Recognition*

Treaty bodies adopt general comments without needing formal state consent. A formal recognition of their authoritativeness ex post does not take place. While the practice of adopting general comments is accepted by the majority of states parties (McCall-Smith 2016: 32), we observe that it is possible that experts on the committee interpret human rights law even in the case of state pushback (Cali and Cunningham 2018). General comments can nevertheless facilitate the normative development of human rights norms and trigger a norm cascade (Sikkink 2011) to support the evolution of legal orders (Helfer 2015).

Recognition by relevant actors is crucial in this regard. Explaining the authoritativeness of general comments moreover requires a discussion of civil society, or the rights holders. Understanding authority as a social relationship between two or more actors always implies a hierarchy: one actor authorizes and the other exercises its authority. As has been noted, limiting analyses of authority in IR to the relationship between the ruler and the ruled, or the commander and deferring actors (Lake 2010), "overlooks the fact that the relational nature of authority (. . .) also relies on the constitutive relation between these and third parties" (Lopez 2020: 7). Domestic courts are important enforcers of international human rights law (Kanetake 2018; Lupu 2013). If judges in domestic courts use general comments in their reasoning and arguments, civil society actors can ground their advocacy work on them, and domestic public actors and institutions, like politicians or NHRIs, lobby for new legislation or policies on the ground of the expert committee's decision, then the committee and its decision gained authority in the community – even against its superordinate's will.[24] A description of human rights treaty bodies as quasi-judiciary organs implies the meaning that for the "judiciary"-aspect the authoritativeness of general comments depends on recognition by other (legal) institutions. The recognition of the interpretative value of general comments by national courts, for example, gives evidence to the "relevance of the perceived authority of treaty bodies and their output" (Van Alebeek and Nollkaemper 2012: 382).

2.3 WHY ARE GENERAL COMMENTS AUTHORITATIVE?

The main reason why general comments are authoritative lies both in their saliency to the normative development of international human rights and in the specific actors who bring them to life after their adoption.[25] The drafting process can anticipate both aspects. The mainly progressive normative development of human rights stems from their vague and ambiguous status as law, or legal norms. Norm ambiguity is, however, a general observation of norms in international law (Chayes and Chayes 1993: 188). Human rights standards that were once agreed on by ratifying a treaty are constantly challenged by

[24] It can be argued for the conceptual differentiation between authority and influence that the addressees in the community do acknowledge the authority of the expert committee to interpret a treaty and hereby set new legal standards. Influence, however, would require the change of their behavior and practices. I assume based on my research for this book that this change usually happens before an interpretation and that civil society actors use general comments as ex post legitimation and/or as basis for advocating political or legal change. Hence, this helps explain why some general comments have a bigger impact than others, and even when they do not change behavior, the committee's authority for interpretation persists.

[25] Following socio-legal scholarship, a legal norm reflecting changed normative orientations by those applying and practicing it "will increase the likelihood of producing changed behaviors, whether of heads of state, high-level officials, lower-level bureaucrats, judges, firms, managers, consumers, ship captains, military personnel, or men in their relations with women" (Halliday and Shaffer 2015: 10).

economic, political, and technical development. The history of human rights on an international level is subject to shifts in international politics and debates on their universality (Donnelly 2007; Goodhart 2003; Schmitz and Sikkink 2013), reflecting interest and power constellations. From this perspective, human rights need interpretation in order to guide states through their obligations when confronted with changing realities. The task is inordinately challenging: indeed while "treaty interpretation in general international law is already a complex matter, the interpretation of human rights presents itself to many as an almost insoluble Gordian knot" (Schlütter 2012: 263), or at least a "knotty issue" (Keller and Grover 2012: 130). As other scholars have emphasized, the requirement for interpretation "results from the fact that human rights norms are (radically) indeterminate" (Wheatley 2013: 85). Norm imprecision is one salient factor undergirding justifications for human rights violations (Jetschke and Liese 2013: 36). This further explains the need for their interpretation, and a dispute about their meaning and application ultimately allows for norm change (Sandholtz 2008).

The normative development of human rights is also crucial to identify their violations. Ambiguous and indeterminate rights, or even a lack of one in a treaty, is difficult to refer to when arguing for violations of human rights treaties. State parties may reject this assessment, especially when no law to be violated exists. Thus, the line separating a treaty body interpreting norms from one creating new ones is thin but crucial. Creating rules is the main responsibility of states and their intergovernmental decision-making bodies. While a monitoring body is not formally a decision-making body, the delegation of functions, which include the interpretation of the treaty, makes them one de facto. Most treaties allow the monitoring body to adopt procedural rules for the interpretation of the treaty[26] (see Appendix A), and the committee alone adopts the interpretation without needing further approval from state parties.

Compliance with general comments provides a further explanation of their authoritativeness. Yet, establishing causality is more than just a methodological issue here. Human rights treaty bodies can adopt general comments, but they cannot force states to comply. Lack of formal enforcement mechanisms is a general phenomenon in international law and global regulation. Yet, even without enforcement means, global rules can still be of consequence (Braithwaite and Drahos 2000) and be complied with (Koliev, Sommerer, and

[26] Procedural rules as secondary rules are defined as "a subset of rules that deal with establishing legitimate processes for taking certain actions" (Raymond 2019: 19). Although no official procedure guides the human rights treaty bodies, they have established several practices for treaty interpretations: information about an ongoing drafting process can be gathered during statements in the sessions, provided that the respective treaty body reports on it.

Tallberg 2020). From this perspective, treaty bodies can be more than just paper tigers (Cassidy 2008) and clarify obligations of the treaties' rules through their general comments.[27] As their relevance then depends on recognition in domestic law, politics, and practice, the obligations must be articulated for the variety of actors composing the human rights community and also take into account the variety of national constitutions.[28] NGOs use the comments as a basis for their advocacy work in different states, domestic courts refer to them when providing reasons for their judgments (Kanetake 2018), and states refer to them in their periodic reports (ILA 2004: 13–27). In addition, specialized agencies that work in related fields to the treaties highlight their valuable contribution to the normative content and their authoritative character (FAO 2004: iii). General comments are an important source for the work of NHRIs, which monitor the domestic performances of states (Kumar 2006). Here, they serve as an update on the scope of the rights states must guarantee. General comments might also be acknowledged by other (legal) bodies of the UN,[29] be included in international declarations and treaties from other policy fields, or play a role for the agendas of international conferences. Furthermore, scholarship on human rights use general comments as a point of reference for illustrating the scope of the norms (Odello and Seatzu 2012; Riedel, Giacca, and Golay 2014).

2.4 CONCLUSIONS

Treaty bodies can develop and establish human rights through progressive interpretation. This process is facilitated by the fact that procedures for the drafting of general comments are less formalized and the number of actors involved is relatively small (Bodig 2016). I offered a typology to distinguish the aim of general comments and argued that only those clarifying norms can potentially be considered as authoritative interpretations. The normative development of human rights informs the work of many actors in the human rights field, and, based on this perspective, I necessarily revisited

[27] Brunee and Toope's interactional theory of law argues that law depends less on force or on possession of authority over others. Law rather becomes authoritative when it is mutually constructed, which "implies that obligation is relevant to compliance because it is not something that is imposed on actors but is an attitude towards the law that is part of actors' identities. Obligation rests in the commitment of actors – their 'fidelity' – to a legal system and its rules" (Brunnée and Toope 2010: 92).

[28] One such example is the variance with respect to the formal status, scope, and nature in national legislation of economic, social, and cultural rights (Jung, Hirschl, and Rosevear 2014).

[29] Most notably the ILC: Draft conclusions on subsequent agreements and subsequent practice in relation to the interpretation of treaties, Conclusion 13 (Pronouncement of Expert Treaty Bodies), A/73/10 2018: 16.

discourse on authority in the ILS and IR literatures to lay out explanation of when general comments are likely to possess authoritativeness and why. The authoritativeness of general comments is argued as resulting from the expert authority of the treaty bodies, while I assume that the varying degrees of impact of each general comment depend on their recognition among the human rights community. While the treaty bodies' autonomy is restricted by state paths of interference (see Chapter 6), their general comments can be authoritative – even without immediate recognition by states. Their authority does not derive directly from their decisions, like the ones of legal institutions like courts, and instead requires further enacting, in NGO practice or via reference in court rulings.

Treaty bodies require a supportive community to buttress their decisions that does not necessarily include state party governments. With this support and the enactment of the decision, the interpretation becomes practiced and the rule brought to life. Hence, the authority of expert committees for law-making depends less on state recognition – which traditional concepts of authority privilege – and more on the commitment of actors to the obligations in their interpretations.

The treaty bodies can extend their given mandate to setting legal standards if their decisions are taken up by key actors of the human rights community. At the same time, a lack of support from the community might explain why some treaty interpretations are not adopted or why they receive varying degrees of recognition after adoption. However, "only time will reveal the true interpretative power of this form of treaty body jurisprudence" (McCall-Smith 2016: 46).

3

Transnational Lawmaking Coalitions

In the past, and continuing into today, the architecture of global governance has seen profound challenge by developments within states and societies and across borders, some of which occur simultaneously in different locations across the globe. Comparing the United Nations today to the organization envisioned in 1945 in San Francisco is but one example bearing the imprint of these challenges. But although global governance institutions like the UN have proven resilient in the face of crises and challenges, they have come to be increasingly subject to contestation by their stakeholders – their member states and external actors – who demand change from, and sometimes even of, the institutions themselves (Hanrieder 2015; Zürn 2018). Whenever such challenges occur, there are a variety of options of how to proceed. One response could be to create a new institution designed to address the needs of governments, as happened in 2009 with the creation of the International Renewable Energy Agency (IRENA), the first international organization (IO) to focus exclusively on renewable energy, established to address challenges occurring in industrialized and developing countries (Urpelainen and Van de Graaf 2015; Van de Graaf 2013). In another option, existing institutions could also be authorized by governments with finding solutions to these new problems or events, therefore expanding their mandates (Sinclair 2017). Think here, for instance, of how the end of the Cold War led to the North Atlantic Treaty Organization's (NATO) reconstitution as a security community (Adler 2008). On some occasions, however, governments are hesitant or undecided on how to react to these challenges, and sometimes they might even prefer to not react at all, hoping for the problem's dissolution or simply to allow themselves more time and flexibility to conceive a path forward.

Transnational lawmaking coalitions (TLCs), as the case studies in the next chapters will show, are typically found in these latter situations. These coalitions of individuals emerge when states decide to not act decisive enough on a given global problem or their negotiations and decision-making processes are in gridlock (Hale and Held 2017; Hale, Held, and Young 2013). In that sense, TLCs are no new phenomenon. Efforts by individuals and organizations from civil society, academia, international institutions, and other public and private spheres to advocate for global solutions and lobby for preferred regulations exist in all places where policies are made (Dellmuth and Tallberg 2017). Yet, TLCs are not focused on persuading governments or intergovernmental negotiations. They deliberately choose international law as a response to these challenges, and their coalition takes place in expert institutions that monitor international treaties (see Section 3.1). Through the instrument of treaty interpretations, these coalitions work on the clarification of state obligations in response to global challenges and crises for agreements that offer "flexibility" to states (Koremenos 2001). TLCs are connected to an expert body through a representative of their group, and the expert body is the formal IO component across whose boundaries they interact, and whose work they partially take over. As actors, TLCs benefit from the semantic indeterminacy of international law and the fact that interpretation of laws "requires agents and agency" (Putnam 2020: 32).

3.1 DEFINING TRANSNATIONAL LAWMAKING COALITIONS

As a concept, TLCs give name to the phenomenon by which "other actors" – namely, non-state actors – influence lawmaking processes *within* international intergovernmental organizations *without* any direct involvement of a government actor, thus cooperating outside the intergovernmental core but within its established institutional framework. With state-empowered entities like expert bodies, non-state actors find a much more direct channel through which they influence the development of international law. Together, individual experts and non-state actors form what constitutes an actor type devoted to developing interpretations of law in global governance, called a "transnational lawmaking coalition."

TLCs are defined – uniquely so – by two distinguishing characteristics. For one, TLCs form around independent experts. To gain membership, non-state actors do not need to pressure, socialize, or persuade governments, but expert committees. For another, their mode of operation is determined by the interpersonal relationships among their constituent members, which necessarily changes the perspective on IOs from a closed system to an open one. By the very nature of the process of *becoming* an expert, the individual maintains connections within professional networks and communities that are not found within the IO but rather at their boundaries.

The lack of resources for a drafting process on the side of the expert body determines how many other actors become members. Actors in a TLC are understood as professionals who can also have ties to advocacy networks and epistemic communities — through their work for international and domestic NGOS, as academics and intellectuals, or as staff of international (and regional) organizations, foundations, and unions.

Empirically, this relationship renders within drafting processes from the following bases – either, externally, via a former professional relationship outside the IO (e.g., colleagues, supervisors, students) or via previous quality work experience directly with the expert body (e.g., former treaty body member or staff member of IOs). The building of their coalition mainly takes place outside or at the boundaries of their organization, as experts are not regular staff of the IO. TLCs thus offer a lens to analyze the key role that expert bodies play in the development of international law, and explain how and by whom these sources were drafted – and ultimately to explain how change in international law and politics is possible.

3.2 STATE-EMPOWERED ENTITIES IN INTERNATIONAL LAW

This book, with its focus on UN human rights treaty bodies, is about actors who feature in the international legal system as those mandated by states to monitor, develop, apply, or interpret law – so-called state-empowered entities (Roberts and Sivakumaran 2012; Sivakumaran 2016). While salient agency in international lawmaking is often attributed to the state for the simple reason that it matters "more than others" (Gilpin 1984: 301), other actors likewise matter, with the substance of their influence increasingly permeating across all areas of international law.[1] This influence is hardly disputed today, with perspectives that skew toward a more global view on law even seeing private regulation (Hall and Biersteker 2002; Pattberg 2005) as effectively governing behavior in states and across boundaries through rules and certification, sans the direct involvement of state actors.

Although states ultimately mediate this legal system in creating and overseeing its constituent parts, state-empowered entities[2] are ceded important roles in making and shaping international law, and exist in a variety of forms.

[1] For an overview, see d'Aspremont 2016.

[2] A better way to talk about the subject of interest, expert committees, is to refer to them as state-empowered entities in international law: "State-empowered entities are entities that States have empowered to carry out particular functions. They include a range of entities, such as the International Law Commission ('ILC'), the U.N. Human Rights Committee, and the International Committee of the Red Cross ('ICRC'). Because States have empowered them,

For some, an explicit lawmaking function is formally delegated: these are international courts and tribunals, like the International Court of Justice (ICtJ), that possess the delegated authority to apply, interpret, and, in some instances, enforce compliance with the law. Others are likewise formally delegated authority to make law, but at a less independent distance: an appropriate example would be the International Law Commission (ILC), a hybrid body[3] officially mandated to progressively develop and codify international law, traditionally understood in its function to draft treaties.[4] And then there are those entities that make law through a formally delegated interpretive function, like the Executive Board of the IMF, which is mandated to interpret the Articles of Agreement,[5] among other tasks, and whose members are by and large trained in business economics and banking, rather than international law.

The delegation of tasks and authority to these entities, however, does not mean that they always act according to their principals' wills (Hawkins et al. 2006a; Vaubel 2006). Indeed the formal mandate of an institution given by states is not fixed but often seems rather fluid and open to expansion (Hall 2016). This feature highlights what a focus on institutions and an assessment of their formal lawmaking mandate necessarily overlooks: that institutions making and shaping international law, like those aforementioned, do not act themselves but rather bear the individual actions of their constituent members, who ultimately are the ones making interpretations and decisions on international law (Birkenkötter 2020).[6]

As it stands, state-empowered entities *can* contribute to the development of international law in going beyond the bounds (or their entire lacking) of

these entities are not truly *non-state* in character. [...] At the same time, they are not States and, given their independence and autonomy from States, they are not simply vessels through which States act. Instead, they fall somewhere between States and non-state actors and constitute a category in their own right" (Sivakumaran 2016: 346).

3 The ILC is hybrid in the sense that it is neither an independent court nor a political body, is highly loyal to international law, and wholly comprises qualified international lawyers with a sense of acuity vis-à-vis the international (political) situation. It has recently been argued that the ILC likewise contributes to lawmaking through their interpretations (Azaria 2020).

4 G.A. Res. 174(II), art. 1(1), Statute of the International Law Commission A/RES/174(II) (November 21, 1947).

5 IMF 2020 Articles of Agreement of the International Monetary Fund art. XXIX(a), December 27, 1945, 60 Stat. 1401, 2 U.N.T.S. 39.

6 In explaining how courts contribute to lawmaking, scholars have taken this perspective on judges, who, by the very nature of their task to apply rules, make choices and decisions ultimately informed by extralegal considerations (Alter and Helfer 2010; Higgins 1995; Yildiz 2020). As clarified throughout this book, courts and judges are different from most expert committees, such as the treaty bodies, by mandate and membership.

a formal lawmaking function. To explore the mechanisms of this more "informal" lawmaking contribution, this chapter – and indeed this book – focuses on the state-empowered entity of expert bodies, and particularly those that comprise the UN human rights treaty bodies. Even without formally delegated lawmaking authority endowed, for example, by a treaty or through state consent, these bodies still manage to substantively influence international law through their treaty interpretations. The reason why they, as well as other state-empowered entities, can go beyond their mandate lies primarily in the ability and willingness of their members to enact change. "Ability" here refers to a certain latitude to act – that is, the members are independent in their choices and decision-making and not constrained by governments and policy considerations. "Willingness" refers to the members' determination to invest resources and risk transaction costs to make decisions that substantially depart from the mere application of rules in pursuance of their further development. Expert body members by the very nature of their membership fulfill the ability criterion,[7] but tougher to explain is *why* they are willing to take the risks associated with activities for which they were not elected. This book's explanation is that expert body members share a causal and moral belief with other actors in the benefits of such activities. Together, they form what constitutes what I call a TLC: an actor type that aims to develop interpretations of law in global governance.

3.3 INTERNATIONAL LAW THROUGH TRANSNATIONAL LAWMAKING COALITIONS

As a concept, TLCs give name to the phenomenon by which "other actors" influence lawmaking processes through expert bodies *within* intergovernmental organizations *without* any direct involvement of a government actor, thus cooperating outside the intergovernmental core but within its established institutional framework (Steffek 2013: 1009). As such, the IO is best seen as an open system where the cooperation among members of the coalition takes place at the boundaries of the IO (Hanrieder 2014).[8] Specifically, TLCs emerge as impermanent, informal collaborations between individuals, comprising necessarily at least one member of the treaty body and aiming to

7 As the empirical case studies will show, the lack of resources in the expert bodies as well as for individual experts further constrains their ability to make decisions and choices without external support.

8 The IO, or more precisely the state-empowered entity such as the treaty body, still holds control over the issue that distinguishes the setting from transnational governance (Seabrooke and Henriksen 2017b).

develop norms through treaty interpretation.[9] Within a TLC, all involved actors coalesce around a like-minded goal of action: to give a certain norm a stronger legal framework. Their interactive structure is thus *temporary* – in contrast to alliances, which operate long term – maintained simply until the desired outcome is achieved.[10] They are defined, uniquely so, by two distinguishing characteristics. For one, TLCs form around independent experts. Their members need not pressure, socialize, or persuade governments, as the targets of their activities are instead expert committees. For another, their mode of operation is determined by the interpersonal relationships among their constituent members. This shift to their personal interactions comes at the cost of reaching the limits of common explanations for transnational actors' influence, which speak only to those aspects of their influence of minimal consequence in lawmaking.[11]

We find expert committees within almost all IOs, some of whom are composed of state representatives, like the subsidiary bodies of the Security Council (Gehring and Dörfler 2013; Sievers and Daws 2014: 460–570), while others are composed of independent experts, broadly understood to be persons of topical and established expertise untied to national interests. Expert committees mainly fulfill monitoring or advising functions, or both, in certain instances. Both functions may be integrated within one body or mandate, for example, when an expert committee is established to monitor states' compliance with a treaty or for country-specific investigations.[12] Furthermore, expert committee "monitoring" efforts typically engender recommendations to equip governments with the means to arrive at a better compliance record – hence, monitoring bodies almost always fulfill an advisory or consultative function, whether explicit in their mission statement or not. Advisory expert committees, however, provide expertise only upon request by intergovernmental bodies, for example, the scientific advisory panels and groups in WHO.

9 This definition excludes treaty interpretations that clarify reporting obligations and applicability of the entire treaty text to specific groups (first- and second-category interpretations, see Chapter 2).

10 Achieving a goal can, however, result in mission expansion, as Haddad analyzed in the case of the NGO Coalition for an International Criminal Court (Haddad 2013). After achieving their advocacy goal of the establishment of the ICC, they became service providers to the ICC: "Mission expansion was not originally intended, but evolved with the perceived needs of the court so that the ICC could become the fair, effective court that the CICC envisioned" (Haddad 2013: 200).

11 Common explanations are the size of an NGO or network, or strategies employed to publicly reach a wide audience.

12 The role of experts was pivotal to the human rights Special Procedures (Domínguez-Redondo 2020), which have become increasingly important for implementation (Golay, Mahon, and Cismas 2011) and monitoring (e.g., Syria or Myanmar).

2006), and the Coalition for the International Criminal Court (ICC); (Haddad 2018: 126–162).

In general, as Figure 3.1 shows, the IO manifests as an open system (Hanrieder 2014; Koch 2015) because the TLC is formed around expert committees. By the very nature of the process of *becoming* an expert, the individual maintains connections within professional networks and communities (Seabrooke and Henriksen 2017b), which are not found within the IO but rather at their boundaries. Tine Hanrieder has highlighted this key role of organizational units in IOs for boundary work by drawing on the AIDS program of the WHO, arguing that a "turn to agency *at* rather than *within* IO boundaries brings to the fore the trans-organisational coalitions that are forged between organisational units and supporters in the IO environment" (Hanrieder 2014: 235). This turn is crucial for understanding TLCs, as well. In organizational units, individuals still act on behalf of the organization, a feature that independent experts do not necessarily share with permanent staff or diplomats. Their main income stems from other sources, and their time serving on expert committees in IOs is usually limited (see Chapter 6).

As Figure 3.1 depicts, the organizational unit or international public administration (IPA) of an IO facilitates the work of a TLC or may even initiate one. That

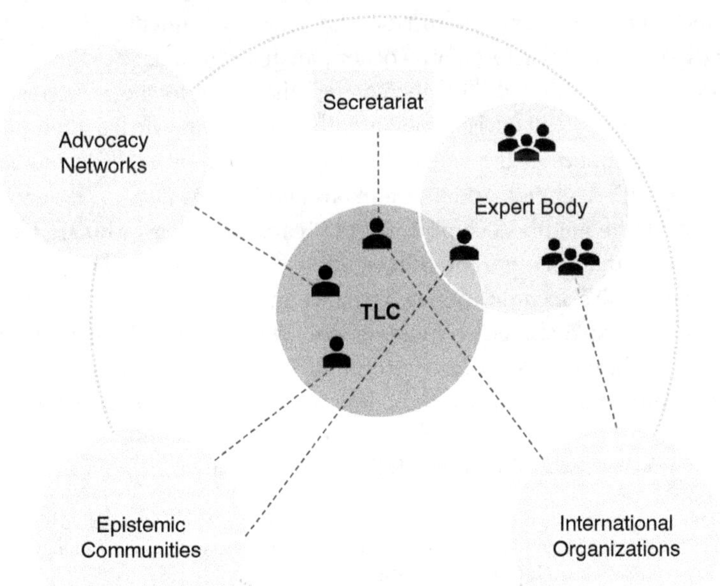

FIGURE 3.1 Transnational lawmaking coalitions (TLCs)

IPAs can take on an autonomous role in policymaking has been well explained for various institutional settings.[15] Their interest in seeing treaty interpretations enacted by expert committees stems from a broader existential quest of changing policies in their favor, which itself stems from a constant "need to acquire material and ideational resources from their environment in order to survive" (Hanrieder 2014: 226). For example, the Office of the High Commissioner for Human Rights (OHCHR) is exposed to serious budgetary constraints, with less than 4 percent of the UN regular budget allocated toward one of its three pillars: human rights.[16] Nevertheless, the IPA has established itself as an actor in the human rights system and seeks to influence the agenda of policymakers through intergovernmental IO bodies by defining problems and raising awareness for human rights challenges. Through this influence, the OHCHR can thus press for initiation of the drafting of new general comments on a topic that benefits its own work.[17]

To set a TLC in the right context, it is important to highlight here that TLCs do not exist as a discrete entity operating alongside these other well-established actors, but rather emerge from and operate *through* these collective entities, albeit for the purpose of lawmaking and without needing to pressure, socialize, or persuade governments. This contrasts with TANs (Keck and Sikkink 1998) and ECs (Adler and Haas 1992; Haas 1992), whose actions target governments as the actors ultimately responsible for making decisions – actors they must convince through causal information or moral arguments. Within those bounds, transnational actors always occupy an outsider vantage to the decision-making process: although "boomeranging" their way to the most receptive government actors and advising policy with facts and knowledge, their participation opportunities in the actual drafting of any output is ultimately left to a government's discretion and thus remains rather limited.

As stated, the members comprising TLCs are individuals who are likewise members of other actor groups. Indeed, each TLC member can be part of one or multiple TANs or communities. To name an exemplar, there is one human rights treaty body member, an international lawyer, who is also part of a TAN on the prohibition of torture, as a result of their time as a junior officer for Amnesty International. During their time as a postdoc in academia, they, as an

15 See, for example, Eckhard and Ege 2016; Fleischer and Reiners 2021; Johnson 2014; Weinlich 2014.

16 The voluntary contributions to OHCHR are, furthermore, mostly earmarked, which "limits the Office's capacity to allocate resources to where they are most urgently required": www.ohchr.org/EN/AboutUs/Pages/FundingBudget.aspx (last accessed February 26, 2021). On IO funding, see also Patz and Goetz 2019.

17 Interactions range from very direct contact between OHCHR staff and treaty body members but can also include actors from civil society and government actors approaching OHCHR first and suggesting working on an interpretation of a particular human right norm.

active member of a TAN committed to a legally binding instrument on business and human rights as well, shared information with NGOs, trade unions, and international bureaucrats, who all promoted the same cause. Before their election to a human rights treaty body, the person worked for a law firm that composed strategic litigation for legal cases on the environment. Not only did all of this experience, and the personal networks it spawned, largely contribute to the election as a treaty body member, but it also makes apparent the way in which experts are inextricably linked with TANs and ECs in their work. Experts in state-empowered entities are experts in their professional communities, but could also be involved in TANs and ECs[18] – actors held as largely distinct from one another (Keck and Sikkink 1998: 1). Broadly speaking, communities, unlike TLCs, are "not organized to fulfill a common task or purpose: that is what organizations, what hierarchies do. [...] But in contrast to hierarchies and to networks as negotiating systems, the effects collectively produced by communities are emergent" (Mayntz 2010: 41). Necessarily, one member of the TLC belongs to the state-empowered expert body, ultimately adopting the outcome a TLC seeks to achieve – which introduces a hierarchy, even if it does not affect the drafting process in practice.

To continue drawing distinction between TLCs and these other collaborative bodies: TLCs operate with fewer actors, and relationships between individual members are often established prior to becoming a coalition, while TANs "operate best when they are dense, with many actors, strong connections among groups in the network, and reliable information flows" (Keck and Sikkink 1998: 206). A TAN's chief focus is on campaigns, thus public activities, while TLCs, in their ultimate need to persuade the involved expert body, must appeal more to a personal level. Advocacy networks, however, are very close to coalitions in their members common grounding in values. As Figure 3.1 depicts, TLC members are often simultaneously members of these networks, across whose duration they never cease being members of the TAN. TANs are "communicative structures" and "political spaces, in which differently situated actors negotiate – formally and informally – the social, cultural, and political meanings of their joint enterprise" (Keck and Sikkink 1998: 3), which is to advocate for policy change. TAN members are not tied exclusively to the

[18] Antonin Cohen has highlighted this by describing the European professional network of lawyers, building on Bourdieu: "Defying the usual categorizations of the national and the supranational, the institutional and the informal, and also the interests and the ideals, the individual agents constituting these networks precisely define themselves by their social ability to cross the borders between the various segments of the European field of power" (Cohen 2010: 108).

network and, especially through its communicative structure that enables negotiations about the meanings of this enterprise, individual members may find these meanings as best materialized in collaboration with other actors. As such, they do not disconnect from the joint enterprise of the TAN, but might just go an additional path to realize it.

Similar to effective civil society coalitions, such as the ICBL, TLCs are characterized by substantive expertise and the ability "to reach outside their comfort zone" (Mitchell, Schmitz, and Bruno-van Vijfeijken 2020: 69). Putting expertise and the process of gaining a shared understanding[19] of it at its center, TLCs are closely connected to epistemic communities. Individual TLC members can, as with TANs, stem from an epistemic community's network of "professionals with recognized expertise and competence in a particular domain and an authoritative claim to policy-relevant knowledge within that domain or issue-area" (Haas 1992: 3). As Eleni Tsingou notes, the epistemic community approach works well "when the experts and the policy community are clearly separated" (Tsingou 2015: 229). For one, TLCs form around the common goal to draft legal interpretations, and not to make policies;[20] for another, the TLC is the contrary of a clear separation of expert and policy community, with members often belonging to the same epistemic community while *also* serving as those they seek to advise. Expertise and knowledge from different communities or advocacy networks are assembled toward the aim to develop strong interpretations of law.

What is more, individuals are willing to reach out and leave the purely advising role of an epistemic community in order to participate in the drafting process. This observation that individuals often leave their collectives in order to more effectively influence policymaking has been made in environmental politics, where collective actors like NGOs have made use of TANs to exchange ideas, but then sought to accomplish their interest through individual actions outside of the network (Orsini 2011). Similar behavior can be found by members of epistemic communities.[21] Within a TLC, individual

19 Renate Mayntz highlights with regard to (policy) communities that a shared understanding does not "imply full consensus; in scientific communities there can be disagreement over the best questions to ask and over the meaning of experimental results, and in policy communities over the measures to adopt in the pursuit of a policy goal. Similarly, while community members are peers with respect to the shared characteristic, they are often different with respect to other properties, such as resources, or, in scientific communities, reputation" (Mayntz 2010: 40).

20 One could argue, though, that through treaty interpretations, TLCs afterward hope to influence policymaking or formed because policymaking was unsuccessful or not wide-reaching enough.

21 The examples of the human rights treaty bodies (see also Chapters 4 and 5) highlight the difficulty of drawing a clear line between epistemic community and international legal scholars. For their interpretations to be recognized as authoritative requires that they stand

academics and scientists share with their collaborators the preference for a particular outcome, the adoption of a treaty interpretation, but they do not approach this aim from the same but rather different knowledge bases (Davis Cross 2013b; Haas 1992: 16–20). As the case studies in the next chapters will demonstrate, input from different epistemic sources is even beneficiary for the drafting process.

Whether international lawyers constitute an epistemic community is a question yet to be answered definitively (see also Chapter 2). With regard to the environment regime, Peter Haas did not see international environmental lawyers as constituting an epistemic community on grounds of their lack of "authority in environmental policy circles that scientists and engineers enjoy directly" (Haas 2008b). The role of lawyers is, however, central to TLCs and cross-cutting for other collective actors. While Haas has seemingly defended epistemic communities against intrusion from lawyers, mirrored by Koskenniemi who feared the law's deference to political expertise (Koskenniemi 2007), the empirical reality of expert committees shows that individuals trained in the legal profession can take on various roles and forms of collective or individual action. Within a "legal complex" for political liberalism, Karpik and Halliday identified structural configurations of relationships among legal professionals through "which legal occupations act collectively, alone, or in alliance with other legal occupations, in the making, implementing, enforcing, or disseminating of law or in leading publics or allying with civil society groups" (Karpik and Halliday 2011: 233). Their skills or practical knowledge might become even more relevant in drafting processes which lack formal procedural rules (Raymond 2019: 20), allowing legal professionals to shape rule-setting more strategically (Quack 2007). Hence, I hold that in TLCs, both a lawyers' expertise and that of other functional experts are needed.[22]

To recap the relation of the TLC as a collective transnational actor to TANs and epistemic communities, several distinctive features are particular to

on technical knowledge of state practice and court decisions (Alston 2001; McCall-Smith 2016). But likewise specific knowledge from other fields is needed, as we will soon see in Chapter 4's empirical example of GC No. 15, where individual experts from epistemic communities of international law (an international law professor) and water governance (an NGO water expert and a WHO health expert) are shown to combine expertise to clarify state obligations for ensuring a human right to water. Collating knowledge of state obligations and the relevant challenges to whatever the right at hand, be it the one to water or another, from as many perspectives as possible, paves way for the most discerning of treaty interpretations.

22 Or, as Anna Leander and Tanja Aalberts addressed this in reaction to Koskenniemi: "However, what is noteworthy about the latter's otherwise perceptive presentation of the politics of expertise is the juxtaposition of law and expertise, of lawyers and (other) functional experts, ignoring the expertise of law(yers) itself" (Leander and Aalberts 2013: 784).

TLCs. First, whereas advocacy networks and epistemic communities intend to change or initiate policies, TLCs form their coalition to develop, interpret, and apply international law. Which is not to exclude policy change from a TLC's broad initiative, but rather to reiterate their purpose: to either preface policy change by establishing the legal standards that should inspire it, or by reacting to policy change which risks watering down already achieved standards. Second, as an entity formed sans official government mandate but within an intergovernmental organization's operations, TLCs are strictly informal in both their membership process and internal links between actors, while networks and epistemic communities manifest in many forms, but membership is more formally organized. In a further difference, TLC members join upon invitation as individuals, rather than en masse, as an organizational body. The operative logic here speaks to the correlation drawn earlier between purpose and membership: while large networks of actors function effectively in the realm of policy change,[23] for entities like TLCs whose purpose coalesces around lawmaking, their efficacy depends on a small group of actors acquainted intimately – that is, on an individual level.

A third difference lies in temporality: a TLC exists solely for the time required to develop or interpret the law of interest[24] and is thus of shorter duration than the other actor types. Although some processes may last longer, once adopted, state parties must ensure the norm's domestic implementation. Once the purpose of the TLC is achieved, some TLC members might then become more active again in their networks and communities and monitor this implementation, for example. A new TLC formed by the same expert committee member would only coalesce around a new specific norm – and thus require other expertise.

Lastly, TLCs are, as aforementioned, distinct in their relationship with the targeted decision-maker: while TANs and epistemic communities turn to governments to enact change or formulate their preferred policies, the TLC instead evolves around the expert committee to adopt an outcome. Important to note here is that at least one committee member is part of the coalition and often the one initiating it. Thus, their individual membership overlaps. The informal character of TLCs has implications for their mode of operation, which, in a further difference, organizes *outside* the strategies and mechanisms

23 Because the decisions are made by expert committees and not intergovernmental entities.

24 TLCs can also end their coalition before achieving their purpose, for example, when it is obvious that this outcome will not be achieved due to a changing opportunity structure or in case an intergovernmental lawmaking process takes place that would supersede the TLC.

traditionally used by transnational networks – namely those that inherit the choice of public communication for pressure and persuasion of their ideas.[25]

3.5 EMERGENCE AND FORMATION

The following sections devote themselves to fleshing TLCs in practice, starting with the *when* and *why* of their genesis. What triggers a TLC's emergence? I argue that TLCs are most likely to emerge when three conditions are given: first, they form around those issues where political and social developments challenge the meaning of legal norms (globally and over time). Second, legal entrepreneurs facilitate the drafting process and provide resources (through time and input, but also by involving others). Third, transnational meetings and conferences provide points of exchange. These three conditions are necessary for a TLC, as the first one provides for their relevance, the legal entrepreneur triggers and coordinates their formation, and the transnational meeting condition facilitates the inclusion of members and their interaction. These conditions make a TLC more likely, yet are not sufficient causes for their existence.

3.5.1 *Political and Social Challenges*

A "good" international agreement regulates behavior at all times and in all places. However, this is more aspiration than normalcy. While many international agreements have endured time and attained (nearly) universal ratification, their application and interpretation nevertheless become necessary in light of political and social challenges. If no actions are taken for clarification of their meaning, norms risk erosion (Panke and Petersohn 2012). Cases of norm contestation through political and social challenges are often made visible through the work of advocacy networks (Keck and Sikkink 1998). Drawing from human rights research, if an issue manifests globally that affects human rights, it is then brought to the international human rights regime by norm entrepreneurs (Finnemore and Sikkink 1998: 896–901), for example, civil society actors, who successfully frame the issue as a human rights issue via

25 The standard strategies available to norm entrepreneurs, such as shaming, pedagogy, or persuasion which have been widely studied with respect to human rights and other issues (Bloodgood 2011; Brysk 1993; Della Porta and Tarrow 2005; Hafner-Burton 2008; Keck and Sikkink 1998; Nelson and Dorsey 2008; Rietig 2016; Risse, Ropp, and Sikkink 1999, 2013; Tarrow 1994). Yet, such socialization and learning mechanisms conceptualized for transnational actors vis-à-vis intergovernmental decision-makers are not easily transferable to expert bodies.

conferences (Joachim 2007; Payne 2001). But even with the issue's introduction, still yet to be conceived is specific human rights law speaking to it – hence, where TLCs come into play.

3.5.2 *Legal Entrepreneurs*

Treaty interpretations are not a fixed item of a committee's work agenda. Someone needs to initiate the process, propose a topic, and present arguments on why a drafting is in order. Among the transnational professionals and communities increasingly acknowledged as influential actors in global governance, of particular importance is "The Invisible College of International Lawyers," which describes an elite professional community of professors, students, government officials, civil servants, and practitioners silently influencing international law (Cohen 2010; Leao Soares Pereira and Ridi 2020; Schachter 1977). International lawyers often employ a hybrid capacity as both academics and members of an international institution. While their activities can be seen as entrepreneurial, legal entrepreneurs[26] do not need to be part of an expert body but can operate from outside of it, be it, in working for an NGO, a think tank or in academia. As such, they remain chiefly committed to their own agenda and are better thought of as issue professionals (Henriksen and Seabrooke 2017).[27]

[26] Work on the roles of individuals within IOs (e.g., as brokers, initiators, or vetoers) (Cox and Jacobson 1973a) remains within the boundaries of an IO and does not explain the role of the legal entrepreneur (Cohen 2010; Dezalay and Madsen 2017). Legal entrepreneurs share many features with the more familiar concept of political entrepreneurs (Joachim 2003; Keck and Sikkink 1998): they actively promote collaborative action, are often experienced with the task (here: of drafting treaty interpretations) from previous engagements, can mobilize material and immaterial resources, and possess in-depth knowledge of the present opportunity structures. While some legal entrepreneurs might be more sensitive toward the necessary politics around progressive norm development through treaty interpretations and engage as political entrepreneur as well, they do not need to be the one doing the political entrepreneur's work in order to get the draft to the adoption stage. In short: A legal entrepreneur is needed for the TLC to emerge and the content-related legal work, but a political entrepreneur will strengthen the mobilizing structure for the draft.

[27] These legal entrepreneurs are area- or field-specific. But even those focusing on a very specific norm can use their networks and professional communities to shape the development of international law. I take the example of a legal entrepreneur in one of my case studies, a human rights lawyer who is specialized in housing, land, and property rights. He has worked with many IOs, funded several NGOs and initiatives, published widely on that topic, and his CV gives a glimpse of the scope of his work on international human rights law and states in his CV that he "has also been very active in the promotion of new international human rights laws and standards since the early 1990s. These include the instigation and original drafting of more than 100 United Nations resolutions, general comments, guidelines, principles, concluding

Often, legal entrepreneurs are located where the targeted institution has its headquarters. Brussels, New York, and Geneva are central hubs for their operations.[28] In contrast to policy entrepreneurs, legal entrepreneurs are less informed by specific domestic contexts than by a global perspective. They are well connected with issue-specific networks and have an overview of legal developments at the international and domestic levels – but not necessarily from experience. Legal entrepreneurs must employ framing strategies to persuade experts of the necessity of a lawmaking process, albeit with less reliance on public strategies (Deitelhoff 2009). They draw on information from multiple domestic contexts where a lack of legal regulation caused problems. When the TLC is formed, they can also be the coalition's entrepreneurial member by way of inviting other experts to join the drafting group. They then resemble the core campaign organizer as sketched out for effective TANs, who "must ensure that individuals and organizations with access to necessary information are incorporated into the network" (Keck and Sikkink 1998: 10).[29] Similarly, becoming a legal entrepreneur for a TLC often follows from experience in a lesser key role in previous lawmaking processes.

3.5.3 *Transnational Meetings*

Before the drafting begins and a TLC is formed, meeting opportunities for the future members are crucial for two aspects: first, every meeting – be it an international conference hosted by IOs on the topic, a workshop organized by TAN members, or an academic conference – adds to the claim that a certain law requires clarification. Second, TLCs often directly emerge out of these meetings by establishing the ties between individuals from different organizations. For example, a legal entrepreneur can meet experts from state-empowered bodies during the Davos Forum, listening to the same presentation by a CEO who points to developments that profoundly challenge the meaning of trade rules.

observations, quasi-judicial decisions and several other international human rights standards. (…) He conceived of and successfully managed campaigns leading to the establishment by the United Nations of several new Special Rapporteurs." CV Scott Leckie, to be downloaded from his NGO website http://displacementsolutions.org/about-ds/scott-leckie/21.11.20.

28 This background is often considered as elitist, symbolizing the means to be close to international power centers and having access to their arenas.

29 Because of their ability to navigate different professional and organizational networks, legal entrepreneurs act like "canny professionals" in transnational governance (Seabrooke and Henriksen 2017a: 5–6) or as "linking pins" to explain interagency cooperation (Schneiker and Joachim 2020).

This might result in the idea to start drafting an interpretation of that rule. During the drafting phase, we can observe a high probability of meetings also outside of the international organization, often organized by transnational actors such as INGOs, political foundations, or other networks. At these meetings, TLC members can test the acceptance of the scope of their draft and calculate the input of their resources accordingly. Additionally, those meetings present an important opportunity for developing or intensifying relationships with other experts and thus enlarge their personal network.

3.5.4 *Formation: Opportunity Structure*

As TLCs arise where expert bodies are empowered by states to make decisions that impact the development, application, and interpretation of international law, a rationalist explanation of their emergence is connected to agency slack – the phenomenon that agents do not always act according to their principals' wills (da Conceição-Heldt 2013; Heldt 2017). Principal–agent theory (Hawkins et al. 2006b; Ross 1973) explains states' delegation of certain tasks to international organizations as a means to reduce transactional costs of policymaking,[30] but "[i]ncorporating the role of third parties (…) is the research frontier" (Lake and McCubbins 2006: 341).[31] TLCs can be seen as the result of an extended delegation chain. To outline this chain briefly: states decide to establish an international organization *(delegation #1)* whose salient purpose concerns the governance of a given issue area. Upon establishment, an intergovernmental body within this organization (*delegation #2*) determines a legal framework in this issue area, a treaty, or other form of agreement, by adopting a resolution. This agreement enters into force upon a sufficient number of ratifications, after which its practical implementation must be monitored; for this, the intergovernmental body delegates responsibility to an expert body[32] *(delegation #3)*, subsequently empowered in matters of the application and interpretation of the treaty's norms. In drafting substantive responses in these realms, the expert body facilitates its drafting processes by

30 For principal–agent theory and informal international lawmaking outside of international organizations, see Andonova and Elsig 2012.

31 This frontier has recently been sought to be overcome by modeling third parties as intermediaries for regulators to reach their targets (Abbott, Levi-Faur, and Snidal 2017; Brès, Mena, and Salles-Djelic 2019; Pegram 2017).

32 As independent experts are elected by state parties and all members serve without a salary, the principal's costs are reduced and governments have control over the monitoring body with elections.

delegating chief responsibility to one of its members (*delegation #4*). Ultimately, the principal's – that is, states' – logic risks to backfire, as the tasks of the expert bodies are too time consuming for members to fulfill the entirety of their functions.[33] Mandated to monitor implementation of the treaty and hereby interpret the treaty's norms, the expert committee engages in this extracurricular task – "slacking," in other words – to strengthen compliance with the treaty. This (arguably) likewise follows a rational, cost-reducing, and utility-maximizing logic: the state-empowered body temporarily must invest more resources to draft an interpretation, but in doing so facilitates the monitoring of the treaty in the long term. This may not have been intended by governments in the beginning, but anyways confirms that extended chains of delegation aggravate principal–agent problems (Hawkins et al. 2006b; Nielson and Tierney 2003; Vaubel 2006) toward a heightened risk for agency slack.

The opportunity structures spawned via the creation of international organizations, and intensified by the delegation of lawmaking to expert committees, are generally assumed to enable transnational actors to act strategically to pursue their interests (Martin and Simmons 2013: 342). Scholars agree that this depends on the openness of international institutions toward them, which also impacts the decision of the transnational actor to target one institution but not the other (Liese 2010; Sikkink 2005). In general, the less state-dominated the decision-making process, the more access points unfold for transnational actors. What remains unanswered, even with this explanation of a TLC's existence from a rational, institutionalist perspective, is *why* the coalition's individual members join, stay, and thus participate as part of it. One may shape an answer by using insights of both rationalist and constructivist perspectives.[34] From a rationalist point of view, a TLC's individual members are goal-oriented people, who evaluate their individual preferences throughout the process and whose relationships are mutually beneficial by way of the exchange of resources, whereby information or operative help needed by an expert body member is given by the individual transnational actor(s). Relying on external actors for assistance without an official mandate puts the committee member in a tenuous position. His or her reputation is at risk[35] when he or

33 This applies especially to experts who are not employed by the international organization but serve voluntarily, like the UN human rights treaty body members in this book.

34 Rationalist models have traditionally informed studies on decision-making in international relations (Allison and Zelikow 1999; Kahler 1998), challenged and complemented by constructivists (Checkel 1998; Haas 2004; Müller 2004; Payne 2001).

35 For instance, the committee member may be omitted from future consideration by states for nomination and election to committees and/or other official positions. At the collective level, the committee is posed risk, if the outcome – the treaty interpretation – is leveled with criticism and fails to meet the expectations and requirements of all stakeholders. The

she, or the entire expert body, is not capable of fulfilling the tasks delegated by state parties. On the side of the individual professional, the benefit of the resource exchange is more difficult to explain. He or she invests a great amount of time to drafting processes for which they are not officially recognized.[36] Yet, informal recognition by the treaty body and other TLC members is, of course, an option. The empirical chapters that follow will show how informal membership often results in prestigious positions within the IO or benefits the professional's career. Academics involved in TLCs, for example, can use their knowledge gained in the TLC for publications and other research projects. Moreover, the professionals involved who are not members of the expert body benefit from the TLC's outcome as it facilitates their organization's work afterward.

Another perspective construes a TLC's members as saddled with more costs than benefits. While altruism could be argued as the motif for all members to participate, it does not explain their collective action in light of the TLC's uncertain promise for an efficient and effective process – an uncertainty that owes itself to the informality of TLC membership. This work, rather, can be explained only by the personal relationships construing the TLC together. These relationships, so goes the assumption, incentivize a pathway toward effective collective action. While this assumption tends to be seen as a hindrance to building and sustaining large networks and movements (Schmitz and Sikkink 2013: 839), for TLCs they are a central feature, and are what open treaty interpretation to the marks of individualized influence. To be more illustrative here: The TLC member who represents the expert body is convinced of the importance of the interpretation and has ideas for the draft's content. These individuals, however, do not only fulfill regular duties for the expert body – for example, monitoring or advising governments, as independent experts – but also as independent experts they retain professional obligations outside of the IO. The need for technical expertise on a particular interpretation comes from professionals not necessarily connected to the IO. The expert body member builds such a coalition in order to free themselves some time from this task, which simultaneously requires that they know the necessary expertise they solicit comes from the "right" professionals. The expert body members thus might themselves choose the professionals they work with, or extend their trust to another collaborator for them to ultimately

committee may, in this instance, suffer a loss of reputation, which may lead to reduced compliance with the committee's recommendations in the state reporting process.

36 Rationally, participation would be justifiable when the individual member gets further benefits once the outcome is adopted, for example, a promotion or at least an extension of duties in its organization.

decide on those best suited to provide input. This "other" collaborator, a non-state-empowered professional, might here have different reasons for proceeding to engage the TLC. For some, their involvement could align well with the overall aims of their professional organization. For example, a human rights defender that is yet to successfully lobby governments and IOs on human rights standards might jump on the TLC as an opportunity to now clarify those standards in an authoritative interpretation. Other professionals, say an engineer, might participate in a TLC, giving their technical input, not necessarily because they seek to influence human rights standard-setting,[37] but because their expert advice is requested by someone they know. Through such conversations outside of the IO, mutual interests crystalize and build the coalition. A plant pathologist, for example, talks at a conference on food security to an advocacy network professional who is involved in a TLC on an interpretation of state obligations on the right to food. The plant pathologist might be unfamiliar with the UN human rights treaty system but sees the opportunity from an authoritative interpretation clarifying states' obligations for the right to food. As the TLC operates informally, the scientist does not risk reputation loss within their community – but has all opportunities to be recognized by a new one and expand their professional network, hence building social capital.

The individuals operate in a trustful and informal way realized within the TLC in the form of top-down reliance: the expert-side member as trustor is willing to rely on the actions of the trustee, the individual non-state-empowered professional.[38] I emphasize hereby the TLC's hierarchical structure, which even if ultimately immaterial to the drafting process,[39] reminds us that it is the expert who must officially justify the decision in front of the expert body before they can adopt the outcome publicly. The expert body member may be less present in the lawmaking process but is ultimately responsible for the draft. If the outcome does not meet the expectations and demands of all stakeholders, the expert committee is confronted with criticism or may suffer a loss in reputation, which may engender a lesser degree of state parties' acceptance with the committee's output. Dense interpersonal relationships enable effective

37 For an overview of the roles of science in human rights, see: Claude 2002.

38 IR's focus on conceptualizing trust in interstate relations (Hoffman 2002; Michel 2013; Ruzicka and Keating 2015; Weinhardt 2015.) has recently also turned to the crucial role of interpersonal relationships (Wheeler 2018).

39 Instead, it is possible that individual members temporarily play a more central and decisive role because they possess the resources. In the end, however, the committee member is responsible for the outcome and is therefore the trustor.

collective action, which, as has been argued, inversely impedes formation of such intimate connections at the transnational level (see Schmitz and Sikkink 2013: 839). But for expert bodies in international organizations and within TLCs these interpersonal relationships are key to their operations.[40]

3.6 HOW DO TLCS WORK?

Continuing on those lines, TLCs primarily work through the interpersonal relationships of their individual members. The focus on the experts' personal professional relationships requires an open-system perspective on international organizations, which conceives interactions and coalition-building to often take place at its boundaries rather than within its structures (Hanrieder 2014). As much of the treaty interpretation work happens outside of the times designated to the committee's work, the experts likely focus on the task in their professional environment.[41]

In general and as stated, all members must share the conviction that a particular norm requires a new or more specific legal framework, as, without it, a TLC holds no impetus for its existence. Their roles within the drafting rules are complementary, with every member bringing in a certain perspective and often different interests in the outcome of the draft. The functional requirements for members are twofold. First, each has specialist knowledge regarding the applicability of the norm that either extends beyond that of the expert body member or complements it when necessary. This knowledge may be purely technical – from a researcher, for instance – or cull from work experience, for example, an NGO employee's knowledge of salient implementation gaps within a domestic context. Ideally, the two perspectives are combined and complemented by an international diplomacy perspective. Altogether, this functionality ascribes great value to the membership of staff from specialized agencies. They possess expert knowledge, have personal experiences in local contexts – or, at least, are informed about them – and are familiar with governments' arguments regarding policy or legal change in the issue area. These qualities are demanded to properly define the scope of the law.

40 What evolves are trust relationships that started as knowledge-based and personalized trust (Börzel and Risse 2016: 152f.) between individuals, but manifest themselves as group trust (Börzel and Risse 2016: 153f.). TLCs are more based on the shared goal of drafting legal standards but may also have a common work history or work language.

41 As the case studies in Chapters 4 and 5 will show, this professional environment is predominantly academic. The research needed for treaty interpretations, especially on state practice, is often carried out by the expert's students in law departments.

Second, at least one member of a TLC must possess legal expertise and be familiar with international law terminology; this is the legal entrepreneur.[42] Practically speaking, this member is crucial for ensuring the coalition stays its course in the drafting stage, able to assume writing responsibility amid the expert body member's absence in meetings, wherein he or she typically ensures that the scope of the norm and the formulation of states' obligations remains at a level where chances of adoption of the outcome by the expert body are likely and states' compliance with the standards are feasible. Without such a stabilizing force, the coalition rather runs the risk of stagnating in the negotiation of political demands instead of working toward a legal framework, which dilutes the ultimate effectiveness of its outcome. In terms of the criteria determining their selection, the individual members of the TLC are, more or less, detached from the reputations and defining features of their source organizations – e.g. the specialist NGOs that employ them. In practical terms, support is typically encouraged and enabled by the international organization itself, be it via an open call for comments on a first draft of an interpretation, or via multistakeholder events, such as days of general discussion on the topic. As most treaty interpretations focus on specific topics, the main determinant in selecting these invitees lies in expert knowledge, rather than necessarily in the "attractiveness of their ideas and values" (Charnovitz 2006: 348). In lawmaking processes, in which ideas must be rendered into specific legal obligations, such expertise needs to be distinctly specialized.

While certainly the established reputation of the institution they work for assumes somewhat of a similar expertise within an individual employee party to the coalition, it is not observable that common denominators for an NGO's success – budget, accreditation, regional outreach, and professionalization – determine the individual members ultimately included in the TLC.[43] The expertise that one acquired in previous positions, scholarly work,[44] or through a specific project at the NGO, often suffices. This can partially be explained with diverging goals of an NGO and the professional working for an NGO. While, for example, one NGO can, in, say, holding the empowerment of rural women in Uganda as their mission, direct all resources to local

42 Even if the expert body member possesses this expertise, the external actor likely needs it as well, if she is delegated the coordination of input for drafting of the substantive provisions. It is assumed that the legal entrepreneur could play such a role.

43 See Chapter 4's narrative of the TLC inclusion of one NGO-employed member who lacked accreditation with the international organization or expertise in the field of human rights. Also, the other members were not working for a "big" and prominent NGO.

44 Recall from Chapter 2 that many members of expert committees are professors. In their role as supervisors, they are likely to have former PhD students who worked or work on a related topic of the draft treaty interpretation.

implementation, a staff member might conclude that an interpretation of an international human rights treaty is needed for this endeavor. Hence, while sharing the mission, the individual might choose to seek other or additional strategies to accomplish it, even if it means doing this work outside the regular working hours. NGO staff is often mission-driven and willing to go great lengths for change. TLCs therefore highlight the role of individuals as actors for collaboration in global governance (Gordenker and Weiss 1995; Schneiker and Joachim 2020). Specialist expertise and familiarity with international lawmaking, as well as the strict informality for their involvement and confidentiality are qualifications that can be met only as an individual. Hence, explanations for effectiveness of transnational actors are more important at the individual level in TLCs, than the internal structure (Hopgood 2006; Wong 2012) or the purpose of an organization.

Beyond the initiative and expertise of a TLC's individual members, a TLC's work further organizes through these members' interpersonal relationships, without any need for official communication channels, regular meetings, or support staff. Personal relationships between decision-makers and transnational actors help to bring norms into an institution (Anderson 2000) through information exchange. The operative logic here is simple: Aware of the base assumption – that drafts will be accepted by the expert body and member states only if they privilege international consensus – experts must trust that an involved actor's input to the process is reliable; an individual, personal relationship is thus paramount here, which, as the case studies in Chapters 4 and 5 reveal, conversely enables influencing both a TLC's drafting process and outcome. Empirically, this relationship renders within drafting processes from the following bases – either external to the IO, via a former professional relationship outside the expert body (e.g., colleagues, supervisors, students), or via previous quality work experience directly with the expert body (e.g., former treaty body member or staff member of international organizations).

With state-empowered entities like expert bodies, other actors have a much more direct channel through which they can influence the development of international law. Because members of these bodies are elected as experts, and not as government representatives, they singularly belong to networks and professional communities, which partially overlap with those of the other members (Seabrooke and Henriksen 2017b; Seabrooke and Tsingou 2014). The possibility to draw from different sources of evidence qua the different trainings and professions of their members for such a body's output is at the heart of what constitutes their expert authority in global governance (Sending 2015). Just as experts in a given field read, observe, talk, and discuss to arrive at an opinion on a particular matter, these bodies' stances are ascribed the status

as "expert opinions" because they derive from persons who likely read, observed, talked and discussed with the "right" people, that is, those relevantly knowledgeable on matters on which their own perspectives are rather limited.

Unlike policymakers', experts' outputs do not stand for diplomatic sacrifices or reflect the will of their governments, but instead represent *independent* expertise, which stands as such solely on the grounds of their individual reputations.[45] Accordingly, although the expert body makes joint decisions, its members will individually prepare and reflect on their input and argumentation. When in doubt or confronted with resistance, each probably gathers more evidence on an issue and talk to people in his or her professional community or issue-specific network. An example for this social practice of rule-making (Raymond 2019) can be found in interpretations by the IMF, which expose a rare case of "power of internal authoritative interpretation" (Gold 1967) among international organizations. The IMF *Articles of Agreement* in Art. XXIX "doubles the IMF organs' powers by according them not only the power to manage IMF resources and advise its members in order to pursue global monetary and economic stability, but also to authoritatively interpret the IMF Articles" (Schlemmer-Schulte 2014: para. 23). Equipped with this power to interpret the *Articles of Agreement*, the Executive Board members of the IMF will present convincing arguments to the Board, which requires the presentation of evidence. As evidence is ideally presented from a variety of sources, the board members will thus reach out to acquaintances in former workplaces – for example, colleagues at a bank, bureaucrats in the finance ministry, and professors from their university experiences – who will then recommend different objects of expertise (books, research articles, statistics, government documents, etc.) to buttress their individual positions. Within the Executive Board particularly, one finds in the sum of opinions much agreement but also leeway to negotiate, stemming from the different knowledge bases of their members. But irrespective of whose individual expertise is incorporated the most in the final document casting the summated interpretation, an expert body's output – be it the IMF or another – derives expert status through the interactions of its members with other actors to cultivate evidence.

The relationship between transnational actors and committee members has various implications for a TLC's internal and external interactions. Internally, the drafting process is characterized by members arguing about the maximum

45 Their personal networks and communities are therefore reliable sources of reassurance of this expertise, having proven to be so in the process leading up to their inclusion as "experts" in the first place.

of achievable standards. As the outcome of the lawmaking process by TLCs is to be implemented by governments, the TLC must carefully consider the acceptable scope of the norm. Externally, in order to prepare that the outcome is accepted, members lobby tactically: The TLC's expert committee member secures the backing of the outcome within their expert body, while the other members apply lobbying strategies according to their respective affiliations. For instance, an individual member who works for an NGO might participate in formal meetings in the international organization, initiate the formation of a network, and present the demands from a civil society perspective to enhance the outcome's legitimacy. Individuals who are members of epistemic communities may present or publish their knowledge and connect it to recommendations that support the TLC's outcome, an outcome that members from international organizations or specialized agencies might likewise leverage within their institutional channels.[46]

3.7 UNDER WHAT CONDITIONS DO TLCS HAVE INFLUENCE?

Once TLCs are formed, their influence can be argued based on whether their draft was adopted or not (see Chapter 5's torture case for a brief discussion of non-drafting) or to what extent their preferred content is achieved. When a TLC is formed but does not adopt an outcome of a drafting process, it is likely that the opportunity structure in the institution changed. In that case, a TLC would temporarily refrain from further drafting until new endogenous events facilitate change in this structure. A successful agenda-setting process can initiate a lawmaking process but must be analytically separated.[47] This differentiation is important because transnational actors have to adapt specific strategies to this phase (Risse 2013: 436) and setting a norm on the international agenda does not mean that it is automatically transferred into policy outcomes, in general, and a legal decision, specifically. Access rights are generally regarded as a precondition for influence. Only accredited actors can, for example, make oral statements in most IO fora (Tallberg et al. 2015: 8). In the

46 The decision to use external strategies can result in a return of the individual member to an advocacy network or the epistemic community. It is possible that the networks see benefits for their own aims and support the purpose of the TLC.

47 The analytical separation from the phase of policy formulation is less clear-cut. It could be that the phase of lawmaking follows policy formulation, for example, when those policies require legalization for effectiveness or when policies have to be adapted for an issue-specific context (as water was created for human rights). It is, however, also possible that lawmaking replaces policy formulation or serves as a phase that initiates further policies.

realm of expert bodies, decision-makers often lack resources to effectively adjudicate a matter themselves and thus recruit or authorize other actors by delegation to assist in the involved lawmaking process (Lake and McCubbins 2006; Zürn 2004). This access, although a tangible entry-point toward influence, does not necessarily guarantee that an actor will actually be involved by the expert body members,[48] but does create an opportunity structure for their *being involved* in the process.

The involvement of other actors, in an important note, does not manifest purely as a resource exchange. Independent experts, in their status as arbiters of the outside sources ultimately consulted, have the power to preclude external influence to the involved lawmaking. Resource exchange can also not alone explain those cases where the involvement of e.g. transnational actors is absent when all criteria for their participation are given. An empirical explanation is that cases can exist where the experts themselves provide all the necessary resources because one is an expert on these standards and/or has extra time for preparing them. Expert bodies at this stage are in control of the process and its possible outcomes. Self-evidently, this opportunity structure allows actors the ability to access the lawmaking process by providing the resources needed.[49] Such resources may be tangible, e.g., in the form of money and/or data, or intangible, for example, in the form of expertise and knowledge (Betsill and Corell 2008; Brühl 2003) or esteem (Baker 2017). Often underequipped with the former, civil society actors typically supply the latter to the efforts of international organizations.[50] In the cases of tangible support,

[48] Some transnational actors can make use of their formal and informal access with the utmost motivation and still not be involved in the decision-making process, for example, speak during days of general discussions and organize site events. But this does not guarantee their involvement, as this depends on an invitation by the decision-maker.

[49] This argument is supported by research on Amnesty International and their strategic change from the intergovernmental to the expert bodies of the UN human rights system. The NGO recognized the opportunity structure in the treaty bodies because of an information gap it addressed: "Instead, AI continued its information provision to the treaty bodies because the NGO considered them better in using its information. The treaty or expert bodies of the human rights system have long been neglected by UN officials as well as by NGOs. Although they are the major bodies for monitoring the human rights treaties, they were becoming more and more peripheral to the UN system as they were not provided with sufficient information. In the past few years, however, these expert bodies have become more and more aggressive in monitoring the human rights obligations contracted by states" (Martens 2004: 1058).

[50] Resource dependence theory assumes that organizations need resources from other actors but are also aware that demanding resources leads to the situation where the other actor can demand something in return. What can be described as "social control" over the organization leads to weighing of the consequences for their autonomy (Raustiala 1997). This, in exchange, influences the organization's authority, following the dual power source of legitimacy and control over expertise and information (Barnett and Finnemore 1999: 707).

sometimes the drafting processes require money that the international organization cannot provide for. Especially in the fields of human rights or environment, field trips are often needed to observe local implementation challenges, and research may require additional resources to reflect universal needs.[51]

The participation[52] of transnational actors in both the public and closed discussions allows for counterarguments on the scope of the right. It is less likely that an expert body alone would publicly argue for the need of a new human rights interpretation. Civil society actors are usually included in these discussions and can hereby shape the scope of the debate. This in turn gives the expert body a litigating function between demands from human rights advocates and governments, which are needed for the legitimacy of the outcome decision.

3.8 CONCLUSIONS

The multitude of state, state-empowered, and non-state actors that together entangle the international legal order, together with numerous processes and objects of law stand as crucial guideposts on the path to creating international law. TLCs differ from other collective transnational actors with regard to their purpose, membership size, and targeted decision-maker. It's particularly this latter aspect – that TLCs target not governments, but expert committees – that distinguishes them from most of the theoretical assumptions on transnational networks, communities, and coalitions (Carpenter et al. 2014; Keck and Sikkink 1998; Mitchell and Schmitz 2014). Acknowledging the increasing role that expert bodies play in the monitoring of international law and that

[51] It is thus insufficient to receive reports on human rights violations or shortcomings of compliance in some countries. For a reliable and universal implementation of treaty interpretations by member states, it is necessary that these adopted standards present global consensus. Only then, the expert body can legitimize its lawmaking activities and expect the states to implement the decision.

[52] Participation is, however, more than formal access rights and includes motivational aspects of participation. Even if actors have opportunities to access the process, it does not mean that they will participate in every process. Also, if they are formally denied access to decision-making, they could still participate informally. I understand participation based on the scope, which includes two dimensions: the transnational actor demonstrates *willingness* to participate in the lawmaking process and is *invited* to do so by either formal or informal invitation. Willingness can be demonstrated by the transnational actor's activity prior to the process, for example, a focus on agenda-setting strategies and instruments, which call for a necessity of new international laws toward states and/or the international organization. This demonstration of willingness can target the institutions directly and indirectly in formal and informal ways. The actor may also indicate his or her willingness once the initiation of a lawmaking process has already been announced.

their decisions can become authoritative sources in the development of international law, TLCs offer a lens through which we are able to analyze and explain how and by whom these sources were drafted – and ultimately to explain how change in international law happens.

In the next chapters, I turn to the empirical level, applying the novel nomenclature of *TLCs* to CESCR'S General Comment No. 15's drafting process. This in-depth study of how water became a human right through treaty interpretation illuminates the relationships of a specific expert body in human rights with other actors, the ways different actors contest new human rights norms, and how these obstacles were overcome by the TLC.

4

How Water Became a Human Right

In November 2002, the United Nations Committee on Economic, Social and Cultural Rights adopted a General Comment on the Right to Water. (. . .) This General Comment may be of some surprise. The word "water" does not appear in the Covenant. (Langford 2005: 275)

With its November 2002 adoption, General Comment (GC) No. 15 on the Right to Water of the ICESCR provided an authoritative base upon which states could better implement their obligations and individuals and communities could more effectively advocate for the fulfillment of their right to water – and, in doing so, closed a significant gap in human rights law (Bulto 2011; Dellapenna and Gupta 2008). Not some twenty years ago, this seemingly basic right stood non-enshrined within UN legalese as a right for everyone.[1] Today, uplifted by the legal framework of GC No. 15's substantive and procedural standards, the right to water enjoys significant attention in the realm of global policy and regulation, as governments, international organizations, civil society, and the private sector cooperate at all levels to provide better water infrastructure and management.[2]

[1] There was a right to an adequate standard of living, which included food, housing, and even clothing in the ICESCR (Article 11), but no reference to water in ICESCR. CEDAW and CRC include mention of water but limited to vulnerable groups like rural women or as a necessity for the realization of children's health.

[2] The right to water entitles everyone to have access to sufficient, safe, acceptable, physically accessible, and affordable water for personal and domestic use. This access is key to human life and health, and its scarcity or poor quality negatively impacts the security of our food, our residence choices, and educational opportunities. Ensuring access to clean water is included in the Sustainable Development Goals (Goal No. 6) and therefore presents a global policy priority for states to achieve universally by 2030. For excellent scholarship on the legal and policy significance of a right to water beyond the GC15, see Baer 2017b; Langford and Russell 2017; Thielbörger 2013; Winkler 2012.

This uptake, however, was no simple act of diffusion, a right defined and then unequivocally advocated for by all stakeholders. Indeed, hence Langford's quote above, GC No. 15's adoption was met with certain surprise, as, to that point, human rights treaty bodies had no formal authority to create norms through their interpretations – their purview, defined by states themselves, lay only in interpreting norms *already explicit* within a treaty (see Chapter 2). Debates thus followed, both within the UN and among legal scholars, that broadly focused on a treaty's body existential role and legal weight: did the CESCR overstep its mandate with GC No. 15? Does GC No. 15 have, or should it even have, any legal significance at all? While such discussions were undoubtedly important in assessing treaty bodies and their pronouncements as sources of international law, they overlooked certain more urgent questions that have significant implications for our present day understanding of the human rights treaty regime: How did the CESCR even *manage* to make water a human right? Who were the drivers for this precedent case of progressive treaty interpretation? Was there contestation along the process and by whom? What can we learn from the drafting process for other attempts of human rights norm creation?

These questions frame our empirical entry point into the TLC in practice. Together, they base an investigation into GC No. 15's drafting process that, in ultimately revealing the TLC as its driving force, will tangibly bespeak a TLC's role and saliency in expert body lawmaking – in sum, an investigation that will give empirical flesh to the theoretical expectations outlined in the previous chapter. This investigation takes the form of narrative reconstruction: that is, this chapter draws on novel data sources from interviews and background talks (see Appendix D) and archival research to reconstruct General Comment No. 15's drafting process – *telling* the story of how water became a human right – to ultimately unearth the TLC and the various aspects of its lawmaking agency in a specific case. To this aim, the chapter proceeds as follows: Based on Chapter 2's argument about the authoritativeness of general comments in international law, I describe why I selected this case for an in-depth study of TLCs. As this is justified also with regard to its importance for the development of international law, I then assess the impact of General Comment No. 15 on international, regional, and domestic legislation and policies, which indirectly mark the involved TLC's influence on international law through this particular treaty interpretation. I turn after to debates into why this gap in human rights law existed at all and outline which initiatives preceded the

CESCR's drafting process. Through this overview, I will illustrate that the pre-environment of General Comment No. 15, in which the human right to water was established on the international agenda, was a crucial precursor to the ultimate success of the TLC operative in this case. Finally, the chapter proceeds to scholarship's first documentation of the drafting process of this General Comment on the right to water, making visible the actors and dynamics behind its creation, and, hence, the TLC.

4.1 CASE SELECTION

I selected the CESCR as the foundation for my empirical study of TLCs for the opportunity structure the committee provides for producing – and involving others in the drafting of – a general comment (see also Appendix C). This opportunity structure, for one, stems from the ICESCR's certain vagueness: As the treaty codifies multiple human rights as enshrined in the UDHR as rather broad and indeterminate norms (Alston 1987), it shows a need for further interpretation and, thus, for production of a GC. For another, the treaty body is composed of 18 experts, all with different professions and specialized knowledge on economic and social rights, for example, on matters related to education, or work, or food and hunger, living or health. The breadth of the ICESCR's norms, both in number and in substance, together with the CESCR experts' diverse perspectives on economic and social rights, creates a situation where – so goes the opportunity structure – the demand for external resources, especially technical expertise on the topic of the draft, in interpretation is high, a precondition for the study of TLCs (see also Table 5.1). Of all GCs adopted by CESCR, this particular case provides sufficient empirical evidence to further refine the TLC concept and arrive at hypotheses that more broadly explain TLC influence and effectiveness across the treaty body system. Given that this evidence is not only recognized by observation but demands case-specific knowledge, it is wise to choose a case that is well documented and where data is accessible. Here again the case proves satisfactory, as the impact of the GC No. 15 and the long-standing advocacy efforts preceding it present the ideal conditions for data collection. Furthermore, it is widely discussed in scholarship and remains "a favorite subject of academic controversy" (Bulto 2011: 3).

4.2 GC15'S IMPACT

As this book's intro prefaces, GC No. 15 has been mapped unequivocally at the level of substance: unmistakable is the far-reaching effect it has had on academia, politics, and law. In academia, GC No. 15's interpretation spurred heated discourse on the practice of dynamic treaty interpretation among legal scholars, who viciously debated[3] whether the CESCR had overstepped its mandate to interpret the ICESCR's norms by ostensibly penning within it an entirely new norm. This existential tension motivated further questions regarding authority, and soon the debate coalesced around whether the treaty bodies even *possess* the authority to create new law. Hereafter, scholarly opinions ranged from appraisal of the CESCR's legal reasoning to criticism that the treaty bodies were putting the credibility of the general comments at risk. While it can be argued from an academic perspective that the creation of new rights through interpretation is in line with provisions for treaty interpretation, the practice remains a matter of contestation. A General Assembly resolution in 2014, for instance, demanded that treaty bodies consult with state parties when drafting general comments. In return, the Chairpersons of the treaty bodies emphasized that they possessed the authority to agree on and apply their own rules of procedure for the development of general comments.[4]

In terms of its impact on international law, GC No. 15 undergirds a number of recent substantive water-centric legislation. To wit, in 2010, the General Assembly adopted resolution 64/292, whose title alone – "The human right to water and sanitation" – speaks to the central basis upon which it stands: GC No. 15. With this resolution, the human right to water was consequently recognized by 122 governments, recognition that responded to the aforementioned debates in affirming the treaty body's authority in the development of human rights norms (Chapter 2). Furthermore, the omission of a right to sanitation in the GC mobilized its supporters among governments, specialized agencies, and civil society, and the resolution finally acknowledged sanitation as a human right (Baer 2017a; Langford, Bartram, and Roaf 2017). In further attestation, the intergovernmental Human Rights Council consensually adopted, in April 2011, a resolution affirming the decision of the General Assembly to acknowledge a human right to water and sanitation. Other treaty bodies have subsequently adopted general comments that reference the human right to water, and treaties adopted after GC No. 15 have included

3 Three years after the adoption, this debate took place in the *Netherlands Quarterly of Human Rights*, wherein one scholar accused the other of "assault" with "Macbethian overleaping ambition" in his critique of General Comment No. 15 (Langford 2006: 458; Tully 2005a.).

4 Report of the Twenty-seventh meeting of chairpersons of the human rights treaty bodies in San José, June 22–26, 2015; in response to GA Res. 68/268, para. 14. Other general comments have substantially developed human rights law as well, for example, General Recommendation No. 19/CEDAW, for instance, has been referred to as "historic" because it framed violence against women as a form of gender-based discrimination in 1992.

the human right to water in their text.[5] The UN's work in global development has also promoted "water and sanitation" in explicit ways – for one, as a target of both the Millennium and the Sustainable Development Goals.

Regarding domestic law and policy, GC No. 15 has had a similarly weighty impact. More than fifty[6] countries now affirm the right to water in their domestic laws, and courts regularly refer to the GC No. 15 when rendering relevant decisions (Brunner et al. 2015). The reframing of water as a basic human need and a right gave leverage to NGO initiatives pressuring local and national governments to adopt policies that provide sufficient, safe, acceptable, physically accessible, and affordable water for personal and domestic use.[7] The GC facilitated the water-related work of human rights, environmental, and development NGOs, and many stakeholders later emphasized its importance for the development of monitoring mechanisms.[8] In terms of effects on human rights law, policies, and advocacy, GC No. 15 has been impactful at different levels; especially in the case of other general comments, it has served as a powerful precedent and tool for treaty interpretation, human rights standard–setting and norm clarification.[9]

Of indisputable visibility to international relations and law scholars, these richly compelling impacts largely frame existing discourse on GC No. 15 itself. As such, certain avenues of research have yet to be pursued. For one, and hence the empirical work to follow in this chapter, little attention has been given to the drafting process and actors that engendered GC No. 15: its origin, its specific language, and its ultimate adoption. The analysis of this information is essential to understand both how norms become rights and, more to this book's purpose, how TLCs collaborate in a general comment's drafting. Here, a process tracing approach proves especially utilitarian.[10]

Accordingly, in conceiving such an approach applicative to GC No. 15, I synthesized a "prototypical drafting process" framework (see Appendix C) that enabled a series of empirical questions, whose constellation expressed,

5 E.g., CRPD Article 28.

6 WaterLex Database (until 2020 here www.waterlex.org now http://humanright2water.org/country-legal-mapping/).

7 UN-Water Decade Programme, www.un.org/waterforlifedecade/unwdpac.shtml.

8 See, for example, the "Manual on the Right to Water and Sanitation. A Tool to Assist Policy Makers and Practitioners Develop Strategies for Implementing the Human Right to Water and Sanitation" published by COHRE 2008.

9 For an overview of other progressive and innovative general comments, see McCall-Smith 2016.

10 For the specifics of the method process tracing see, for example, the following works: Beach and Pedersen 2013; Collier 2011; Ricks and Liu 2018. Please refer also to Appendix C for the analytical framework of this chapter's analysis.

and thus provided pathways to answer, gaps in our existing narrative understanding of GC No. 15's drafting. What follows is my synthesis of those process-traced answers, cast as a linear narrative that, in detailing exactly how GC No. 15 came to pass, weaves a single story of TLC lawmaking.

4.3 A PROCESS-TRACED NARRATIVE OF HOW WATER BECAME A HUMAN RIGHT

4.3.1 *Political and Social Challenges, Legal Entrepreneurs, and Transnational Meetings: Water Enters the International Human Rights Agenda*

As Chapter 3 outlined, three conditions are necessary for a TLC's emergence and subsequent collaboration. The first speaks to the coalitions' originating impetus, whereby they form in contexts, and around those issues, where political and social developments challenge the meaning of a law globally and over time. The second concerns the certain contribution of a legal entrepreneur, who facilitates the drafting process and provides resources through time, input, and by involving other experts. The third can be found in transnational meetings and conferences, which provide points of exchange.

From the perspective of human rights, the fear behind the first condition is that such political and social challenges will destabilize the meaning of human rights, to the extent that the norms become misinterpreted or ignored. Needless to say, however, is that neither every new nor modified political and social reality requires that international law be adjusted accordingly. Rather, for change in international law to become manifest, these challenges must affect the norm's substance with a potentially long-lasting effect. The key entity for detecting these kinds of challenges are transnational advocacy networks (Keck and Sikkink 1998), who are knowledgeable about local implementation problems and domestic contexts, are familiar with governments' justifications for not adapting their behavior and can quickly share information with actors in other countries and activate network members to set the issue onto the agenda of international organizations.

As agenda-setting usually precedes decision-making, this section will preface its empirical narrative of GC No. 15's drafting process (see Appendix C for a timeline) by addressing the following question: How did water enter the international human rights agenda? The fact that a right to water was not included in any of the international human rights treaties was and is puzzling for human rights scholars and practitioners alike. Many background talks with treaty body members and staff at OHCHR confirmed that the CESCR in the early 2000s shared the "startling" view (Craven 2006: 39) about the lack of a human right to water in the covenant (see also: Riedel 2006).

For the human rights community, it became "disquieting that a right so basic and fundamental for bare human survival had not been given explicit expression in the major UN human rights treaties" (Bulto 2011: 2). Rather unconvincingly, one position puts it down to a lack of foresight that water could become a scarce resource through drought or pollution. However, long before 2002, numerous events in the field of development and environment had already confirmed an international acceptance of the basic global need for access to clean drinking water. In 1977, the same year the ICESCR entered into force, the UN Water Conference produced the *Mar del Plata Declaration*, which, in its explicit reference to the right to drinking water,[11] provided first steps for the right's eventual codification into an international norm. NGOs thereafter took up the cause of agenda-setting, mainly focused on development-related aspects of water. While the developed world took clean water as a matter of course, more than one billion people in the Global South lacked access to this resource. This was regarded as "one of the most fundamental failures of 20th century development" (Gleick 1998). Development cooperation NGOs demonstrated how their work in health, agriculture, and nutrition was hindered or even at risk of becoming nullified by a lack of access to water. These NGOs' facilitated calls for state action on the international level. Other international conferences followed, like the *UN Conference on Environment and Development* in Rio in 1992 and *Habitat II* in Istanbul in 1996, which crystallized consensus regarding the centrality of global access to drinking water and extended the scope of a potential right to water to include water for sanitation.

These multilateral events and meetings facilitated the establishment of transnational advocacy networks in the 1980s and 1990s, comprising actors from civil society, who organized to advocate for water issues in the field of sustainable development. Despite their efforts, the human right to water remained without acknowledgment by any organ of the UN into the millennium. The reasons for the standstill of the norm's development were complex, but a key factor lay in the shift of the development paradigm during the 1980s and 1990s, whereby "water for all" became no longer regarded as a public obligation only. Supported by bilateral development cooperation and the programs and policies of the World Bank and the International Monetary

11 "All peoples, whatever their stage of development and their social and economic conditions, have the right to have access to drinking water in quantities and of a quality to their basic needs" (United Nations 1977).

Fund (IMF), this new perspective saw visibility in the Dublin Principles – the codified result of a 1992 expert meeting regarding global water-related issues – in which water was deemed with economic value, something to be advocated for as a commodity. This emphasis on water's economic dimensions, rather than its status as a human right, spurred heated debates at the international level, propped by NGOs from different fields, who coalesced to advocate a dissenting angle (Reiners 2021). From a norm evolution and agenda-setting perspective, water as a human right emerged through the diffusion of the water-related problems by different collective and individual actors in international development, environment, and humanitarian affairs who hereby transformed water quality and scarcity problems into a problem-solving norm[12] – water as a human right.

Heading this network were primarily NGOs working in the field of humanitarian aid and in developing countries, though further support came from specialized agencies of the UN, like the WHO and FAO. Their activism targeted the water commodification policies of the World Bank and, more broadly, the argument around the efficiency of privatizing water supply (Bakker 2007; Goldman 2005; Simonson 2003). Public–private partnerships in this sector were of particular interest to companies, as risks remained with the government and profits were high. The TAN lobbying for a human right to water was concerned that water's scarcity in many of the world's regions would lead to an increase of its value that companies might capitalize on to demand new terms for their public–private partnerships; as such, the risk of cutting the water supply as a means of applying pressure was high. Furthermore, advocates for a human right to water were afraid that this basic need would be subject to affordability. The network of actors supporting a human right to water therefore spread the idea of water as a basic need instead of as a commodity – pressing, by way of awareness-raising, for water's acknowledgment as an international human right – in order to effectively advocate for water policies at the domestic and international levels (Nelson 2015; Nelson and Dorsey 2007, 2008).

However, their advocacy had to be channeled into strategy, and debates into options, of which there were several, ensued. Should a human right to water be codified in a new treaty or an optional protocol? Or, conversely, should it be declared in a resolution of one of the intergovernmental UN bodies? For NGOs experienced with the UN human rights system, these considerations resulted in the agreement that a human right to water would be best situated in connection to the ICESCR, which included explicit mention of two rights practically contiguous to the right to water: a right to food, and a right to the highest

12 For this model of norm emergence, see Rosert 2019.

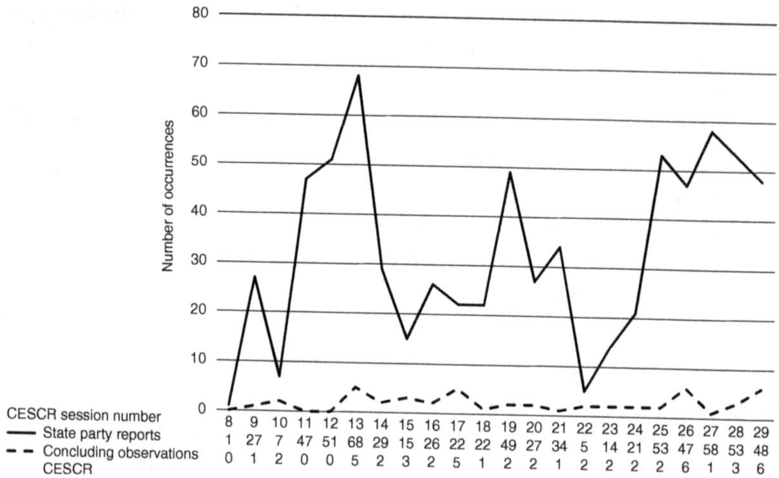

FIGURE 4.1 "Water" in CESCR sessions (1993–2002)

attainable standard of health. The operative logic herein sought to make use of the general comment, which, although an instrument to that point solely used to interpret a treaty's existing provisions, seemed a substantive pathway to codify, and ostensibly create, new obligations. When members of the network approached the committee and its members, the latter were generally open to the idea, but felt that the time was not yet right for such a bold venture (Riedel 2006).

As depicted in Figure 4.1, a content analysis of all state reports and the CESCR's concluding observations considered between 1993 and 2002 indicates that water had indeed been an issue related to the ICESCR even before it was interpreted as a right inherent to an adequate standard of living under article 11.[13] Ultimately, though, the figure also depicts that the treaty body did not integrate the states' concerns on water with the same intensity in their concluding observations.[14]

[13] For this purpose, all state party reports and concluding observations by the CESCR have been downloaded from the treaty body database (Search: Treaty Body "CESCR" / Document Type "State report" and "Concluding Observations," date "01/01/1993 – 31/12/2002") and coded for "water" and "eau" (as some documents are available in French only).

[14] The committee pointed, however, to this frequency as an incentive for the GC No. 15. It was justified as the consequence of the CESCR's consideration of state party reports, which to that point had "frequently commended, or expressed concern, as to steps taken with respect to water" E/C.12/2002/11 2003. An accompanying note cited specific numbers: "In 32 of 120 concluding observations issued between May 1993 (8th session) and November 2001 (27th session), the Committee commended, or expressed concern, as to steps taken with

The findings of this analysis of the sessions between 1993 and 2002 reveal that the issue of water was addressed by states in their reports to the treaty body before GC No. 15 was drafted. States here acknowledged the connection between water and human rights by including water policies and issues in their report addressed to the CESCR, which itself can be seen as indirect confirmation of the treaty body's competency to deal with all issues connected to water.[15]

Empowered with a window of opportunity in the realm of popular opinion – and with transnational meetings like the World Summit on Sustainable Development in 2002 and the Third World Water Forum in 2003 sitting on the horizon – the ICESCR then mobilized to draft GC No. 15, giving water its first explicitly substantive status within the human rights agenda. Water thus entered the human rights agenda thanks to decades of advocacy work of development, environment, and humanitarian actors.

4.4 THE EMERGENCE OF A TLC: "HAD BEEN ASKED TO CONSIDER THE ISSUE"

When GC No. 15 was adopted, the drafting process was recapped as follows in an opaquely insightful statement by the rapporteur Eibe Riedel: "In 2001, the Committee had been asked to consider [the human rights dimension of water] in preparation for the International Year of Freshwater in 2003 and the World Water Forum that would be held in Japan in March 2003" (E/C.12/2002/SR.50 2002). While scarcely revealing, these comments do imply that the issue had been brought through external means to the attention of the treaty body. Upon the initiative of COHRE, a now-defunct NGO (1994–2012) that played a seminal role in the legal development of economic and social rights, GC No. 15's drafting process began on two levels. On an informal level, COHRE's founder and director, Scott Leckie – an "international human rights pioneer," then-recognized as such by leading human rights scholars (Displacement Solutions 2016) – approached then-CESCR member Eibe Riedel in 2001 to broach production of a general comment on the right to water, to be ready

regard to water." These numbers were ultimately wrong, as Figure 4.1 depicts, and thus later absent from GC No. 15's final version. The citations nonetheless show that CESCR heeded the guidelines on drafting general comments as a response to the consideration of state reports.

15 The absence of sanctions or persuasive means to enforce human rights vis-à-vis states further supports the deference-based model of treaty body authority discussed in Chapter 2, as states nevertheless address CESCR with a right to water in their reports, although such a right did not exist at that time.

within a year. Both had prior professional experience – COHRE had already collaborated with Riedel and the CESCR on General Comment No. 12 on the right to food – and Mr. Leckie himself knew Mr. Riedel and the committee to be generally open toward his idea.[16] Through a more formal channel, Mr. Leckie wrote a similarly entreating letter, dated November 28, 2001, to the CESCR's Chairperson. Penning an official appeal from civil society, which the committee indeed considered, the content of this letter contoured Leckie's broaching of Riedel. In it, he welcomed the CESCR's initiative to develop a general comment on the right to water,[17] offered his support, and cited the same urgency he did to Riedel regarding an adoption timeframe (i.e., within the next year),[18] which would capitalize on the window of opportunity afforded by the soon-upcoming World Water Forum[19] and the UN Year of Freshwater in 2003.[20] One might here already attribute Leckie, a human rights lawyer with vast experience in drafting legal frameworks with UN bodies, as this case's TLC-facilitating legal entrepreneur, on grounds of his issue-raising initiative, which laid the initial groundwork for the TLC's eventual formation. But, as this story will later reveal, this role was ultimately laid to claim by another individual, a colleague, who was part of Leckie's own network at COHRE.

With the UN environment indeed ripe for such a right to water (see preceding section), Mr. Riedel realized a certain confluence of perfect timing to go ahead and initiate the drafting process as its rapporteur.[21] The impetus for

16 The committee and individual members had expressed at several formal and informal occasions that they saw a right to water as part of ICESCR (see also Figure 4.1).

17 Which, at that point, was not brought up in the public records of the committee.

18 "We, therefore, urge you to move forward the process of developing a General Comment on the right to water to ensure its adoption during 2002." Letter from COHRE to the CESCR/OHCHR, retrieved from the UN archives on November 4, 2015.

19 In attendance at the forum were a number of stakeholders there to gather information and engage in discourse. NGOs likewise organized a parallel forum and mobilized for the right to water (Simonson 2003: 8–12). It is very likely that paths crossed between treaty body members, OHCHR staff, and right-to-water advocates during one of the events prefacing the Kyoto forum, for example, a water meeting which took place in July 2001. This "first international civil society conference to respond to the commodification of freshwater resources" brought together "more than 800 people from 35 countries," Simonson 2003: 9.

20 The 2003 World Water Forum in Kyoto – a debatably successful meeting (see: Biswas 2004; Gleick and Lane 2005) that was, to date, "the largest … ever organised on water" (World Water Forum 2003: 5) – was framed as a salient trigger for the CESCR to begin moving on a draft and capitalize on a window of opportunity in international politics, marked, for one, by the UN's 2002 inclusion of access to safe drinking water as one of the eighteen targets of the Millennium Development Goals.

21 The rapporteur is one, sometimes two, committee members who are responsible for the drafting process of a general comments. Note that all info regarding general treaty body procedure for drafting GCs is consolidated in Appendix A, for your reference.

Riedel here was explained, by the involved actors and CESCR colleagues, on account of his willingness for the role and certain pressure from NGOs who were familiar with his work on other general comments.[22] Indeed, the rapporteur is not an elected position, but rather someone who takes the role via voluntary proposal – that is, as "someone [who] has interest and the time."[23] But his qualifications were also substantive. For one, Riedel was established, among colleagues and beyond, as a seminal contributor to the legalization of the ICESCR's norms. For another, since his election to the CESCR in 1997, the professionalization of the instrument of general comments, whose drafting he was already experienced in, had been given utmost prominence as part of his personal mandate; and with regard to GC No. 15, he felt a personal obligation to the issue.[24] For yet another, Riedel was part of the group that had developed an outline for the coherency of the CESCR's future general comments, four years earlier.[25] Further yet, he possessed legal expertise as an international law professor, which granted him the authority to trustfully lead his fellow committee members in the drafting process to follow. His autonomy was enhanced by the fact that the committee only meets biannually, and members only get a per diem for the sessions in Geneva. They serve in their individual capacity as independent experts and therefore work in their professions the rest of the year. The additional task of drafting a general comment is not covered in the schedule of the sessions and the per diems, and instead must be carried out without payment and meeting time (see Chapter 2). As such, the organization of the drafting process, and thus the initiation of coalition-building, was transferred from the collective to the individual level and outside of the inner UN-system (see Chapter 3). Hence, with Mr. Riedel's assumption of responsibility for the subsequent process, the committee left it to him to present a first draft. As an independent expert, he had to assume this

22 "[The rapporteur] was particularly keen on the right to water. He sort of claimed that – and I don't mean that in an inappropriate way. Someone has to go with one interest – and he was interested in this. He's been very instrumental in General Comment No. 14, where he's been able to ensure some consistent analytical approach" – interview with a former CESCR member.

23 Interview with a treaty body member.

24 See his scholarly work on the drafting process: Riedel 2006.

25 "At its twenty-first session, the Committee adopted the outline for drafting general comments on specific rights of the Covenant. (. . .) The Committee emphasized the importance of ensuring that general comments are reader-friendly and readily understandable to a broad range of readers, primarily States parties to the Covenant. The outline will assist in ensuring consistency and clarity in the structure of the general comments, thus promoting their accessibility, and strengthening the authoritative interpretation of the Covenant provided by the Committee through its general comments." E/C.12/2002/SR.28 2002: 21f.

responsibility on top of numerous professional obligations,[26] facilitating the formation of a TLC.

4.5 PREPARING A FIRST DRAFT

In the case of GC No. 15, the resources Riedel needed were expertise on the ICESCR's particularities – for one, Article 11 on an adequate standard of living and Article 12 on the right to health – and in-depth knowledge about water and its relationship with economic, social, and cultural human rights. For Mr. Riedel, configuring those resources was what constituted the next step: consultation with known experts from civil society, understood here primarily as "personally known," reflecting the collegiality that characterizes a TLC's manner of work. In this instance, Riedel turned to individuals with whom he shared work experience within his capacities as a treaty body member and professor on account of his collaborative work with their NGOs on previous general comments. One was Leckie, and the other Michael Windfuhr, the UN representative of the Food First Information and Action Network (FIAN), who worked with Riedel on the General Comment 12 on the right to food and was thus known to the committee and present in Geneva. This selection of inputters was at this stage solely the decision of Mr. Riedel. From here, Mr. Leckie directed assumption of his role to his colleague, Malcolm Langford, as he himself was already involved in other projects. The representative from FIAN, similarly busy with other projects and thus unable to assume responsibility for the drafting process, only engaged with the group from time to time.

In a next stage, sometime between the end of 2001 (the time of Leckie's letter) and July 29, 2002 – the first date attributed in an official document to any GC No. 15 draft[27] – Riedel and Mr. Langford jointly discussed several draft

[26] His CV, at the time of interest here (2001/2002), not only lists his CESCR membership but also that he was simultaneously a Full Professor for German and Comparative Public Law, European and International Law at the University of Mannheim (until 2001 also the Pro-Vice Chancellor), he was Director of Studies for International Law and examiner for the German Foreign Office in Bonn/Berlin.

[27] The following text – "The Chairperson invited [the] Rapporteur on the right to water, to introduce draft General Comment No. 15 on the right to water and explain the changes that had been made in the version of 29 *July* 2002 [italics mine]" (E/C.12/2002/13 2003) – marks the first surfacing of any draft and according time stamp to GC No. 15. This July 29, 2002 version, hereafter referred to as the "first draft," remains a subject of mystery, going unmentioned among sessions preceding the final draft's adoption, and the summary records. From a formal-facing front, the only thing clear was – hence the quote – that it heavily informed a later iteration presented in November 2002. See also Appendix C for the questions guiding my data collection to reconstruct the drafting process of this first draft.

versions,[28] which they prepared based on topical discussions regarding the scope of the right to water. Interviews with treaty body members, representatives from other international organizations, and civil society actors who were affiliated with the right to water all identified Mr. Langford here with the leading role.[29] While his COHRE colleague Mr. Leckie appealed to CESCR to start the drafting process – an idea Eibe Riedel, in his capacities as a law professor and CESCR member, furthered among his treaty body colleagues – Mr. Langford, in serving as the draft's principal orchestrator, ultimately played the role of the process's legal entrepreneur. To facilitate this drafting, Scott Leckie expanded the threads of the TLC in seeking out a secondary outside collaborator – Virginia Roaf, herself an expert on water and land issues, of recent employ at a development aid organization specialized on water issues, and notably with *no* prior experience in human rights work.[30] She was approached by Mr. Leckie while discussing another project of her NGO,[31] who took this opportunity to invite her to contribute to GC No. 15's drafting process – a revealing instance of TLC dynamics and, particularly, the initiative with which its members engage at the behest of the official decision-makers, namely, the treaty body. To round out the coalition's core members, the WHO's representative Jamie Bartram was included, who was then amid drafting of a WHO booklet[32] on a right to water and sanitation with regard to the Millennium Development Goals and thus could further speak to the issues at hand.

As stated above, in its approach to crafting a general comment, the Langford-led TLC decided on different drafts for further consideration: To

28 "We went through several rolling drafts, as I remember [, taking] two or three." Interview with an NGO professional.

29 For example, a WHO representative recalled: "The principal protagonists were the NGOs. The person who got the politics around the general comment in particular was Langford." An NGO professional involved in the drafting added: "Langford was the main drafter and we commented. (...). It was quite a small group. It did expand obviously, but he was the main drafter."

30 "He just said: 'But don't you want to write a general comment with us on the right to water?' And I said: 'What is that?' – You know I'm not from a human rights background, I've had no experience of human rights at all in development work," interview in September 2015.

31 "I was working at WaterAid in London (...). My experience was land, land as a particular problem for access to water in formal settlements. (...) I contacted Scott Leckie of COHRE because I met him previously and I thought he would be up to help me think through some of the issues"; interview in September 2015.

32 As a result, this booklet was finalized after the drafting process and published with a wider scope of rights but referring to General Comment No. 15 as the basis. This mutual reinforcement of institutions and individuals (OHCHR and WHO; WHO and NGOs; OHCHR and individual, WHO and individual) continued after the drafting process and the members of the TLC all ended up in the acknowledgments of a WHO booklet in 2003 (WHO 2003: 40).

consolidate these into a first draft, and work through key subjects and issues, the coalition sans Riedel met several times in the Geneva offices of COHRE. It was not possible to retrieve these rolling drafts,[33] not all of which were written in the form of a general comment. Mr. Riedel initially received those "rolling drafts" and forwarded them to Mr. Langford with his comments. Upon Riedel's authorization, the document ultimately cohered from their input and the COHRE-based meetings became the official first draft of July 29, 2002.

To this point in GC15's drafting process, the role of the treaty body has shown itself to be less central than expected, with the draft's facilitation carried out more or less autonomously, often even without the presence of Mr. Riedel. This only further underlines the key role the legal entrepreneur occupies within the TLC. Although the CESCR through Mr. Riedel's status as rapporteur was designated with chief responsibility for the draft, the drafting process itself appears mostly a coordinated effort of Mr. Langford, who predetermined (1) invitees to the draft meeting at COHRE's premises, (2) which feedback was directed to the rapporteur, and (3) which points advanced in draft discussions ultimately held merit. This previous experience of COHRE with the CESCR undoubtedly fostered the high degree of autonomy with which Langford was able to operate within the drafting process – an autonomy COHRE's director Leckie later, in his public CV, lauded in reference.[34] In any case, the special relationship between him and the rapporteur Mr. Riedel was implicated and made explicit in several interviews, demonstrating again how TLCs operate in large part through the interpersonal relationships among its members, which makes it hard for less-personally acquainted external actors to insert themselves substantively into the drafting process.[35]

[33] One TLC member explained that with the analogue nature of the process in 2002: "And it was before we had the easy access of sharing files we have now. I mean we didn´t have Dropbox and you know I´ve got lots of the drafts and the handwritten comments (…). So there was more face to face probably then we would have now." This testament to the changing nature of transnational advocacy in the face of digitalization (Hall, Schmitz, and Dedmon 2020) adds further to the book's argument that transnational coalitions do not operate solely within the boundaries of IOs.

[34] In which Scott Leckie stated he himself "*drafted and instigated* [italics mine] the (…) General Comment No. 15 on the Right to Water (2002), General Comment No. 7 on Forced Evictions (1997) and General Comment No. 4 on the Right to Adequate Housing (1991)." This account reads not only self-confidently, but also raises – in its claim of leadership in the crafting of these general comments – questions on the instrument's very legitimacy, given his lack of formal association both within the UN system and the represented state parties. See Chapter 3, fn 27.

[35] It was taken as a matter, of course, that an individual officer from an admittedly small NGO was in charge of the coordination of the drafting process of such a key document. One NGO

Both individuals, Mr. Riedel and Mr. Langford, benefited from the collaboration on the draft, individually and as members of a professional community now with a much-needed framework to facilitate their work on the right to water. Given the tight window for adoption, it was likely the case that the TLC held little interest in receiving a score of diverse feedback as they worked – hence the insular behind-the-scenes meetings at COHRE, involving only a small few, and the lack of public events during the sessions or outside the UN prior to the adoption session (see below). Speaking further to this disinterest for feedback comes directly from a TLC member, who expressed their sense of role as being purely "technical" for the drafting process and their involvement generally as only a result of the legal entrepreneur's explicit interest to invite other individuals to provide input.[36] Assumedly, draft revisions were inputted under Mr. Langford and Mr. Riedel's sole purview, whereby the latter gave explicit consideration to the applicability of the GC No. 15. Simultaneously, Mr. Langford's drafting lens appeared particularly colored by his NGO affiliation, an entity with previous history in the creation of convincing general comments. Indeed Mr. Langford himself, as a legal expert well familiar with both domestic court decisions on water issues and fundamental human rights, took an economic and social rights advocacy perspective and included wide-ranging standards in his draft versions.

4.6 DISCUSSING AND REVISING THE DRAFT

Once rendered in paper, the draft was circulated, at Mr. Riedel's discretion and by the secretariat of the CESCR, among selected UN agencies and academics, who were solicited for their feedback. As the date for adoption was envisaged for November, therefore extremely soon, it was a tactical decision to keep the draft non-public and make no open call for statements. For one, given the urgency for adoption before 2003, it would not have been possible to wait for statements and to then consider them. For another, as the issue saw contestation among stakeholders – on, for example, the right to water's scope and the obligations of states when water provision infrastructure

professional had no objections in describing that a draft was already "prepared by Eibe and Malcolm. I was one of a small number of NGO experts who then worked with the both of them." A representative from an international organization recalled in an interview how he needed Mr. Langford to meet the rapporteur Riedel, describing Langford a gatekeeper to the treaty body (for the different roles of individuals in NGOs, and gatekeepers in particular, see Schneiker and Joachim 2020).

36 "We [the other civil society actors] were just technical. Helping them [Mr. Langford and Mr. Riedel] with the technicalities." Interview with an NGO officer.

is privatized – a public call would have sparked inundating sticking point discussions on the side of states and legal scholars, which their reactions post-adoption made clear.[37]

Draft revisions are likely not borne from a particular revealing event – for example, a formal day of discussion during a session, or more informal events outside the UN in which contrasting positions debate the draft's content – but rather reflect the sediment of direct-to-rapporteur input from actors pre-selected to comment on the draft. Nevertheless, interviews reveal that a single meeting *did* take place in Geneva after circulation of the comment's first draft, held in one of COHRE's offices for only a select few of the TLC's members, plus additional resource persons.[38] Some interviewees distilled the makeup of the resource participants further, stating this help included civil society actors and an expert from WHO. One TLC member said that she had not even met the rapporteur before this meeting shortly before the adoption of GC15.[39] To parse the draft's content in person, the solicited experts, along with relevant stakeholders, were invited to participate in a day of general discussion, contained within the CESCR's 29th Session on November 22, 2002. This day was split in two parts: one public meeting, organized for the stakeholders,[40] and one non-public in the afternoon that catered to the more critical voices.

The chairperson of CESCR opened this discussion by clarifying the committee's impetus to draft a general comment as a matter of significant topicality: highlighted by the upcoming International Year of Fresh Water and the March 2003 World Water Forum in Kyoto, she opined, "water had probably

37 Several states issued statements denying the existence of such a right altogether; for example, the United States openly criticized the CESCR for this general comment in a view submitted to OHCHR in June 2007: "The United States does not share the view that a 'right to water' (. . .) exists under international human rights law." This is a remarkable intervention given that the United States is only a signatory state to ICESCR, but to date has never ratified it. Thus, the general comment does not apply to them anyway. For scholarly critiques on the GC15 and a human right to water see Baer 2017a; Brunner et al. 2015; Clark 2017; Langford and Russell 2017; Tiboris 2019; Tully 2005b.

38 "We had one meeting which must have been six, you know, seven or eight people. I remember in the COHRE offices." Interview with an NGO officer.

39 "I mean Malcolm [the legal officer] would have had very direct contact with [Eibe Riedel]. I'm trying to think whether I've even met him [Eibe Riedel] before." Interview with an NGO officer.

40 "At its 46th and 47th meetings (twenty-ninth session), held on 22 November 2002, the Committee considered, under agenda item 3, a draft General Comment on the right to water. In addition to the members of the Committee, representatives of the United Nations specialized agencies, non-governmental organizations and individual experts actively participated in the discussion of the draft. (. . .) The Committee expressed its great appreciation to those experts who provided comments on the draft general comment both before the session in writing and orally in the course of its discussion" (E/C.12/2002/13 2003).

become the most important issue of the day ... [, something which] the Committee had a compelling reason to discuss"[41] – a statement that reflects the initial urging of the chairperson advanced by the founder and director of COHRE in his 2001 letter. Thereafter came statements by the aforementioned participants, who, in advancing their perspective, directly responded to points of concern raised by the rapporteur, Mr. Riedel.[42]

The participants who spoke during the public meeting on the day of general discussion represented all relevant stakeholders, of whom Japan, as host of the upcoming 2003 World Water Forum, was the only state party.[43] The WHO and World Bank represented the international organizations, and the UN comments were delivered by the respective United Nations Sub-Commission on Promotion and Protection of Human Rights Special Rapporteurs on the right to water, the right to housing, and the right to food. The private business sector was represented by the Senior Water Advisor of SUEZ, and academia was represented by the Indian Institution of Public Health Engineers. Mr. Langford and Audrey Chapman[44] from the AAAS allegedly provided input to the discussion as representatives of civil society.[45] There were other

41 E/C.12/2002/SR.46 2002: para 2.

42 "The question was whether a minimalist approach should be taken that focused solely on drinking water or whether the issue was inseparably linked to sanitation, household and agricultural use and its impact on the realization of human rights. From the outset, it had been clear that the Committee's emphasis was not on water allocation, but on the effects of strategies, legislation and practices on human rights." E/C.12/2002/SR.46 2002: para 2.

43 Given that the human right to water and sanitation was highly contested among state parties on various dimensions, it is a surprise to see that not more states made use of their formal opportunity to give a statement on the draft general comment. Either states underestimated the potential impact of such a general comment at that time or they did not see any necessity to take a position on it because of their non-binding nature.

44 "Ms. CHAPMAN (American Association for the Advancement of Science (AAAS)) said that AAAS was a large and multidisciplinary NGO that had no links with the United States Government and operated at the international level. In October 2002, it had invited various human rights and environmental NGOs to participate in an informal consultation in Washington to discuss and offer suggestions on the draft general comment. The participants had reached a general consensus that the scope of the right to water should be extended beyond the right to drinking water to encompass other personal and household uses of water, including water for cooking, bathing and sanitation, which would, of course, subsequently entail changing its designation from the right to drinking water. It had also been agreed that the draft general comment did not pay sufficient attention to sanitation." E/C.12/2002/SR.46 2002: para. 32.

45 This input, however, might have entered the summary records for different reasons. My research could not find any evidence on the content of Ms. Chapman's input. The time frame from the meeting in Washington to her presenting input would have been remarkably narrow: the NGO meeting was said to take place on October 30, and the CESCR session in Geneva began a week later. Audrey Chapman in 2006 left the AAAS for work in academia and does not recall such a meeting (information based on e-mail exchange in 2015), a surprising

invitees, not all of whom attended. One, a scholar solicited for input on October 6, 2002, by the treaty body's secretariat but unable to attend this day of discussion, provided comments by e-mail. These comments included no novel points but contoured aspects of the draft. Nevertheless, the inclusion of the scholar in GC No. 15's acknowledgments ensured greater credibility for the document – suggesting that it was more the name, rather than the content, which was sought after. This is further supported by other acknowledgments of other well-known academics in the footnotes of the final draft; unclear, however, is whether or not they provided additional input to the drafting process. A general search for the biographies of all such individuals – honored "for their valuable and long-standing cooperation with the Committee and contribution to the drafting of the general comment" – reveals all were experts in the field of water, had previous work experience with the UN and/or the CESCR, and, in large part, cull from the rapporteur Mr. Riedel's epistemic community.[46]

Overall, all present agreed on the necessity of a general comment focused on a human right to water, and generally perceived the right's absence of explicit mention in the ICESCR as unproblematic, given the right's tacit interrelation with, and therefore sublimation within, the rights to health and food. In a further fleshing of discourse, the World Bank representative "agreed that water must be considered a public good,"[47] but emphasized that, as a good, water is simultaneously a commodity that requires a delivery structure. Hence, the responsibilities of the private sector were obviously connected to

answer, given her tangible involvement in the general comment's public discourse. Even more confounding, further interviewees identified as involved in the drafting process similarly reported no memory of this Washington meeting. Ms. Chapman explains the NGO connection to the right to water as follows: "Subsequent to the adoption of the general comment on the right to water, [we] sponsored a project on developing a manual to monitor the right to water. We had several meetings in conjunction with that project" (quoted from the e-mail exchange). In sum, given her lack of recollection alongside zero involvement by treaty body members and civil society actors, the tacit assumption here is that this meeting in Washington had no connection whatsoever to the drafting process of GC No. 15. That it is mentioned in the summary records of the UN raises additional questions: Who authored the report's quote? Why was this information not verified? More broadly, what was this statement's rationale: who was it intended to benefit, and in what ways? These fascinating questions, whose answers are not yet available, reiterate the saliency of this book's directive: that beneath the surface of formal rules, processes, and actors of IOs is where the scholarly meat is with regard to prying open processes of decision-making.

46 In his publications on the right to water, he also presents the work of two such colleagues as taking a similar view as the committee. Making references to scholars as resource persons in a decisively nonpolitical document assembles knowledge perceived as objective, highlighting it as an object of expertise able to "speak truth to power" (Haas 2004).

47 E/C.12/2002/SR.46 2002: para 59.

a right to water, but in his view a "human rights-based approach offered a unique opportunity to societies needing protection from [water's] commercialization."[48] Not every speaker seemed to be familiar with the draft general comment to the same extent.[49] Some gave very general input, while others proposed specific additions or modifications; Mr. Langford of COHRE, for instance, using the occasion and his status as main drafter, pushed strongly on a series of present omissions.[50] The Special Rapporteur of the Commission on Human Rights on the right to food sent written statements to the rapporteur and was pleased with the preliminary outcome.[51]

Following this public discussion was a closed afternoon meeting,[52] which centered on the substantive issues of ICESCR's implementation. The closed meeting, which gathered together CESCR members alongside representatives of civil society[53] and the WTO,[54] revealed hard-lined points of a disagreement on how to proceed. The closed meeting was attended by more civil society

48 Ibid.

49 A note here: unclear is whether this discussion was based on the first draft, or if a revised draft was circulated among the participants to frame discourse.

50 "However, as it stood, the draft general comment failed to address three important points: the scope of the right to water, sanitation and the role of local governments." E/C.12/2002/SR.46 2002: para 28.

51 He "expressed his appreciation to [the rapporteur] for his excellent work in preparing the draft general comment and to the other members of the Committee for their contribution. He was pleased to see that the empirical and theoretical comments he had submitted to [the rapporteur] had been taken into account." Ibid.: para 43.

52 Such meetings are usually reserved for debates among the treaty body members on concluding observations. In some cases, closed meetings are also held with other actors when the subject of the discussion requires confidentiality. Closed meetings are therefore not documented for external use.

53 The closed meeting was more a political discussion on a human right to water than a diplomatic exchange of opinions or a legal argument on the normative content of such a right.

54 The WTO, hence their presence at the *closed* meeting, appeared apprehensive toward strongly endorsing a right to water. To this point, the WTO at the time had been leveled with harsh criticism by civil society regarding the GATS (see, for example, GATSwatch.org and Alliance for Democracy), to the extent that they had even published a counter-responsive article titled: "GATS: Fact and Fiction. Misunderstandings and scare stories: The WTO is not after your water," World Trade Organization n.d.

The WTO had been invited to give a public statement at the CESCR's 29th Session, in supplement to their participation in discourse. But they declined officially: "with regard to the draft general comment on the right to water to be considered by the Committee on Friday 22 November, the WTO has no specific comment to make on this text" (Letter to CESCR found in the UN archives in November 2016) Given this context, it appears the WTO's reluctance could stem from one of three reasons: it was either a diplomatic move to avoid further criticism when presenting their position to the public; the result of possessing nothing of substance to add to the draft (acceptance); or just simply because they did not regard the

actors than the public one earlier this day. Overall, the main points of discussion debated were the inclusion of a right to sanitation, quality of drinking water, and the states' obligations in case water provision is privatized (for an overview: Langford, Bartram, and Roaf 2017; Riedel 2006; Salman and McInerney-Lankford 2004; Winkler 2012). With regard to the water-related problems of developing countries, due mention was advanced only by international organizations and civil society. As the only present state party on the speaker's list, Japan was contrastingly unaffected, already a follower of progressive water policies. Given minority attention, critical government voices were essentially dismissed and (seemingly) purposely excluded in the invitation to provide commentary. On the paper of the summary record, all stakeholders provided input within discussion, amalgamating to a strong criterion for process legitimacy.[55]

The closed meeting furthermore revealed the political roles assumed by some TLC members in the process. To be exact, some interviewees highlighted the fact that they were there only to give technical input than to serve a political role. This second meeting followed a different dynamic of representation and line of argument: no state party was present, but there were representatives from WTO and more civil society actors. In this meeting, the strong opposition from WTO (see fn. 54) was debated and civil society actors and committee members alike tried to advance counterarguments.

This day ended with an invitation-only dinner hosted by the Friedrich-Ebert-Foundation, bringing together the core drafting group, the rapporteur, other treaty body members, and civil society actors, some of whom met for the first time amid the drafting process. As this foundation archives their documents for only ten years, I could not obtain the full participant's list, but interviews with individuals who were present confirmed the general tenor of the informal meeting: that it was, in effect, a dinner discussion of the draft general comment.[56] The informal

draft, and the right it aimed to codify, as important to their work (ignorance). That, however, contradicts the general interest in the WTO's participation in the closed afternoon meeting.

55 In a caveat, however, the committee did not exhaust all means available to engender transparent and fair discourse. First, it did not publish the first draft on the website. Second, it did not openly call for comments on the draft or at least announced a general call for statements on a human right to water. Third, it did not discuss the draft in a paragraph to paragraph reading, which limited the statements of the participants to be of a more general nature.

56 The foundation traditionally has close ties to the committee and the norms of the ICESCR. They actively support and facilitate meetings with the committee members and civil society. As they have countries all over the world, the legalization of economic and social rights is described as their focus work in Geneva. On their website, it states that it "works in cooperation with Geneva based international organizations and their staff. Our partners include both non-state actors (NGO-activists, trade unionists, journalists, academics and parliamentarians)

meeting served less as a general discussion of the draft than as a constructive dialogue for the TLC on what to include, exclude, and how to justify changes. The substantive, and ultimate, revision of the draft took place immediately after, over the weekend at the COHRE offices. Again, the actors here were primarily the core drafting group, whose leading coordinator Mr. Langford – the legal entrepreneur – consulted simultaneously with the rapporteur who then presented the changes made to the first draft to the committee members and only minor changes were suggested, mainly centering around formalities, and not the content.

4.7 THE TLC'S SUCCESS: ADOPTING GENERAL COMMENT NO. 15

On the day of GC No. 15's adoption, during which the committee met in public, Mr. Riedel was asked to present the revisions of the July 29 draft. Per the chairperson's announcement, "members of the Committee would discuss any final changes in [the aforementioned] closed session later in the day, before adopting the final draft general comment in public session that afternoon."[57] In this meeting, Mr. Riedel took the opportunity to thank all those who helped him in drafting,[58] but distilled mention by name to only two actors: Mr. Langford of COHRE, which supports the notion of his role as perhaps *the* salient resource person for the draft, and the WHO representative Jamie Bartram. With regard to everyone else involved, Mr. Riedel's commendation referred simply to their respective contributions on the day of general discussion, implying this last day to be the only on which he received the input he ultimately considered to make

and representatives of governments (including members of diplomatic missions). We organize conferences, seminars, workshops and dialog sessions, training and information programs with international participation, and provide studies, consultancy reports, and other publications."

57 As this public meeting started at 10:00 am, the closed session's discussion of final changes consequently must have been very short.

58 "When preparing the final draft general comment, he had paid particular attention to the valuable comments put forward by the members of the Committee. He could never have completed his work without their help. He had also taken account of the opinions expressed by non-governmental organizations (NGOs) and United Nations agencies during the day of general discussion held on 22 November 2002 (E/C.12/2002/SR.46). He thanked all those who had contributed and was particularly grateful to Mr. Langford of COHRE and to the representative of the World Health Organization. Many thanks were also due to the secretariat drafting group. He welcomed the fact that four of the special rapporteurs of the Commission on Human Rights had been present during the discussion." E/C.12/2002/SR.50: 2.

draft changes.[59] Tacit in the quick move toward adoption, Mr. Riedel chose not to heed the issue raised by most participants on the day of general discussion, this inherent connection of a right to water to a right to sanitation; thereafter, the other committee members discussed the comment's title, with some highlighting the importance of the clarification of water as a public good.[60]

Then, in a direct proceeding, GC No. 15 was adopted during the CESCR's 51st meeting on November 26, 2002.[61] Only three days passed between the discussion of the comment's revised draft and the adoption of its final iteration. No official documents are available that speak either to the content of draft versions or to a change of recommendations after the July 29 version. In its introductory paragraph, GC No. 15 clarifies water as both a limited resource and a public good; here, sanitation is also included,[62] and later given frequent

59 Regarding the changes, the summary records proceed: "With regard to substance, he said that many suggestions had been made on the title of the document. Although he would leave the decision in the hands of the Committee, he was personally in favour of the simple title 'The right to water'. The fact that it was a human right was very clearly explained in the paragraphs that followed. The core focus of the document was water for personal and domestic uses. It had been difficult to include a reference to water for agricultural purposes, owing to the widely varying amounts of water needed for crops; the solution had been to include the questions of subsistence agriculture and the right to adequate food in the introduction. On the sensitive issue of privatization, or third-party activities, the draft general comment took a neutral stance on whether private sector involvement was good or bad. However, paragraph 23 made it clear that States parties had to regulate the private sector to ensure the right to water for the entire population. Only Governments could decide whether water services were to be operated by third parties; the Committee's objective was to monitor how Governments' decisions affected the human rights situation." E/C.12/2002/SR.50: 3.

60 The final discussion before the adoption meeting was further legitimized by the approval of the High Commissioner himself. Mr. Vieira de Mello attended this meeting and explicitly put the general comment in a broader context of the work of the treaty bodies in general, namely as an emphasis of the rule of law: "Water was an essential prerequisite for human existence and he therefore congratulated the Committee on formulating draft general comment No. 15 on the right to water (...). With a view to achieving equality, dignity and security for all, he had made the rule of law the cornerstone of his agenda. In his role as High Commissioner for Human Rights, he shared the responsibility of the Committee and the other treaty monitoring bodies to act as custodians of the human rights legal framework, of which the Covenant was a key component. States had a primary responsibility for the well-being and security of their citizens, as well as for the promotion and protection of their human rights. The treaty monitoring bodies did not merely have moral or political authority: they had legal authority. They were, after all, monitoring compliance with legally binding agreements to which States had freely and willingly become parties. At a time when human rights were being eroded and attacked, it was essential to emphasize the rule of law." E/C.12/2002/SR.50: 4f.

61 E/C.12/2002/13 2003: 99.

62 The general comment acknowledged that water supply must be available for everyone for personal sanitation and includes a paragraph under the heading of states parties' legal obligations to fulfil "Ensuring that everyone has access to adequate sanitation is not only

mention through the text in footnotes, although never being denoted explicitly as a right itself, as the NGO members of the TLC had wanted.

4.8 A TLC FOR WATER

While the previous part of the chapter aims at reconstructing the drafting process of GC15, the following brief part interprets the process with regard to the meaning of this book's key concept, the TLC. To provide a first such investigative foray, I will briefly discuss the specifics of the formation and work of the TLC for water, where the TLC was successful, and why some of the TLC's preferences were not entirely included in the outcome.

One area in which civil society demands substantively and successfully affected the ultimate draft language concerns the quality of drinking water, which GC No. 15 includes as a factor applicable under all circumstances[63] in a paragraph[64] accompanied by a footnote reference to WHO guidelines on the topic. This inclusion stems from Jamie Bartram, who was part of the core drafting group and working for WHO at the time, prior to which he was a well-known expert on water; later, the Chair of UN-Water, and now, a Director of the Water Institute and Professor of Environmental Sciences and Engineering at a university (since 2009), he confirmed that he was satisfied with his impact on the outcome.[65]

fundamental for human dignity and privacy, but is one of the principal mechanisms for protecting the quality of drinking water supplies and resources. In accordance with the rights to health and adequate housing (see general comments No. 4 (1991) and 14 (2000)) States parties have an obligation to progressively extend safe sanitation services, particularly to rural and deprived urban areas, taking into account the needs of women and children." UN Committee on Economic, Social and Cultural Rights (CESCR), General Comment No. 15: The Right to Water (Arts. 11 and 12 of the Covenant), January 20, 2003, E/C.12/2002/11 2003: para. 29.

63 The ICESCR includes a progressive realization clause which is for some states a welcomed provision to connect their fulfillment (or lack thereof) of obligations to their economic situation.

64 "*Quality*. The water required for each personal or domestic use must be safe, therefore free from micro-organisms, chemical substances and radiological *hazards* that constitute a threat to a person's health. Furthermore, water should be of an acceptable colour, odour and taste for each personal or domestic use." UN Committee on Economic, Social and Cultural Rights (CESCR), General Comment No. 15: The Right to Water (Arts. 11 and 12 of the Covenant), January 20, 2003, E/C.12/2002/11 2003: para. 12 (b).

65 "Certainly, with regard to the normative elements there was a lot of comfort around 'safety' (quality) because there was an international position on it in full detail (the WHO Guidelines on Drinking Water Quality) and I certainly advocated for that. And a few years before, I had recognized the need for a more formal position on water quantity (or service level) and we were finalizing that. Both ended up referenced in the GC and so from a WHO perspective, I felt I had done my job and got the formal normative aspects recognized and maximized

Privatization was unsurprisingly the chief sticking point within the committee's drafting considerations. While the public discussion of the draft raised private water provision as a general concern vis-à-vis the obligations for states, the classified summary record from the closed meeting revealed the full scope of the posed risks to the implications for the committee's taking any kind of stance on the topic. In light of this scope – or even without it – the empirical fact is that GC No. 15 approaches the topic of private water provision obliquely, if not entirely evasively. To wit, the general comment only mentions private companies together with civil society as *addressees* of states to inform and collaborate with on a right-to-water strategy. On the states parties' obligation to fulfill affordability, the comment states: "Any payment for water services has to be based on the principle of equity, ensuring that these services, whether privately or publicly provided, are affordable for all, including socially disadvantaged groups."[66] The TLC was accordingly unsatisfied with this outcome.

Another of the drafting process's debates centered around the meaning of sanitation, whose inclusion in the ultimate GC No. 15 as a conjoined right with the right to water was unsuccessfully advocated for by certain participating civil society actors from the field of development – namely, NGOs and health experts. Indeed, sanitation was included in the text of the GC No. 15, but not as a right in and of itself. The CESCR's reservations came as skepticism in the right as having a broad appeal, with committee members indicating that they did not "believe there was sufficient international support in international law" (Langford, Bartram, and Roaf 2017: 356). Speaking to their skepticism, at the time of GC No. 15's drafting, sanitation was regarded as too contested, due to the breadth of obligations it would impose as an enshrined right.[67] Hence, although sanitation is frequently mentioned throughout the document, its reference takes a secondary position, with its mentioning put mostly in footnotes. Even so, GC No. 15 nevertheless acknowledged that water supply must be available to everyone for the purpose of personal sanitation, included in a paragraph under the heading of state parties' legal obligations to fulfil (paragraph 29). As a result, these efforts led to the establishment of the

coherence across international instruments." Jamie Bartram (quoted from written response to a questionnaire).

66 UN Committee on Economic, Social and Cultural Rights (CESCR), General Comment No. 15: The Right to Water (Arts. 11 and 12 of the Covenant), January 20, 2003, E/C.12/2002/11 2003: para. 27.

67 Access to a clean toilet, for instance, which requires serious state party investments to provide, would target the poorest countries of the world, where this access is predominantly restricted Satterthwaite, Mitlin, and Bartlett 2015.

office of the first UN Special Rapporteur on the Human Rights to safe drinking water and sanitation in 2008 whose policy advisor became Ms. Roaf.

Overall, the actors involved in the TLC, all of whom have pursued remarkable careers after General Comment No. 15's drafting,[68] agreed it was a major success simply to stipulate a human right to water as a core obligation for states through implementation of Articles 11 and 12 of the Covenant, a significant boon for the water-related work of all human rights, environment, and development NGOs, and highly important for the development of monitoring mechanisms and the codification of a right to sanitation thereafter (Langford, Bartram, and Roaf 2017). The members helped implementing the General Comment individually and with other actors in domestic contexts, but also jointly developed indicators to monitor its implementation.[69]

4.9 CONCLUSION

How did the CESCR manage to make water a human right? Who were the drivers for this precedent case of progressive treaty interpretation? Was there contestation along the process and by whom? What can we learn from the drafting process for other attempts of human rights norm creation? This chapter enhanced our understanding of how TLC-led treaty interpretation comes to pass by articulating a detailed reconstruction of the drafting process of General Comment No. 15. Its impact on human rights law and policies on the international and domestic level and on legal scholarship qualifies this general comment as one that contributed substantially to the further development of international human rights law. Its adoption came to many stakeholders as a surprise, because water is not included in the Covenant and also because its drafting process went quick and without further notice to the public. I revealed that there is a story beneath the visible procedures and

68 The rapporteur was a professor for public law with a specialization in socioeconomic rights and a well-known advisor to UN bodies, governments, and civil society. The NGO officer involved with expertise on water, who admitted that she was rather uninformed about the UN human rights system when she was asked to join the drafting team in 2002, later became the advisor to the first UN Special Rapporteur on the Human Rights to safe drinking water and sanitation. Another expert consulted is now a committee member himself.

69 Virginia Roaf and Malcolm Langford co-edited a paper introducing a framework for the monitoring of implementation of a human right to water. This paper was based on the proceedings of a workshop held in October 2004 and organised by the German Heinrich Böll Foundation, Brot für die Welt (Bread for the World) and the Centre on Housing Rights and Evictions (COHRE) which was also attended by Eibe Riedel: www.boell.de/sites/default/files/assets/boell.de/images/download_de/internationalepolitik/righttowaterindicators.pdf.

outputs of the human rights treaty bodies, one which can be traced to the collaboration of a few individuals, the TLC.

The timely, if not expedited, adoption is seen as saliently responsible for the less comprehensive inclusion of sanitation,[70] a key goal of TLC members, and in general explanatory for the ultimate omission of some important discussion aspects within the final iteration of the comment. In further attestation: *all* involved members in interviews – those with drafting experience and those that were involved for the first time – remembered the drafting process as incredibly quick. This speed attests to the efficiency of TLCs, who can deliver a successful adoption process within a short amount of time, but gives food for further investigation into whether this speed is self-defeating by way of diluting the content ultimately reflected in the later outcome. It was possible because one member of the CESCR, Eibe Riedel, took responsibility for the draft in front of his committee and was willing to entrust the drafting process to economic and social right professional Malcolm Langford. The rapporteur as the well-known senior expert opened a lot of doors to younger advocates, scholars, and practitioners throughout his career.[71]

In the case of GC No. 15, a TLC occurred in a treaty body composed of members with broad expertise — members with legal training, an academic background, and/or experience working in government, civil society, and international organizations, alongside those without — tasked to monitor a treaty whose spectrum of norms likewise spanned diverse, requiring the assessing of rights to education, housing, and social security. As the analysis revealed, stakeholders pointed to the time crunch of GC No. 15's drafting and the lack of relevant expertise among the CESCR's own members as crucial impetuses for outside involvement in the drafting process, and hence, to the involved TLC's formation. Yet, time was more important for the scope of the

70 "You know there was definitely some jockeying. And the one problem with that was that we wanted (. . .) to have sanitation in that but the speed of the process went so there was no time to prepare the committee to accept something as tabooed as sanitation. And now even a few years later would it be no problem at all but then it was seen." Interview with an NGO officer. For a critical take on the GC15's stance on sanitation, see Cahill 2005.

71 Many people working in Geneva for NGOs or OHCHR count among his doctoral candidates and within the economic, social, and cultural rights community, his network is particularly dense. A testimony to his network is an edited volume in his honor ("Festschrift"), which highlights his personal ties in policy, practice, and academia and summarizes his long term on the CESCR as one in which his roles as academic, diplomat, and philanthropist was combined in the most fruitful way (Hanschel et al. 2013). The dominantly male editorship and contributions in this volume (Birkenkötter 2015: 2) prompts further questions on the exclusiveness of this network – and therefore on equal opportunities to become a member of a TLC.

final output, reflecting TLC members' need to having to make compromises in the process, and less important for the formation and the interactions of the individual members. What can be learned from this in-depth case study about TLCs and whether the observations can be made in other cases of treaty interpretation across the treaty bodies will be covered in the next chapter.

5

Interpretation across Treaty Bodies

Diving beneath the surface of formal access rules, procedures, and actors of the UN treaty body system, the previous chapter's in-depth study of the drafting of CESCR's General Comment No. 15 rendered the TLC concept – the close knowledge- and trust-driven, law-influencing collaboration between treaty body members and other non-state actors that underline a treaty interpretation's drafting and adopting – visible in a singular empirical instance. But while an exemplar, the story of GC No. 15 is no single or exceptional case of TLC-driven collaboration on treaty interpretations. Indeed, the TLC casts a wider empirical net across the human rights treaty body system, which this chapter will argue for by demonstrating the TLC concept to be applicable to drafting processes in other treaty bodies, even where their formation is unexpected.[1]

As stated previously, TLCs are neither necessary nor sufficient conditions for general comments. Instead, they present one explanation for how and by whom these interpretations are developed, given the resource constraints on the side of the treaty bodies for such a task. As such, the scope conditions for the application of the concept need further refinement to be of analytical value for other cases. This chapter marks the bounds of this applicability specifically by way of explaining the likelihood of TLCs to occur across treaty bodies. To this explicative end, I start by formulating assumptions regarding the transferability of the concept to other cases, a formulation I bear through summation of all treaty bodies' member compositions and working

[1] TLCs are expected to occur in a setting where resources for the expert bodies are scarce. As elaborated in Chapter 2, this scope condition applies to all treaty bodies because of their collective workload and their individual members' obligations. Based on the process analysis in Chapter 3, these conditions will be further specified below.

procedures. Guided by hypotheses derived from Chapter 4's process analysis, I then turn to three case studies to test their probability.

All three case studies are hence understood as a plausibility probe for the TLC concept. In the following, I suggest how its analysis could be extended to shed light on why they occurred (or not). The first case centers on the Human Rights Committee-adopted (2018) General Comment No. 36 on the right to life – a hard case for TLCs, on account of the committee's court-like composition – whose inclusion of abortion against internal and external contestation shows dynamics which bespeak the existence of a TLC. The second follows the drafting process of the CAT-adopted (2008) General Comment No. 2, also a hard case for TLCs, given the pertinent treaty's narrow scope on the prohibition of torture and the CAT committee's high degree of collective expert knowledge. Although both aspects make the TLC-facilitating demand for external expertise less likely, this case nonetheless unearths the marks of a TLC's influence in showing the comment's inclusion of rape and gender-based violence in its text to have spawned from an external legal entrepreneur and a committed committee member. The third and final case investigates CERD, a committee that regularly drafts general comments notwithstanding its monitored treaty's single norm focus,[2] and its interpretation of the obligations of states to take actions against newfound challenges such as (online) hate speech. Here, empirical research reveals committee members to not only have closely collaborated with another treaty body, the Human Rights Committee, but also to have solicited and incorporated expertise from their respective professional networks – the markings, again, of a TLC. Together, these cases will contribute to a specification of TLC's scope conditions and success factors for the development of human rights.

5.1 CAN TLCS MAKE IT EVERYWHERE?

Are my findings on TLCs generalizable to contexts differing from the one on the genesis of the human right to water? To begin my answer, I return to Chapter 4's in-depth analysis of GC No. 15's drafting, which identified the extent of professional diversity among a treaty body's membership and the breadth of the pertinent treaty's core norm(s) as what chiefly prefaces the need for external input in drafting a general comment. In order to make assumptions vis-à-vis the particular cases where TLCs are most likely to be found, I take these findings as a starting point for articulating a typology of treaty

[2] To be more specific here: the ICERD, the treaty the CERD monitors, focuses acutely on one UDHR norm, the prohibition of racial discrimination.

bodies with regard to their demands for external expertise. Such a typology could distinguish the scope of the treaty (single–multiple rights) and the scope of knowledge as represented by its members (homogeneous vs. multi-perspective) (see Table 5.1).

The scope of a treaty considers how specialized it is, assuming that the need for interpretation is less likely when a treaty has a rather narrow scope. To render it, within the typology, as a tangible variable, I used the reference point of the Universal Declaration of Human Rights (UDHR), as the universal core of human rights,[3] to categorize the treaties as single or multi-norm. Every article in the UDHR counts as one norm, making CAT and CERD single-norm treaties, whereas CEDAW and CESCR are considered multi-norm. Moreover, based on scholarship on non-state influence in international negotiations (e.g. Betsill and Corell 2001), I assume that the necessity for external input in a treaty interpretation process is more likely when the decision-making body lacks knowledge on a particular issue. As such, the knowledge of the collective decision-maker treaty body may be cast as the sum of the expertise of its individual members.[4] To assess the scope of knowledge of the various treaty bodies, I analyzed their memberships' diversity of education, professions, and relevant experience.[5] The CCPR, for example, features expertise that skews rather homogenous as it is composed only of lawyers. CAT and CRC likewise possess specialized knowledge; although their members hail from more diverse educational backgrounds and professional positions, they all bear biographies that reflect a clear specialization on the subjects at play: torture, children, youth, and family affairs.

The TLC-spawning committee featured in the case of GC No. 15, for instance, falls in the latter category, with the CESCR composed of members representing *multi-perspective* expertise[6] and the ICESCR a treaty featuring a spectrum of rights that likewise spans diverse, requiring the assessing of rights to education,

3 This is a pragmatic decision for the moment in order to compare the scope of treaties and be able to select cases. A helpful overview of the scope of rights covered by the treaties can be found in the appendix of Posner 2014, adding that "[l]ittle weight should be placed on the exact number of rights; the number will always be controversial."

4 This knowledge, of course, might be "sufficient" for one general comment, but not the other. The typology thus only aims at showing a broader picture of the composition of the treaty bodies and not a qualitative assessment of their intellectual capacities to work on specific general comments.

5 Data available for members from 2008 to 2020. See also Truscan 2018.

6 That is, CESCR members *with and without* legal training (educational background evaluated as provided in the committee members official CVs), and their profession during the time of appointment, for example, they are academics, have experience working in governments, civil society, and/or international organizations; see also Figure 2.3.

housing, and social security. The following table provides a typology of the treaty bodies[7] according to these institutional features:

TABLE 5.1 *Treaty body typology*

		Treaty	
		Single Right	Multiple Rights
Members	Multi-perspective	CERD	CESCR CEDAW
	Homogenous	CAT	CCPR CRC CMW CRPD

One note on time. We can assume that the scope of a treaty remains rather stable over time, for self-evident reasons. On the subject of composition, while membership can change with elections, we nonetheless find the professions and educational backgrounds represented among the treaty bodies to have varied minimally (see Chapter 2 and Truscan 2018)). So long as treaty body members are elected for a fixed term, with their pay commensurate only with the time they are present for meetings, academics and (former) government representatives will be those most likely to take on this role. Individuals working for an NGO, by contrast, have higher hurdles to clear, as their election requires their leaving an advocacy role for some weeks of the year, plus many human rights NGOs would not be able to compensate for their leave. But regardless of *who* becomes a body's expert, the very notion of time and budget constraint remains a condition stable across all treaty bodies, as all experts serve in their individual capacities and not as regular staff of the UN (see Chapter 2). Their presence in official sessions chiefly centers on dialogues with state parties on their implementation of the treaty, with additional tasks, e.g. the drafting of treaty interpretations, designated as extracurricular, playing no part in the sessions' schedules. This creates a situation whereby the tasks must be carried out when the experts are back in their regular occupations and thus at a loss for time. As CESCR stakeholders noted (see Chapter 4), this kind of time crunch, combined with the lack of relevant expertise among the committee's own members, was a crucial impetus for outside involvement

[7] CED and SPT are not included as the former does not make use of treaty interpretations so far and SPT is a sub-committee, thus "a *sui generis* body, whose functions are wholly unlike those of the other treaty bodies and so cannot be considered as a normal part of the 'system'" (Rodley 2013: 623).

in the GC No. 15 drafting process,[8] and, hence, to the involved TLC's formation.

My case selection therefore casts these empirical observations into a wider hypothesis, building from the assumption that the scope of the treaty (singular–multiple rights) and the scope of knowledge as represented by its members (homogeneous vs. multi-perspective) determine the need for external collaborators. With the multi-norm, multi-perspective quadrant of the typology already covered by Chapter 4's in-depth exploration of the formation and existence of TLCs within the CESCR, and its drafting of the GC No. 15, what follows here are case studies that probe the plausibility of the TLC concept from the angle of the other three. In order to account for a convincing assessment of TLCs in the treaty bodies, I chose these three illustrative case studies based on data availability and previous knowledge. All general comments are arguably visible in the broader human rights community, generating some form of impact among the legal community, academics, and in other entities of the UN. For all three case studies, my analysis draws on a combination of data: documents and existing scholarship, as well as interviews and, in the case of CCPR, personal observations during the committee's meetings.

5.2 GENERAL COMMENT NO. 36, HUMAN RIGHTS COMMITTEE (2018)

Among the UN human rights treaty bodies, the Human Rights Committee (CCPR) stands as somewhat of a unicorn, with its members almost all lawyers. This compositional quirk is oft-justified on the grounds that the ICCPR itself stipulates for it – indeed, the Covenant simply states that the CCPR's 18 members must be "persons of high moral character and recognized competence in the field of human rights," with "consideration given to the usefulness of the participation of *some* persons [italics mine] having legal experience" (United Nations December 16, 1966b) (ICCPR, Article 28). Relative to those of the other treaty bodies, the CCPR's interpretations are considered as especially authoritative contributions to the development of international human rights law (Keller and Grover 2012; Roth-Isigkeit 2012). As this authority rests on the committee's high degree of expertise vis-à-vis the ICCPR's legal interpretation – *because* all members are lawyers – TLCs are

[8] A former committee member made it clear in an interview that "without other actors, (. . .) the committee can't write these general comments," as such actors necessarily provide "the expertise" requisite in their drafting.

assumed unlikely to form, with legal documents like general comments, in theory, easily crafted among members themselves, that is, without the need of TLC-spawning outside help. But given the breadth of articles the Covenant covers and the human rights treaties' certain idiosyncrasy as "living instruments" (Moeckli and White 2016) – which saddles a requirement to account for political, social, and economic developments on the CCPR's interpretations – consultation with actors external to the CCPR nevertheless constitutes an important part of the committee's work processes. Indeed, the CCPR regularly invites interested stakeholders to provide written and oral comments on their various drafts (Keller and Grover 2012). In light of its members' increasing workloads and external work obligations, how exactly the committee proceeds to weigh and give consideration to this input follows no general rubric but is rather left to in-house discretion, that is, is decided in each instance by an internal decision-making process. In light of these burdens, it is not unlikely that external actors, on account of their expertise, should provide the impetus for a general comment's formulation.

Demarking the first of the three probability probes for TLCs is a case from the CCPR's recent past, centered namely on General Comment No. 36, a wide-ranging interpretation of the substantive provisions of the ICCPR Article 6 (the right to life) (Joseph 2019), which was adopted by the CCPR on October 30, 2018, after a 3+-year drafting process. In it, the CCPR's eighteen independent experts together identify the obligations of the Covenant's 172 states parties, speaking with great specificity to the right to life in light of environmental threats, to how the right should be defended in times of war, and to the measures that should be taken when the right is threatened by circumstances of extreme poverty and homelessness.[9] It became a general comment of special public interest foremost because of the polarized advocacy of pro-life and pro-choice groups, and I will focus in my analysis on the general comment's stance on a right to life and abortion. Adopted unanimously, the document reflects the CCPR's consensus on the scope of the right to life, which the CCPR – in a surprise to many observers of the committee – interpreted with exceedingly precise detail, particularly with respect to the right's relation with abortion. To that latter point, this new comment expanded upon the committee's earlier comments on reproductive rights, in recognizing a woman's autonomy to choose as a human right in and of itself.

9 CCPR/C/GC/36 2018.

GC No. 36 had two rapporteurs: Yuval Shany und Sir Nigel Rodley.[10] According to his colleagues on the committee, the latter served as the interpretation's initiating legal entrepreneur but passed away during the drafting process, which Mr. Shany then continued alone.[11] Upon its circulation in April 2015, the comment's first draft received harsh reactions from civil society, who, as one member of the International Commission of Jurists (ICJ) recalls, were "surprised, disappointed and profoundly concerned" with what the draft "set out [regarding] the thinking of the then Committee's two rapporteurs as to (. . .) the applicability of the right to life to 'the unborn', "[12] among other things. Before this draft could see the public light of day, the ICJ's legal experts collaborated with other civil society organizations to prepare a joint statement for the upcoming day of general discussion aimed to cement the rapporteurs' stated positions, "urging the Committee to seize the opportunity of the new general comment to reaffirm that Article 6 rights accrue at birth and do not extend prenatally."[13] However, as has been nicely put, "the proverbial genie was out of the bottle, and worse was to come[, as the] half-day of general discussion [then] generated 115 written submissions, many from anti-abortion groups."[14] This created a situation whereby progressive development on the right to life and abortion could less convincingly point to civil society as legitimizing input. The rapporteurs relied on assistance from the secretariat to summarize all input for the other committee members. The entirety of this input was read by the rapporteur himself, who found a number of submissions to be highly political and unattended by legal arguments, which lessened their utility to the drafting process.[15] The strong counter-mobilization by anti-abortion networks could not be ignored by the CCPR;[16] moreover, that the

10 Both rapporteurs were widely known beyond Geneva for their substantial expertise on human rights law through scholarship and practice. Yuval Shany was member of the committee from 2013 to 2020 and is a professor for public international law at Hebrew University. Nigel Rodley had been on the committee since 2001 and until his death in 2017. He held several positions in the UN human rights branch and was also a professor for public international law in Essex.

11 www.ohchr.org/EN/NewsEvents/Pages/DisplayNews.aspx?NewsID=23797&LangID=E.

12 Zilli 2019.

13 Ibid.

14 Ibid: "Some hailing from the anti-abortion camp described how during the half-day of general discussion the Committee had been confronted with a '*deluge of requests urging it to resist pressure to declare abortion a human right*'. Over 30 organizations, out of the 40 entities and individuals who took the floor at the half-day of general discussion, urged the Committee '*to recognize the right to life of unborn children, or at least not recognize a right to abortion*'."

15 Interview with Yuval Shany.

16 On a further note, this case exposes a further risk that individuals take when serving as independent experts on human rights treaty bodies. The heavy mobilization by antiabortion groups resulted in a surge of e-mails (some of them striking as "Stop killing babies") sent to the university accounts of the rapporteurs and other committee members. Thereby, the work on

majority of individuals and organizations speaking at this day of general discussion came from these networks inculcated the impression at Palais Wilson in Geneva, the grounds of the UN human rights treaty bodies, that they presented the majority view of civil society.

How did the committee respond and find a path through these opposing demands? The CCPR began the half-day of general discussion during its 114th session on July 14, 2015, to which it invited interested members of national human rights institutions (NHRIs), civil society, and academia. The two rapporteurs here took the ICJ's urgings with regard to the informal first draft seriously, by including in the revised draft's beginning a statement that excluded the unborn child from Article 1's protection of the right to life, as well as the distinction that the unborn child's right to life was superseded by that of pregnant mothers.[17] The Committee later made its change of direction transparent by stating that "proposals to include the right to life of the unborn within the scope of article 6 were considered and rejected during the process of drafting the Covenant."[18] In order to counter the seeming majority of the antiabortion civil society camp, the ICJ had joined forces with other organizations to pressure the CCPR prior to this day of general discussion to change its course.[19] ICJ organized this network of progressive civil society organizations also as a substantive homage to the legacy of its late president and co-rapporteur, Nigel Rodley.[20]

At the next session (115th), the CCPR began its first reading of the draft, a review that spanned until its completion at the 120th session in July 2017, to which the Committee invited all interested stakeholders to provide input on the draft. The subsequent commenters included states parties, other UN and regional human rights bodies, UN and specialized agencies, NHRIs, NGOs,

the committee intrudes their professional life for which they are not compensated by the UN or state parties.

17 CCPR/C/GC/R.36/Rev.2 2015: para. 7.

18 CCPR/C/GC/R.36/Rev.2, fn 9.

19 "The ICJ and other CSOs worked hard to persuade the Committee to delete from the draft any express references, such as 'the rights of the unborn children', or any other turn of phrase that may have implied that the right to life under the ICCPR applied before birth. We called on the Committee to reaffirm that the rights protected under the ICCPR begin at birth, and that the protection of article 6 does not extend prenatally. (. . .) In July 2017, the Committee finalized its first reading of the draft and commenced a formal consultation process with a wide-range of stakeholders, such as States, CSOs, academics and UN agencies, on this *new revised draft adopted by the Committee at first reading*. The joint CSO strategy and efforts had already begun to pay off. This draft no longer featured any reference to the unborn, let alone to the idea that article 6 protected prenatal interests" Zilli 2019.

20 ICJ 2017.

research institutions, and scholars,[21] whose feedback led to amendments to the draft's wording. Then, in October 2018, GC No. 36 was officially adopted by the CCPR. Included in it was paragraph 8 on abortion.[22] The article associates the deprivation of access to abortion with violations of women's and girls' right to life; calls for legal access to abortion in situations where pregnancy would endanger the life or health of the mother, or where the completion of the pregnancy would cause significant pain or suffering, for example, in contexts of rape or incest; and insists on states to decriminalize abortion and provide confidential health care after one takes place.

The general comment's progressive stance vis-à-vis abortion can be primarily traced, in light of the committee's internal controversies (Reiners 2019) and critical legal scholars' voices (Stevens 2018) and certain confirmation by his fellow committee members, to the driving role Sir Nigel Rodley played in the comment's drafting. His credentials spanning many – he was a human rights professor, an author of a number of the field's seminal works, a 20+-year legal advisor to Amnesty International, the former UN Special Rapporteur on

[21] Input can be found here: www.ohchr.org/EN/HRBodies/CCPR/Pages/GC36-Article6Righttolife.aspx.

[22] The finals paragraph on abortion reads as follows: "Although States parties may adopt measures designed to regulate voluntary termination of pregnancy, those measures must not result in violation of the right to life of a pregnant woman or girl, or her other rights under the Covenant. Thus, restrictions on the ability of women or girls to seek abortion must not, inter alia, jeopardize their lives, subject them to physical or mental pain or suffering that violates article 7 of the Covenant, discriminate against them or arbitrarily interfere with their privacy. States parties must provide safe, legal and effective access to abortion where the life and health of the pregnant woman or girl is at risk, or where carrying a pregnancy to term would cause the pregnant woman or girl substantial pain or suffering, most notably where the pregnancy is the result of rape or incest or where the pregnancy is not viable. In addition, States parties may not regulate pregnancy or abortion in all other cases in a manner that runs contrary to their duty to ensure that women and girls do not have to resort to unsafe abortions, and they should revise their abortion laws accordingly. For example, they should not take measures such as criminalizing pregnancy of unmarried women or applying criminal sanctions to women and girls who undergo abortion or to medical service providers who assist them in doing so, since taking such measures compels women and girls to resort to unsafe abortion. States parties should remove existing barriers to effective access by women and girls to safe and legal abortion, including barriers caused as a result of the exercise of conscientious objection by individual medical providers, and should not introduce new barriers. States parties should also effectively protect the lives of women and girls against the mental and physical health risks associated with unsafe abortions. In particular, they should ensure access for women and men, and especially girls and boys, to quality and evidence-based information and education on sexual and reproductive health and to a wide range of affordable contraceptive methods, and prevent the stigmatization of women and girls who seek abortion. States parties should ensure the availability of, and effective access to, quality prenatal and post-abortion health care for women and girls, in all circumstances and on a confidential basis." CCPR/C/GC/36 2018: para. 8.

torture and a board member of numerous NGOs – Sir Rodley had already attracted attention in many of the CCPR's state report proceedings with his stark views on state's obligations and abortion.[23] Nigel Rodley can well be considered the legal entrepreneur for abortion in this GC No. 36; nevertheless, he needed the expertise of his colleagues at ICJ to push through the backlash from antiabortion organizations, which outnumbered those supporting the right to life beginning only after birth. In other words, the legal entrepreneurship with regard to adoption and the right to life needed the power of an advocacy network in order to be effective. In that sense, the coalition at play in this case not only needs to account for pushback by state parties, but also by other civil society groups.

5.3 GENERAL COMMENT NO. 2, COMMITTEE AGAINST TORTURE (2007)

CAT, the smallest of the UN human rights treaty bodies (ten members), is composed of specialized experts, all with demonstrated knowledge on torture, and monitors a single-norm treaty. While these members occupy several professions relevant to the work of the committee, for example, medical practitioners, the committee is restrained to take a multi-perspective stance in its interpretations, with its small number of members posed the treaty body system's highest number of ratifications and, thus, state reports and individual complaints to consider. On the subject of scope of norms, the treaty CAT monitors is a single-norm treaty, a feature assumed to make a TLC's formation less likely (see section 5.1). At first glance, this assumption appears to follow empirically, given the small number of general comments adopted over time by CAT relative to the other treaty bodies. Indeed, only four general comments have been adopted in the over thirty years since the treaty's entering into force, with only one coming in CAT's first twenty years of existence.[24] Many actors within and outside the committee have tried to convince CAT for years to more often make use of general comments (Evans 2002), and the committee itself has internally discussed several proposals for such comments, but none have ever really taken off.[25]

23 For example, during the state review on Ireland in 2014: UNHRC, CCPR/C/IRL/CO/4, August 19, 2014: para 9. His close ties to civil society organizations were further reflected in the Abortion Rights Campaign NGO's #NotAVessel campaign, which was borne from a statement Rodley made to the Irish government (De Londras and Enright 2018: 50).

24 CAT had a more specific mandate for general comments (Gaer 2020: 145–148) but revised its rules of procedures and adopted the language of other treaty bodies in CAT/C/3/Rev.6 2014; CAT/C/3/Rev.5 2011: Rule 74.

25 CAT/C/SR.435 2000: paras. 11–13 and CAT/C/SR.439 2000: para. 12.

In the few instances CAT has made use of the instrument, the responses of civil society actors to potential violations of CAT by state parties have proven highly influential to the committee's internal decision-making to go ahead and draft a general comment.[26] As an example, one issue long debated by CAT's members for a potential draft concerned the distinction between torture as defined in UNCAT's Article 1 and the obligations of states parties to prevent ill-treatment (Article 16). Coupled to the question of non-derogability of the prohibition of torture and ill-treatment, two of the UNCAT's state parties – Israel, in the 1990s, and later the United States, in 2006 – used the interpretative room left by the Convention to justify their interrogation techniques in the fight against terrorism (Lesch 2020: 312–331; Liese 2009). The committee was willing to jump on this interpretative room by drafting a general comment clarifying the definition of torture and ill-treatment in Article 1 of CAT. Civil society's opinion mattered in this context: When the proposal for a general comment on Article 1's definition of torture was brought up in 2002, it was firmly and publicly rejected by committee member Felice Gaer,[27] precisely because an earlier "proposal had caused consternation among the NGOs, which feared that a revised definition would either water down the definition of torture or narrow its focus."[28]

Accordingly, the CAT committee decided to drop the drafting of a general comment on the definition of torture and, upon the initiative of Felice Gaer, instead aim for an interpretation of state obligation with regard to the prevention of torture, as laid out in Article 2. This general comment was a progressive endeavor for CAT and laid the ground for, and in itself reflected, path-breaking developments in international human rights law. For one, it "outlined a long list of categories of such vulnerable persons that go well beyond usual UN categorizations, including in particular explicit references to sexual orientation and transgender identity long before other such bodies did so" (Gaer 2020: 148). For another, it highlighted, in its para. 18, the prohibition of rape and gender-based violence as obligations under CAT, notwithstanding that gender-related aspects of torture are entirely absent from CAT itself.[29] The drafting process of a general comment on this particular article was preceded

[26] Malcom Evans, then member of the APT NGO and later Chairman of the SPT, wrote: "Members of the CAT were present at an informal seminar on the definition of torture organised by the Association for the Prevention of Torture in Geneva in Nov 2001 (at which a version of this article was distributed and discussed)" (Evans 2002: 368, fn. 18).

[27] Felice D. Gaer is director of the American Jewish Committee's Jacob Blaustein Institute for the Advancement of Human Rights. Ms. Gaer served on the Committee from 2000 to 2019.

[28] CAT/C/SR.532 2002: para. 71.

[29] Note that the rapporteur for this General Comment, Felice Gaer, was at that time the only female serving on the committee but successfully convinced the treaty body to adopt this

by the advocacy work of women and human rights lawyer Rhonda Copelon, whose biography stands on years of related experience using means of advocacy and international cooperation to integrate rape and domestic violence within criminal law's definition of torture (Copelon 1993, 2000). To preface the case of GC No. 2, Copelon joined forces with a women's rights law clinic and strategically submitted reports to CAT, and also the Human Rights Committee, to convince them of sexualized violence as a human rights issue.[30] The general comment reflects the advocate's knowledge on the wide-ranging implications of privately inflicted violence and clarifies that domestic abuse is not just included as against women, but also explicitly mentions gender transgressors including nonconforming women and lesbian, gay, bisexual, transgender, and queer persons (art. 18–24).

The GC No. 2's drafting process can be argued to date back to 2003, following the events on September 11, 2001, and the subsequent War on Terror (Davis 2007: 180). Ongoing conflicts within the committee prolonged its drafting process. At CAT's 30th session in 2003, the Special Rapporteur on Torture, the aforementioned Sir Nigel Rodley, and the World Organization Against Torture (OMCT) recommended CAT to adopt a general comment on Article 2, a call supported by the NGO Association for the Prevention of Torture (APT), who entreated CAT to take "a strong position on the principle of the absolute prohibition of torture and ill-treatment."[31] The drafting process's next steps followed the individual initiative of committee member Fernando Mariño Menéndez, a professor for public international law and committee member since 2001, who presented a first draft on Article 2 during the CAT's 31st Session in 2003. This preliminary draft was met with strong procedural and substantive criticism by fellow committee members, with particular condemnation leveled at Menéndez's dispersal of the draft to

document. After she joined the treaty body, there was a new opportunity to take up gender issues under CAT and "the Committee began frequently to question States parties regarding various forms and incidences of gender violence both in official custodial situations, in institutional contexts beyond prisons, and in situations of non-State violence, including rape, female genital mutilation, forced sterilization and abortion, trafficking, and domestic violence. Ms. Gaer also played a critical role as co-rapporteur on the General Comment, by which time the Committee had two more female members and at least one male member with expertise in issues of gender violence" (Copelon 2008: 231).

30 "Rhonda Copelon and the IWHR Clinic also pressed for recognition of the gravity of officially inflicted sexualized violence as well as privately inflicted gender violence where the state does not intervene to exercise due diligence to prevent it. Subjects raised in these NGO submissions ranged from the sexualized abuses of women detainees at Abu Ghraib prison to coerced interrogation of women seeking medical services for incomplete and life-threatening abortions in Chile" (Gaer 2011: 295).

31 CAT/C/SR.560 2003.

NGOs and the Special Rapporteur on Torture, Sir Rodley, prior to his discussing it with the committee.[32] From his perspective, pressure to draft a general comment mounted significantly in light of post 9-11 developments and the subsequent War on Terror,[33] which risked rolling back a number of the CAT's accomplishments. Accordingly, the rapporteur looked for drafting support outside of the committee and found it in experts in the UN and NGOs (Menéndez 2014). Following a partially public, lively debate among the committee members of CAT, the treaty body then opted to establish a working group for a draft general comment.[34] The working group raised further procedural issues with the committee in 2004, but then the drafting process appeared to stall until 2006, when, at the CAT's 36th session, Menéndez – following up on an earlier request of other CAT members and states to finalize the process – proposed to quickly move forward and complete the work within a year.[35] During the time between, former CAT member Felice Gaer recalls that her fellow CAT "members expressed a heightened sense of frustration with the reporting process as a means of advancing the prevention of torture" (Gaer 2020: 146). This frustration with the reporting process was translated into an expedition of the drafting process of the general comment on Art. 2. The committee agreed that members Menéndez and Gaer would develop a joint proposal of the existing drafts; the two eventually were assigned as the rapporteurs for the drafting process, whose discussion was pushed to the next session.

The first reading of the consolidated draft thus took place in November 2006.[36] The drafting and revising process went forward without further calls for input or public debates, so that state parties felt the need to specifically ask whether and when they would be involved in the drafting process.[37] During the same session, the committee made considerable progress on the draft, which it sent out to NGOs, other UN bodies, and states for comments. Whereas the committee members described their engagement with non-state actors as quite productive at this stage, it was noted that the committee seemed less responsive to the input by states (Lesch 2020: 321). After

32 CAT/C/SR.638 2004: paras. 30, 32.

33 On a symposium on the General Comment held at CUNY, the panelists "discussed [that] the General Comment closes the holes bored by counter-terrorism policies – especially those approved and used by the Bush administration – into the absolute and non-derogable prohibition on torture" (Copelon 2008: 230).

34 The members were Mr. Gubril Camara, Ms. Felice Gaer, Mr. Grossman, and Mr. Fernando Mariño Menéndez (rapporteur).

35 CAT/C/SR.717 2006: paras. 1 and 2.

36 CAT/C/SR.752 2006: para. 14.

37 Switzerland, the United Kingdom, and Canada: CAT/C/SR.775 2007: paras. 19, 45, 69.

three meetings of paragraph-by-paragraph debates of the draft, the committee concluded the process in two sessions, formally adopting General Comment No. 2 on November 23, 2007. The Special Rapporteur on torture praised "its authority by providing guidance to States parties and all other organs of national and international society as to the meaning and implications of the Convention as an instrument of international law" (van Boven 2007: 211). The legal significance of this general comment was further underlined during a symposium at CUNY, leading to a special issue of its law review in 2008.[38]

With the drafting narrative clear, I now revisit my core assumption of CAT to move discourse toward the case's empirical revelations regarding TLCs, finishing the "test" of the plausibility probe. To remind, a TLC was assumed to be less likely to arise in the CAT, on account of the committee's high internal degree of specialization on torture, which lessens the need to solicit the expertise of external actors, and the clear-cut nature of CAT, whose exacting clarity on the meaning of a single human rights norm (the prohibition of torture) appeared to make any need for the treaty's interpretation essentially moot – a view supported by CAT's relatively infrequent adoption of general comments. But even in this less likely case, we still find the empirical imprint of a TLC, which here shows in the ways in which individual CAT members worked in unison with actors from civil society organizations and the Special Rapporteur on Torture to affect an outcome with substantive implications on human rights law. To name their contributions specifically: these individuals, organized through the rapport of the expert members with the others, together facilitated not only CAT's drafting of GC No. 2 but also the dissolution of the initially planned draft general comment on CAT's Article 1 in favor of a new drafting course focused on interpretation of its Article 2. This turn to Article 2 further exemplifies the *why* of interpretation of human rights treaties: CAT's Article 1, as a very precise provision on the definition of torture, was enough well delineated to make any degree of further interpretation unnecessary (Lesch 2020), hence shifting lawmaking efforts to the less-clear provision of Article 2 on the distinction between torture and ill-treatment.[39]

Further refining the particulars of this case's TLC, we may point to General Comment No. 2's innovative and progressive stand on rape and gender-based violence as sign for the legal entrepreneurship of Rhonda Copelon, a women's

38 The symposium special issue (New York City Law Review Volume 11, Issue 2, 2008) can be found here: https://academicworks.cuny.edu/clr/vol11/iss2/.

39 This shift also affected the dynamics within the committee and general comment leadership: Committee member Menéndez consulted with individuals first before he had his colleagues on the committee read his draft, resulting in internal discussions and a revised drafting procedure.

rights advocate well experienced with bringing these issues into legal frameworks. Felice Gaer herself attributed "intellectual leadership in the evolution of the norm of torture and the recognition of its negative gendered origins" (Gaer 2011: 293) to Copelon. Upon her successful work advancing the matter within courts and tribunals, she turned to the treaty bodies for a similar inclusion in the human rights framework. Through Felice Gaer as the CAT's only female expert on the committee, who at the time was pushing CAT to include more gender-related aspects of torture in their work, and Rhonda Copelon, who was directly experienced in the drafting of international legal frameworks, there arose the opportunity to initiate a drafting process on exactly the distinctions Gaer was pushing CAT to clarify. The intimate working ties of the TLC orienting this new course were so insular that not only states but even fellow committee members demanded inclusion throughout the drafting process.

How can we explain this TLC's occurrence against the backdrop of minimal likelihood? While answering this question goes beyond the scope of this short case study,[40] I regard the lack of coherent decision-making within the committee to be an important player here, intensified by the high workload of the committee to share on fewer shoulders as compared to other treaty bodies. Additionally, internal dissonances about the right way to proceed temporarily blocked the committee, while individual committee members see these disputes as a missed opportunity to make the most of its member's certain expertise and jointly draft more powerful general comment.[41]

5.4 GENERAL RECOMMENDATION NO. 35, COMMITTEE ON THE ELIMINATION OF ALL FORMS OF RACIAL DISCRIMINATION (2013)

The Committee on the Elimination of All Forms of Racial Discrimination (CERD) is the longest-standing among the UN human rights treaty bodies.[42]

40 9/11 was an external shock for CAT which changed the views among committee members but also state parties that the committee should take more action and thus facilitated the general comment drafting process, yet not necessarily a TLC (Lesch 2020).

41 Then former committee member Fernando Mariño Menéndez published papers in which he argued that his fellow committee members were "blocked" and "paralyzed" and did not take sufficiently into account the advances that had been made in international law (Menéndez 2014: 32).

42 "The drafting of the CERD was initiated within the context of the seemingly endless process of drafting the two covenants [ICCPR and ICESCR]. In fact, it was modelled on the draft of what a year later would become the ICCPR" (Rodley 2013: 622). He further notes that CERD became a precedent for the establishment of other treaty bodies.

Established in 1970, five years after ICERD was adopted in the General Assembly, the CERD and its eighteen members have adopted more than thirty-five general recommendations to date, accounting for one of the highest numbers of interpretations adopted by the treaty bodies. The high number can be attributed both to CERD's status as the oldest treaty body and the ICERD's especially imprecise language, a result of the treaty's hasty adoption.[43] To recall the CERD quadrant assumption about TLC formation: TLCs are hypothesized as less likely to emerge in bodies like CERD, that is, broadly specialized bodies that monitor a single-norm treaty from multiple perspectives. But as the high number of general recommendations adopted by CERD makes evident, there is certain caveat to the latter feature in CERD's case. While the ICERD is indeed concerned with a single norm of the UDHR, namely, freedom from racial discrimination, the multidimensionality of this norm – and moreover, the "imperfect text"[44] of the ICERD – has fostered a need to better clarify its meaning. As this multidimensionality likewise levels on the according interpretative process a requirement for relevant expertise, the expert members of CERD represent multiple perspectives on racial discrimination through their education, profession, and personal experiences – a diversity further reflected in the committee's unusual practice to attach the dissenting opinions of individual members to its decisions as a treaty body.[45] As such, CERD's approach to treaty interpretation is widely casted as "creative" (Keane 2020: 255).

The particular case study detailed here centers on General Recommendation No. 35, entitled "Combating Racist Hate Speech," which was adopted in 2013. Reflecting a similar instance of dynamic treaty interpretation as seen with General Comment No. 15 (see Chapter 4), the GR conceives "hate speech" as a particular species of racial discrimination protected under the ICERD, although the term itself never appears in the Covenant. General Recommendation No. 35 takes Articles 4, 5, and 7 of the ICERD as its interpretive foci.[46] Article 4 in particular, which condemns propaganda and organizations that either attempt to justify discrimination or are based on the idea of racial supremacism, had already been subject to several prior general

43 "The speed with which the Convention was considered and adopted, the robustness of the political forces that pushed its formulation and adoption, and perhaps a certain impatience with the niceties of legal drafting are among the factors that underlie some of the problems discussed in this study" (Meron 1985: 316).

44 Ibid.

45 Eiken 2020. www.ejiltalk.org/breaking-new-ground-the-cerd-committees-decision-on-jurisdiction-in-the-inter-state-communications-procedure-between-palestine-and-israel/.

46 CERD/C/GC/35 2013: 8.

recommendations adopted by CERD, namely, in GR 1, 7, and 15. General Recommendation No. 35 thus represented the CERD's *fourth* structured attempt to elucidate the meaning of hate speech, "an unclear term ... alien to the Convention, but governed largely by [its] most convoluted and controversial article" (McGonagle 2017: 246). A committee member summarizes the GR35 as "a rounded articulation of the Convention, subsuming elements of earlier readings by the Committee into a fresh normative synthesis, upgrading the anti-racist currency through clearer integration with libertarian speech principles" (Thornberry 2015: 139).

As is often the draft comment (and TLC) impetus, political and social challenges spurred the necessity for CERD to clarify state obligations, that is, measures to be implemented, on combating racist hate speech. At the center of these challenges was hate speech's wide colloquial use as a term but total absence in international law (McGonagle 2017: 247). In 2001, the World Conference against Racism, Racial Discrimination, Xenophobia and Related Intolerance in Durban, South Africa, took place. Hopes were high within the UN and the human rights bodies concerned with racism that a conference in post-Apartheid South Africa would finally bring progress and it was now the time "the 'globalised' world paid attention, first and foremost, to the structural manifestations of contemporary racism" (Alves 2003). It was a controversial meeting, to say the least, even academic publications deeming it the "Durban debacle" (Lantos 2002) and "Disaster in Durban" (Camponovo 2002). The US and Israeli delegations both left the conference, and the parallel NGO meetings likewise ended in a quarrel over language contained in documents condemning the racist practices of Zionism.[47] The final document adopted contains no language accusing Israel of racism, but many states were unhappy with the outcome for different reasons. These were the circumstances under which the UN had to organize and implement follow-up procedures in its fight against racism and hatred. In 2006, the Intergovernmental Working Group on the Effective Implementation of the Durban Declaration and Programme of Action recommended that CERD would be the right institution to "develop early warning indicators, including on hate speech."[48] While this endorsement was certainly not an invitation for CERD to work on a general recommendation, CERD members Raghavan Vasudevan Pillai and Patricia January-Bardill participated in this meeting[49] and likely discussed options of the committee to address such a recommendation.

[47] Swarns 2001.
[48] A/61/18 2006: 501; E/CN.4/2006/18 2006: para. 45.
[49] E/CN.4/2006/18 2006: para. 6.

Several transnational meetings preceded the adoption of General Recommendation No. 35, most of which were organized and facilitated by OHCHR. In 2008, an expert seminar on the links between Articles 19 and 20 of the ICCPR with regard to freedom of expression and incitement to hatred marked the GR's starting point. Here, the later rapporteur of General Recommendation No. 35 Patrick Thornberry, professor of international law and committee member since 2001, jointly explored legislative patterns, judicial practices, and policies with the High Commissioner, treaty body members, academics, IO staff, and civil society representatives. Papers addressing the meeting's theme had been circulated in advance.[50] Between February and October 2011, expert workshops on freedom of expression and the prohibition of incitement to national, racial, or religious hatred as reflected in Articles 19 and 20 of the ICCPR were held in Vienna, Nairobi, Bangkok, and Santiago. These workshops were communicated as follow-ups of the Durban Review Conference outcome document[51] and led to the adoption of the Rabat Plan for Action.[52] The small group of individuals present at these events quickly facilitated preparations for the GR, and the results of the expert workshops influenced the drafting process (Thornberry 2015: 139).[53] This facilitation features most visibly in the suggestion advanced by Patrick Thornberry at CERD's 79th session in August 2011 to "draft an updated general recommendation" on broader issues, including hate speech, and the committee's subsequent decision to hold a thematic discussion on racist hate speech during the next session.[54] However, the committee eventually decided to discuss the matter in a closed meeting first.[55] The thematic discussion on racist hate speech was postponed to the next session,[56] for which CERD committee members Ion Diaconu and Patrick Thornberry were appointed rapporteurs.[57]

The thematic discussion took place as agreed in the next session in August 2012, supplemented by written and oral input from CERD members,

50 A/HRC/22/17/Add.4 2013 and www.ohchr.org/Documents/Issues/Expression/ICCPR/Seminar2008/CompilationConferenceRoomPapers.pdf.

51 OHCHR 2009. www.ohchr.org/EN/NewsEvents/Pages/DRCAdoptsFinalOutcomeDocument.aspx.

52 www.ohchr.org/EN/Issues/FreedomOpinion/Articles19-20/Pages/ExpertsPapers.aspx.

53 Ten to fifteen individuals, among them the Special Rapporteurs on Freedom of Expression and Opinion, on Freedom of Religion or Belief, and on Racism, Racial Discrimination, Xenophobia and Related Intolerance, as well as members of the Human Rights Committee and CERD participated in the workshops.

54 A/66/18 2011: 93.

55 CERD/C/SR.2126 2012.

56 CERD/C/GC/35 2013: 1.

57 A/67/18 2012: 62.

representatives of permanent missions to the UN, NHRI, NGOs, and academics.[58] The discussion evolved around the concept of racist hate speech and its evolution over time; previous work of CERD on combating racist hate speech; how racist hate speech and freedom of opinion and expression are related; and racist hate speech in political life and in the media, the latter including a focus on the Internet.[59] The only academic speaking at this event was Tarlach McGonagle, a law professor, who received his PhD a few years prior with a dissertation on the interface between minority rights and freedom of expression under international law. His dissertation committee included Patrick Thornberry, a fact that indicates the TLC mechanism at work of a treaty body member closely collaborating with individual(s) to whom he or she has previous ties.[60] At the meeting, Patrick Thornberry noted the entreating from certain stakeholders regarding a need for CERD to craft a general recommendation, while also addressing others' countering skepticism for combating hate speech through legal regulations.[61] It was after this discussion that CERD publicly announced the initiation of a drafting process of a general recommendation on racist hate speech.[62] General Recommendation No. 35 was then adopted one year later.

As stated, the formation of a TLC is less intuitive for a broadly specialized, single-norm treaty body like CERD, especially in such a backlash-provoking context as one that involves drafting an interpretation on a term not included in the actual text of the ICERD. Nevertheless, some professionals involved in the drafting process featured in this case as connected to the professional network of individual treaty body members – Tarlach McGonagle and Patrick Thornberry providing one such example. Beyond legal entrepreneurship for the drafting, we find that once the political and social challenges of hate speech heightened to what may be considered an inflection point, a series of expert meetings came to pass between 2011 and 2012, attended by CERD

58 A/69/18 2014: para 71.

59 McGonagle 2017: 254.

60 Also in line with observations from other cases is that he held several appointments as advisor with other IOs following his work on GR35 and also published widely on CERD and GR35 in particular: www.uva.nl/en/profile/m/c/t.mcgonagle/t.mcgonagle.html.

61 Creatively, he suggested that the title of such a general recommendation would not entail the term: "Noting that the NGOs present would have liked the Committee to draft a general recommendation on racist hate speech, he emphasized that the organized Committee's thematic discussions did not necessarily lead to a general recommendation. The Committee had not yet decided on the matter but would probably do so before the end of the current session. Whatever the outcome, if a new general recommendation were issued, the term 'racist hatred speech' would not appear in the title because it did not appear in the Convention." CERD/C/SR.2197 2013: 25.

62 A/68/18 2013: 83.

members, that directly preceded CERD's drafting of a general recommendation on combating hate speech.

5.5 TLCS ACROSS TREATY BODIES

The three cases detailed above served as plausibility probes for TLCs to occur in other treaty bodies beyond the in-depth case study of CESCR's GC No. 15. While the TLC-specific dynamics were found in all three aforementioned drafting processes, certain observations culled from these cases allow us to parse the concept further. What, then, can we learn from these case studies regarding TLCs as an actor coalition occurring across treaty bodies?

For one, the TLC in each of these cases built on well-established personal relationships between a treaty body member and at least one actor external to the committee that began prior to the former's joining of the committee. In line with the observation in Chapter 2, the sizeable number of professors serving as experts facilitated the drafting participation of their former students, with other external participants likewise worked in on account of their past association with an individual draft member (as prior work colleagues, or as those who crossed paths working within a particular civil society context). To extend these observations into a TLC scope condition: treaty body members' connectedness in a professional network is crucial for a TLC's formation. The inner circle of treaty body decision-making thus often coalesces around a common past, its members comprising a select few whose paths cross at several occasions. The operative framework of such a circle heightens the role of the individual, who is regarded as autonomous and disconnected from his or her professional affiliation,[63] and thereby of the same trustworthiness even when, say, switching NGO employers.

For another, formal access opportunities to international institutions now emerge to be less relevant to TLCs' ultimate success, as their transnational-side members have other pathways to channel influence. The literature has emphasized repeatedly that formal access is key for non-state influence in international politics and formal access is a strong argument for democraticizing IOs.[64] But in treaty interpretation, and thus lawmaking processes, this creates problems: On the surface, only specialized NGOs accredited for the treaty body session can access a draft's

[63] What is more difficult to explain is the motivation for individuals without organizational affiliation to invest their time and possibly other resources into the drafting process without officially garnering reputation for it.

[64] For example, Tallberg, Sommerer, and Squatrito 2013; Tallberg et al. 2015.

public discussion, which, in turn, first requires that the treaty bodies formally announce the drafting of a general comment and publicly invite comments on a draft. Hence, access is determined by two constraining factors: first, formal access is only granted to NGOs, the organized actors of civil society, and in a further distillment, only to those with specialist accreditation; second, and in terms of actual contribution, written and oral statements may be made only if a draft general comment is published or circulated among these specialized NGOs. Such circulation generally delays the process. Formally, there are no opportunities for NGOs to actively and publicly inform the treaty body about their perspective on the scope of the substantial provisions, if not specifically invited and encouraged to do so. Oral statements during days of general discussion are not organized by all treaty bodies and not for every general comment. Furthermore, input required for the draft of a general comment differs from parallel reports: the focus is per definition not on human rights violations by a single state, and traditional monitoring strategies by human rights advocates are thus less suited for a legal debate on the scope of rights. NGOs that want to influence general comments thus have to shift their perspectives toward a more editorial slant: from naming and shaming states' human rights violations in single cases to the broader, more diplomatic goal of preparing a legal opinion on the scope of a particular right, which necessitates determining to what extent it needs interpretation to allow for states' full implementation. From this perspective, NGOs are less successful in drafting general comments if they operate with violation-based arguments instead of law-based arguments, an empirical fact which might consequently narrow down the circle of NGOs with access to those that are specialized in human rights law. The norm subject to interpretation is a further part of the explanation of when and why TLCs are successful. TLCs seemed to be highly likely in drafting processes for norms not included as such in the respective covenant, for example, water or racist hate speech. At the same time, the challenges this norm is facing risk a weakening or a redefinition of human rights, for example, right to health or freedom of expression.

Moreover, the actors in support of a TLC (or even members themselves) are individuals who work for NGOs, as academics or by occupying positions within IOs themselves, with some holding prominent mandates as Special Rapporteurs for country or thematic mandates. What arises through these interactions at the individual level is interinstitutional cooperation, able to overcome "institutional roadblocks" (Anthes 2019), which infers that the norms drafted in treaty interpretations are growing in their immediate

relevancy for the wider international community. The crucial role of these external collaborators or the treaty body members seems especially relevant in cases where the treaty body itself is more polarized around the pertinent issue, for example, abortion. TLCs could thus be argued to increase a general comment's impact through their involving of relevant stakeholders in the issue area.

In a last observation, we find TLCs to foster learning processes in expert committees. Committee members were open and willing to change drafts, include or exclude certain terms, and listen to external expertise. In turn, they also had to make compromises. For those cases where members of the TLC did not see their desired goals included in the adopted general comment, they often successfully chose new pathways to enact norm change afterward.

6

Lawmaking without Governments?

Establishing a normative framework for a human right to water, clarifying states' obligations to prevent rape and violence as a form of torture, combat racist hate speech, elucidating what a right to life encompasses – these are just some of the outputs marking TLCs' active and vivid contribution to the development of human rights through the UN human rights treaty bodies. As the case studies have shown, these contributions reflect the substantive influence of non-state actors on the setting of international law's standards, a domain traditionally regarded as exclusively intergovernmental and to which these actors have access through the collaborative channels of TLCs. In observing their shaping of law, what is striking is that TLCs enact these contributions within the realm of a formal intergovernmental organization, the UN, while at the exclusion of government actors. This inspires certain questions pondering the implications of TLCs' broader embedding in the human rights treaty body system as lawmaking agents – Do TLCs affect the monopoly of states in the making of international law? Do they represent an increasing skewing within formal intergovernmental institutions toward transnational decision-making? How do states react to TLCs? To what extent are TLCs actually a case of international lawmaking sans government involvement? – whose answers frame the heart of this chapter's discourse.

IR scholars have long sought to determine the full range of the actors of global governance, with some earlier works having intuited the agency of transnational actors like TLCs, seeing "a plausible scenario marked by 'governance without government'" (Rosenau and Czempiel 1992). While the international system is traditionally understood as governed *by* states, global governance can indeed manifest in hybrid forms where private or other public actors govern together *with* governments (Beisheim and Liese 2014), or entirely *without* governments, the latter featuring especially in private regimes (Mattli and Büthe 2005; Pattberg 2005) or in areas of limited statehood

(Krasner and Risse 2014). That governance can take place outside the sole hand of government is a fact widely accepted, with alternative modes of governance now recognized as a tangible part of international politics. But more complex to explain, and hence less assented to, is whether governance without a state can even work (Börzel and Risse 2010), as most governance structures are embedded in hierarchies and private or transnational lawmaking is shaped by the rules and structures of public lawmaking (Halliday and Shaffer 2015). For IR research especially, which has already spoken substantively on private rule-making and transnational governance, moreover tricky is the special phenomenon TLCs present in the more intermediary space they occupy as law-shaping agents within formal international institutions where states are rule-makers and -takers (Abbott, Levi-Faur, and Snidal 2017) – a space of alternative governance that sits outside those IR research has already spoken to substantively: that is, private rule-making and transnational governance (Dingwerth 2007; Roger and Dauvergne 2016).

In this space – the space of expert body lawmaking – states, although not entirely absent, are neither directly involved, nor are their contributions very visible; indeed, they are rather targets of outcomes than actual participants, omitted from expert bodies' decision-making processes and precluded veto or voting rights regarding the final draft of the bodies' general comments. While this autonomy of the treaty bodies and the who and how of their decision-making on treaty interpretations has been the main focus of the previous five chapters, this chapter takes a closer look at the opportunities of governments to limit this autonomy and substantively shape the treaty bodies' work. Even from the periphery, states, as the human rights system's founding actors, still occupy a top-level vantage from which they can press their thumb on the operations of the treaty bodies. Explaining how states have proceeded to do so in recent years, against the backdrop of a human rights system increasingly under stress, construes this chapter's answers to its defining queries about the state–TLC relation.

To this end, this chapter turns to the ongoing Treaty Body Reform 2020 initiative to illustrate states' attempt to regain control over the operations of the treaty bodies, in general, and the drafting processes of treaty interpretation, in particular. This precedes a summary of the formal roles of governments in the UN human rights system, before focus turns to the treaty body system, whose growth and expansion have put the chronically underfunded human rights system under enormous stress. More states have become parties to ever more treaties, which has meant more submitted reports to report on implementation and more submitted statements from nongovernmental actors on a lack thereof, all of which require the committees' consideration. Hence, the pressure on the Geneva-based OHCHR is immense, and even further burdened by a lack of support by UN member states. As argued in the previous chapters, a combination of a lack of financial and ideological support by governments helps to facilitate TLCs in the treaty bodies. I then sketch the different formal, informal, treaty body-related and external pathways for how states, in spite of the aforementioned peripheralizing of their involvement, can potentially influence the treaty body system by way of, for example, elections, ratifications, budget, willingness to participate in the procedures, and compliance with their obligations. The ultimate argument I put forward through these sketches is that TLCs are in no way to be seen as a mode of international lawmaking without governments. They are instead a product of an international institution left without adequate resources and support by its members, whose delegated expert body makes use of the instrument of treaty interpretation to regulate state behavior.

6.1 STATES AND THE UN HUMAN RIGHTS SYSTEM

What role do governments play in the international governance of human rights? As the issue area human rights traditionally provides many points of access and participatory opportunities for non-state actors, one might assume states to be actors sidelined, those who must make room for numerous others; but reality shows no zero-sum game. As it stands, states have established, coined, and contested the development of the international human rights regime – and continue to do so. Within the UN human rights system,[1] their formal roles span broad; they are financiers, agenda-setters, mediators, decision-makers, monitoring actors, all while monitored themselves for human rights compliance. Additionally, the UN human rights mechanisms assign states further roles – some formal, others less so – which the following briefly discusses in the context of the UN human rights system's charter-based bodies.

6.1.1 *The Human Rights Council*

In 2006, the Human Rights Council (HRC)[2] replaced the Commission on Human Rights, following the observation of the UN Secretary-General that "the Commission's capacity to perform its tasks ha[d] been increasingly

[1] For a complete overview, see Alston and Mégret 2020.

[2] For an insightful and up-to-date overview of the functions, activities, and sites of the HRC: Tistounet 2020.

undermined by its declining credibility and professionalism."[3] The HRC is the principal intergovernmental forum of the UN human rights system and a subsidiary body of the General Assembly (GA). Its forty-seven members are elected by secret ballot by the majority of the GA's members, and their membership is based on equitable geographical distribution for a period of three years (A/RES/60/251 2006). Three regular sessions per year allow government representatives in the HRC the opportunity to discuss ten agenda items, such as procedural matters, considerations of urgent human rights situations, and reports from UN mechanisms. Special sessions can be held on specific human rights violations, if one-third of the members require it. The HRC fulfills a monitoring and a lawmaking function.

One monitoring instrument is the Universal Periodic Review (UPR), the most visible change in the human rights system after its institutional reform and a direct response to the partiality reproach of the Commission. It is the instrument HRC utilizes to review the actions of every UN member state and assess the extent to which they fulfill their human rights obligations. A UN member state currently goes full circle through the review process every 4.5 years, which starts with an assessment of its domestic human rights situation, followed by recommendations by the HRC on measures to be implemented, which are subsequently accounted for over time, before reassessment of the country's situation (FDFA 2015). In allowing governments both to serve as monitoring actors and be subject to monitoring, this universal peer-review process is an example of horizontal, peer-review monitoring (Carraro, Conzelmann, and Jongen 2019; Elizalde 2019).

The HRC may adopt, upon request from states, a resolution on a particular thematic issue or country situation and choose to create a mandate for an independent expert to conduct further analyses into the human rights violations of concern. These mandates, better known as Special Procedures and defined in the respective resolutions, are enacted through independent experts, special rapporteurs, or working groups, who must report to the HRC annually. While states both create their mandate and elect the mandate-holders, the experts selected generally work as independent experts, often using the mandate to push human rights agendas (Domínguez-Redondo 2020).

The HRC may also establish open-ended, intergovernmental-composed working groups (OEWG) explicitly mandated to develop international law and standards of human rights, such as an international regulatory framework

3 A/59/2005 2005 report, "In larger freedom: towards development, security and human rights for all" UN Secretary-General, Kofi Annan.

on the regulation, monitoring, and oversight of the activities of private military and security companies, or an international legally binding instrument on transnational corporations and other business enterprises with respect to human rights. Successful OEWG have, for example, driven toward the development of optional protocols to the CRC and the Declaration on the Rights of Peasants (A/RES/73/165 2019). Governments are afforded numerous opportunities to shape human rights by, for example, sponsoring resolutions and working groups, supporting candidates for the special procedures, and/or actively participating in events and processes supporting the HRC's causes. But even so, research on the HRC has a rather pessimistic view on the effectiveness of the institution for the advancement of human rights, with some scholarship bespeaking the widely made claim of the HRC as politicized (Carraro 2017; Freedman 2015; Terman and Voeten 2018) and other works giving explanation to why different framings of human rights norms are more likely leading to stagnation than to progressive development (Voss 2018).

In sum, governments showcase as the salient actors in all human rights operations of the UN's charter-based body, featuring with the most leverage in all aspects of human rights governance. They can directly shape the development, application, and compliance with human rights law in the HRC and its mechanisms, while also holding capacity to orient the work of the human rights system's other branches through the discretion they exercise on matters of budget, staff, and the other actors they consult with.

6.1.2 *The Treaty Body System*

This particular subsection builds upon the previous empirical chapters' presentation of the respective functions and procedures of the UN human rights treaty bodies in discussing several pathways through which states can influence their various operations. As government actors are not formally involved in expert committee deliberations, this task – and, indeed, any evaluation of states' role vis-à-vis the treaty bodies – requires first considering what serve as preconditions to the bodies' autonomous decision-making processes.

The first and foremost line of influence lies in states' status as the originating source of human rights law, whose treaties would not exist without the states who draft, ratify, and implement them and establish the monitoring institutions that clarify their bounds. Although studies have shown how nongovernmental actors can initiate, and exert pressure on governments to conclude such treaty-making processes, as well as educate states on the benefits of a new legally binding instrument for human rights (Anderson 2000; Clark 2001), the ultimate existence and design of the instruments of the human rights system remain sovereignly decided upon by governments themselves. Accordingly, states are not obligated to delegate the monitoring of a treaty to an independent expert body and could just as easily opt either for an intergovernmental expert monitoring body, or to reform the whole system to be oriented around peer review. Moreover, they could include rules of procedures to treaties or at least formally inscribe a role for themselves in the drafting or adoption of such rules; they might also ex ante incorporate mechanisms that serve as checks and balances to treaty bodies' processes. To some extent, that shows in opting for expert bodies authorized to consider individual complaints but then their decisions have no legally binding force. For another, the CESCR was not established by the treaty itself but an ECOSOC decision in 1985. That states can indeed effectively pursue certain interests when making human rights treaties shows in the numeral differences that distinguish the treaty bodies' respective memberships,' which range from ten to twenty-three members. Without formal rules defining when such an expansion should take place and the number of members needed for the monitoring of treaties, the "only explanation" for why some bodies have expanded membership while others have not "is that each decision reflected a tension between states' desire to keep costs down and the strength of their commitment to the subject matter of the convention" (Rodley 2013: 625). These various formal agencies we may umbrella under the term *treaty-making*.

A second pathway for governments to influence the course of human rights law is to become party to it – by actually *ratifying* a particular treaty – even while dissenting from the content of the treaty's norms content by making a *reservation*. This has already become a widely used instrument for governments (Goodman 2002; Neumayer 2007; Zvobgo, Sandholtz, and Mulesky 2020) and evinces the perception of "window dressing": only ratifying human rights treaties to signal commitment externally, without any real intention to comply with obligations (Hafner-Burton and Tsutsui 2005). And indeed, such moves hold merit, with it arguably the case that states can exert more influence on the development of a treaty through status as state parties, which enables their involvement in constructive dialogues with the treaty body, than if they remained outside these processes and thus without credibility when criticizing the treaty body for overstepping mandates they have not acknowledged in the first place. Relatedly, the state parties to the treaties could further prevent the need for a general comment by actively *participating* in the system. A timely submission of comprehensive reports avoids the impression that there is a need to clarify the content of treaties, which is often preluding the general comment. As such, a comprehensive report and a constructive dialogue that does not omit certain norms and information on their implementation is another path of governmental influence in (avoiding) human rights lawmaking.

Agent selection via elections or judicial appointments is a powerful tool for governments to exert influence at the international level (Elsig and Pollack 2014; Voeten 2007). Against this backdrop, states may thus use elections as a (third) pathway to determine the progressiveness of a candidate prior to making him or her a treaty body member (Carraro 2019). Only state parties have the authority to nominate candidates, with other ways of application not possible. States indeed often nominate and ultimately elect only those individuals they regard as well suited to be independent experts (Carraro 2019: 844). These selective skew features in the data on treaty body membership (Truscan 2018), which shows candidates-turned-elected-experts to only infrequently hail from activist backgrounds – for example, those previously employed with a human rights NGO, or prior human rights advocates in other organizations – despite their suitability, expertise-wise, to serve on these bodies. States have rather preferred their experts to be academics, diplomats, or government officials, the latter two, although not the most active in drafting general comments or in monitoring activities, particularly important to state parties' relationship with treaty bodies.[4] Notwithstanding that academics may be chosen for their flexibility to spend a significant amount of time away from university, these choices of states arguably reflect a preference to nominate and elect experts who are less likely to take strong positions on human rights obligations and thus formulate less demanding standards.

The treaty bodies need funding to hold their sessions, acquire and exchange information, and work on additional tasks extracurricular to meeting time, such as the drafting of general comments. Hence, unsurprisingly, *budget approval* constitutes a (fourth) pathway for governments to facilitate or disrupt a treaty body's lawmaking efforts. The OHCHR is the administrative branch of the UN human rights system,[5] whose bureaucrats, highly skilled human rights experts in their own right, often play key roles in the politics of treaty body

[4] One former treaty body member explains: "When I used to observe the committee before I was on the committee, I was always some more critical of committee members who were passengers. They didn't seem to be doing anything. And I was always some more critical of them. And then I became a member of the committee and actually, I became a bit more appreciative of these passengers. Because they were passengers in a sense that they didn't do a lot of work, but they were very important politically. So, because of their status, their position, their association with their government or whatever, they were able to create a political space for work for those of us who were doing most of the work. From inside I realized that these people were not working hard, but they were playing a very useful and important political role." Interview with a treaty body member.

[5] For more information on its functions and activities visit their website www.ohchr.org.

drafting processes, becoming involved themselves. In its regular operating, the OHCHR holds the marks of state influence: For one, states approve the office's regular budget in the GA and can make individual voluntary contributions to it, which they may earmark – an increasingly common practice in the UN system to influence political agendas (Patz and Goetz 2019) – to press OHCHR in a particular policy direction. For another, states play a key role in staffing the office, an administrative power they can leverage to fashion the branch's composition toward their liking (Parízek 2017).

Necessary for the OHCHR's effective administration of the human rights pillar of the UN's work, financial support is specifically provided through assessed contributions from all member states. Here we find certain disruption, as the states can skew stingy: indeed, the human rights pillar recently received only 3.3 percent of the 2020 regular budget from the General Assembly (OHCHR 2020: 24). Additionally, the rise of aforementioned earmarked voluntary contributions to the budget by states limits the flexibility of the office to allocate resources to where they are most urgently needed (OHCHR 2020; Patz and Goetz 2019). Their logistical challenges are many: With more states ratifying the human rights treaties and the optional protocols, the OHCHR must coordinate an increasing number of meetings for more and more treaty bodies, while also administering support for more state reports. The specific requirements of these stresses – to supply translators for the meetings and documents for the reporting system – pose considerable challenge both to the budget and to the day-to-day operations of the treaty-based human rights system. As the case studies have shown, this has opened a pathway for treaty body members to invite, and then justify, support by other actors in their processes. Against these backdrops, this pathway of government influence may thus be rendered in two ways: either by providing the OHCHR and the treaty bodies with a more substantive and flexible budget to preclude TLCs' formation and thus external influence on treaty interpretations; or, by restricting the budget, in hopes that this will drive the experts entirely away from any motivation to engage in an additional task in excess of their capacities, that is, one not already part of their regular meetings budget.

The final and most powerful way for governments to influence treaty bodies' operations, while also precluding the lawmaking contribution of TLCs, is to actually *comply* with the treaties. While this might sound naïve and give further substance to critics of a human rights "utopia" (Moyn 2012) given the current global human rights situation, this is the ultimate aim to which the treaties aspire. Of course, new social and political developments require a constant dialogue about what the implementation of the norm requires;

but that does not automatically necessitate that a general comment be drafted and adopted.

Further pathways for governmental influence – those more external to the treaty bodies but still within the human rights system – can be found in *states' approval of UN staff* on human rights. States have made recent use of this pathway, in killing the positions for the Secretary-General "Human Rights up Front" initiative at the UN's NYC headquarters (Lynch 2018). States can moreover go the route of the ECOSOC path[6] to formally restrict the access of specific civil society organizations to the treaty bodies, an instrument they have increasingly utilized in target of organizations from established democracies, such as the Konrad-Adenauer-Foundation in Germany, to provide a recent example.[7] States' exercising of this pathway technically precludes organizations without accreditation to attend meetings or make statements; but even so, their influence here is somewhat muted, mattering less for TLCs, some of whose members are not accredited anyway. Lastly, states can influence the development of human rights law by both *sponsoring mandates* for special procedures and *actively supporting* candidates. As these individuals often set agendas in the treaty bodies, governments can put their thumb on the individuals' candidacies and elections, preventing both.

A leading incentive for states to exert influence on treaty bodies' operations is to use the mechanisms to foster cooperation with other states. Indeed the UN's treaty-based bodies can impact interstate relations both directly and indirectly. Direct impacts are rendered through the role treaty bodies themselves occupy in interpreting the respective treaties. To influence the lawmaking borne from these processes, states may group together and submit joint statements on drafts. What may be deemed the *group of friends*, these states push forward discussions and debates, either with the aim of establishing a new norm or, on the contrary, to prevent a too rigid outcome.[8] Additionally, small states or developing countries assist each other in preparing the periodic report.[9] Indirect impacts of the international human rights treaty regime on interstate relations, and facilitated by human rights NGOs

[6] ECOSOC is the organ of the UN approving accreditation status for NGOs.

[7] In 2018, the Committee on Non-Governmental Organizations recommended in a rare vote to the Council that it not grant consultative status to the Konrad-Adenauer-Stiftung e.V. (Germany), by a vote of ten against to five in favor, with two abstentions. www.un.org/press/en/2018/ecosoc6923.doc.htm.

[8] The term is, of course, meant for those who are interested in new legal human rights norms, like for the Optional Protocol to the ICESCR.

[9] E.g., the Pacific Community's Regional Rights Resource Team's activities https://rrrt.spc.int/about/what-we-do.

and TANs, come in the opportunities it gives states for cooperation in the fields of trade, development, environment, and, foremost, on security.[10]

6.1.3 *Summary*

To sum up, states have numerous pathways at their disposal to exert influence on the design, operations, and dynamics of the treaty bodies. But do these pathways likewise prevent TLCs? The answer is not so clear-cut: While states can indeed exercise considerable influence on the opportunity structure of the expert committees by nominating and electing the experts, unintended consequences may nevertheless arise from tactical nominations and elections. It may be the case that, contrary to the intent behind the election, a more neutral perceived expert, like an academic, drafts and adopts stronger standards when on the committee than an NGO advocate, given that the individual academic expert enjoys autonomy from the government[11] for their work and therefore can benefit from their perceived neutrality when pushing new standards, whereas an NGO member would risk having their arguments rejected as too biased against the government.

But states can nevertheless set the terms of the opportunity structure needed for a TLC through its resource-based pathways of influence. There are multiple reasons why the experts themselves lack the resources – the additional time, money, expertise, and/or connections – to perform the research and work requisite in creating substantive interpretations. All treaty bodies are composed of independent experts not formally employed by the organization, whose pay – prepared on a per-diem basis – directly relates to their time present within the official sessions of the committee. This scheme typically leads to a lack of resources in two regards: in the form of (a) time constraints, as committee members work in their regular jobs the rest of the year and therefore lack time to rigorously prepare the sessions; and (b) missing additional information on state reports, as committee members will not be paid for extra preparation on states' reports and fact finding, such as costs for travel and participation in workshops and conferences. Simultaneously, the secretariats for every treaty body are understaffed for the increased workload this implies,

10 IR scholarship has provided rich accounts for the effect human rights violations have on a state's opportunities for cooperation in other fields, specifically through shaming from NGOs (Murdie and Davis 2012; Peterson, Murdie, and Asal 2018). Similarly, the work of treaty bodies like CESCR has profoundly shaped developments in the trade regime (Desierto 2015).

11 For a comparison of academic freedom see Aberbach and Christensen 2018; Grimm and Saliba 2017.

lacking the necessary personnel to assume duties that go beyond, for example, organizing the sessions, assisting the many countries reporting every year and any supporting of the committee members.

This lack of resources can easily be solved by the state parties. In general, all treaty bodies require budgetary support for their work, which is either approved by the GA or via voluntary donations by governments to the OHCHR. Regarding material resources, it is possible that governments pay more for the institutions of expert bodies by providing additional allowances and per diems for tasks like drafting general comments. States could also agree on more staff within the international organization's responsible secretariats to assist the expert committees or the independent experts. This support could also include nonmaterial resources that provide the decision-making body with expertise and knowledge on the subject of a decision. In these opportunity-structure-related areas, states could exercise their influence to the extent they interrupt the mechanism leading to a TLC prior to its very beginning.

Moreover, as the previous empirical analyses have shown, state parties can intervene in TLC-involved drafting processes to influence outcomes. In GC No. 15's case study, for instance, informal discussions on the privatization of water revealed the experts in CESCR to be subject to pressure by WTO, with governments acting through other international organizations to push their points. This is a further pathway of state influence by pressuring or creating strategic conflict through other IOs (Ranganathan 2016).

6.2 SEEKING TO REGAIN CONTROL: THE TREATY BODY REFORM 2020

Given that states' lack of commitment to support the work of treaty bodies adequately was identified as a salient impetus for TLCs, the recent treaty body reform[12] can be seen as states' attempt to countervail the spoils of their laissez-faire approach and regain control over the bodies' procedures. As it stands, states have tried to diminish the authority granted to the committees to develop treaty interpretations by pushing drafting processes to exclude non-state actors in favor of consultations with the state parties themselves.[13] States thus appear to know about the power of TLCs, an argument this sub-chapter hence establishes. But rather than use the multiple institutional pathways that

[12] The process was finished in 2020 and is now subject to review by the GA.

[13] The GA "encourages the human rights treaty bodies to develop an aligned consultation process for the elaboration of general comments that provides for consultation with States parties in particular and bears in mind the views of other stakeholders during the elaboration of new general comments," A/RES/68/268 2014: supranote 14.

would render their existence unnecessary – by, for example, expressing stronger commitment to the treaties, sticking to the reporting procedure, and adequately funding the system – they have rather sought to regain control by putting additional pressure on the system through year-long reform processes with possibly limited effect.[14]

The first legs of an actual push for reform came from within the human rights system already in 2009, when the former High Commissioner for Human Rights Navi Pillay published a report, in which she drew attention to the grievances in the OHCHR and initiated the so-called Treaty Body Strengthening Process. This process afforded all interested stakeholders the opportunity to submit proposals for reform and to react to others. To this end, the High Commissioner coordinated several formal and informal meetings for committee members, UN institutions and specialized agencies, states parties, NHRIs, NGOs, and science representatives. The breadth of the actors involved, as well as the detailed documentation of the meetings showed the process as inclusive and transparent. In 2012, the High Commissioner presented the initiative's final report, which highlighted the main challenges of the treaty system, made recommendations for improving its effectiveness and found the system to be "at a critical juncture" (Pillay 2012). Although referring to the growing workload of treaty bodies, these words had further significance for the global human rights community: at the initiatives of China and, later, Russia, the General Assembly passed a contested resolution in February 2012 that also commenced a process to strengthen the human rights bodies – only this time exclusively intergovernmental.[15]

Criticism from civil society followed immediately, leading the network of treaty body advocates in Geneva to inquire whether the General Assembly even had the power to intervene in the working methods of the treaty bodies (Alkarama et al. 2014). Nevertheless, the 2014 General Assembly passed Resolution 68/268, which included various proposals and recommendations to strengthen the effectiveness of the treaty bodies. In this particular resolution, the General Assembly made clear that the procedures for treaty interpretation should run in closer coordination with the states and recommended that the committees reform their work processes accordingly. The implicit reform to exclude civil society actors from these processes sparked criticism (Reiners 2018), with the committees themselves responding with a joint statement, highlighting their authority to interpret the treaties (Grossmann et al. 2014).

14 For a detailed analysis of the history of treaty body reform attempts from an enterprise transformation perspective, see Egan 2020.

15 A/RES/66/254 2012, see also www.asil.org/insights/volume/18/issue/16/reform-united-nations'-human-rights-treaty-bodies#_edn6.

This resolution heralded the "Treaty Body Reform 2020" process (Geneva Academy 2018; OHCHR n.d.), which includes two mechanisms: first, the preparation of a biennial report by the UN Secretary-General on the state of the treaty body system and second, an overall review of the effectiveness of the measures taken pursuant to resolution 68/268 no later than 2020. Academic assessments and recommendations were coordinated by the Geneva Academy's "Academic Platform on Treaty Body Review 2020" initiative, in close collaboration with the Geneva-based human right bodies.[16]

During the process leading up to 2020, the gap widened between those actors supporting the treaty bodies and those who view their growing importance more skeptically. This prompted certain actors outside of the UN to begin building bridges by investing in new initiatives and innovative forms of exchange to truly find solutions for a strong treaty body system.[17] Nevertheless, civil society's perception as the reform process reaches its end is rather pessimistic: in their view, the strengthening of the treaty body system runs contrary to the interests of many states "who are actively seeking to undermine the system in order to avoid human rights scrutiny."[18]

The High Commissioner Bachelet presented a statement at the GA in June 2020[19] in which she highlights the need for an open, transparent, and merit-based process for election of candidates and the need for adequate budgets for OHCHR to secure the success of the treaty bodies. But, she also clearly defended the autonomy of the treaty bodies, by rejecting needs to reopen treaties for signature and by highlighting that the treaty bodies themselves are best equipped to take steps to implement the proposed reforms. While finishing this book, the GA needs to review the proposals and agree on a resolution.

6.3 LAWMAKING OUTSIDE THE INTERGOVERNMENTAL CORE

The steady growth of the UN human rights treaty body system in size and its relevance for international and domestic human rights law – and international law more generally – has led to rifts between Geneva and New York, and the

16 See www.geneva-academy.ch/geneva-humanrights-platform/initiatives/detail/70-treaty-body-review-2020.

17 Most notably the Geneva Academy and the Human Rights Platform organized numerous meetings and facilitated exchange in networks beyond the professional smaller circles: https://www.geneva-academy.ch/geneva-humanrights-platform.

18 GI-ESCR 2020. www.gi-escr.org/latest-news/ensuring-human-rights-accountability-in-the-context-of-the-covid-19-pandemic-opportunities-and-challenges-of-online-work-for-the-un-human-rights-treaty-bodies-kwly3.

19 www.ohchr.org/EN/NewsEvents/Pages/DisplayNews.aspx?NewsID=25917&LangID=E.

UN human rights system and the GA. Such rifts have conjured discourse of the existence of a "war on human rights" (Lynch 2018). In light of this discourse: how do the developments presented in this chapter impact the structure of international law (Krieger, Nolte, and Zimmermann 2019)? Will the future of the human rights treaty system change from an international to a transnational one, or will states take back control? What do TLCs tell us about the human rights regime and the state – is it the "persistent power of human rights" (Risse, Ropp and Sikkink 2013) that prevails in the end?

States may be the founders and addressees of the treaty regime, or the regulators and targets (Abbott, Levi-Faur, and Snidal 2017), but they have delegated the monitoring and interpretation of the standards to independent expert committees, who are expected to act as international intermediaries (Pegram 2017). However, as the existence of TLCs confirms, these intermediaries do not always act in the spirit of their principals, with some exceeding their given mandates with progressive general comments. Particularly the role that civils society actors (can) play – and particularly TLCs, who change "the bilateral and formal nature of the interstate monitoring regime in significant ways" (De Búrca 2017: 310) – has provoked significant backlash from governments and international lawyers. Nevertheless, states technically hold the power to end the practice of the treaty bodies, as well as numerous ways to shape their bounds.[20] For one, they can elect the members of the expert committees at their discretion, and thereby choose candidates more or less strict in a treaty's application or those with more or less expertise in a given legal field. For another, they can exercise their particularly powerful thumb on budgetary support in contexts where the authority and decisions of a committee exceed their tolerance.

The interpretation of human rights by the treaty bodies and through TLCs is essential for their universal protection and, given the scarce resources of the UN human rights system, also without an alternative. The assessment of the causes and extent of changed political, economic, and social conditions for human rights protection requires special knowledge by civil society actors, for example, on implementation difficulties of human rights at the local level – for which there remains no substitute in most cases. States should rely on these experts' judgment, rather than challenge or curtail their expertise, and work together with treaty bodies to standardize procedures.

At the same time, there can be no implementation of the general comments without political will, and consensus with states on the reform of the treaty system should be achieved for this aim. Most treaty body members are aware

20 Intergovernmental frameworks remain furthermore important for transnational cooperation (e.g., Hickmann 2015).

that overstretching their discretion in treaty interpretations would lead to ignorance or denial of the treaties' obligation by state parties and thus harm the treaty body system. Delegating the interpretation of the treaty to expert committees without further regulation forced state parties to struggle between reclaiming their sovereignty over human rights development through general comments and showing commitment to the treaty bodies' decision on human rights.

The question of the future of the treaty system can be answered functionally, that is, with regard to the effective protection of human rights for all. States, however, become detrimental to this strengthening, if they cut budgets and reject specific additions to the regime. The fact that the treaty bodies are nevertheless able to continue their activities against state resistance is based, on the one hand, on the importance of their outputs for the work of many actors in human rights policy and, on the other, on the fact that states do not actually have to ratify the general comments. Further playing a role is the constant power of human rights itself, which attests to the treaty regimes fitness for the future. States may disagree with committee procedures and budgetary pressures, but an exit and thus the shunning of universally shared values of the international community will continue to be something difficult to justify in the future, especially in the face of global civil society.

Indeed, if state parties do not equip the committees with sufficient resources, or even reduce them, it becomes harder for the experts to work on new drafts and to spread information on an adopted decision; and accordingly, a community is less likely to use the new standards when no material information is accessible. Furthermore, the power of states in international law is simply exercised by either not obeying it or by leaving the regime. In this case the committee proves to be powerless. It can only be argued with the power of the legal regime itself and high reputation costs if state parties prefer to remain in the regime against their interests.

The debate around the treaty body reform and who the treaty bodies may consult for the elaboration of general comments shows two things: first, that states acknowledge the effect general comments might have on human rights protection as a cause for their skepticism on who might have a say in the process; and second, that the treaty bodies oppose any interference in their working methods, arguing that the treaties authorized them to adopt their own rules of procedure. As such, the outcome of the reform process remains to be seen and whether it might actually deliver on its promise of a more efficient treaty body system or whether the reform politics between the entities in New York and Geneva end up fragmenting the human rights system only further.[21]

[21] For IO reform effects see Hanrieder 2015.

7

Conclusion

At a moment where the human rights system is permeated by pessimism regarding its health, future and efficacy – where it is fragmented in reform politics, challenged by state- and civil society–led human rights regression, and generally pervaded by the sense that it just does not work anymore (or never has) and its foundations are wrong – my aim to write a book about this system's inner workings might seem a lost cause. But my acute focus here was always less to comment on the system's present sticking points than to figure out the forward progress of one its actors: the treaty bodies, where we see expert committees capitalize on their autonomy to adopt interpretations, the general comments, that work around any stagnation of formal lawmaking. Indeed in teasing beneath that practice – in figuring out how and by whom these interpretations come to pass – I discerned a vein of promise underneath the pessimism in TLCs, coalitions that arise, at least occasionally, to push for and then create general comments that fill some pressing gap in human rights law.

And filling gaps they do: While admittedly not all treaty body (whether TLC-led or not) interpretations change the course of global human rights governance, general comments can, and often do, come alive as substantive, even progressive constructs of law. To give an example: In 2010, the High Court of India ruled that there had been a "complete" and "systemic failure" on the part of the Government to effectively implement pre- and post-natal services to reduce maternal and infant mortality.[1] The Court found that this failure of providing access to health services for the lower castes severely affected not just the two women on whose behalf the petitions were brought – one of them died as a result of the lack of access to these services – but also a large number of

[1] *Laxmi Mandal* v. *Deen Dayal Harinagar Hospital & Ors*, WP(C) 8853 of 2008, and 10700 of 2009 (2010), India, High Court of Delhi, Judgment of June 4, 2010.

women and children placed in similar positions across the country.[2] Additional to compensation for the claimants, the Court determined that maternal health schemes in India themselves needed reform. Its argumentation on the meaning of the right to health relied upon General Comment No. 14, adopted by CESCR in 2000.[3] The decision "influenced subsequent judicial decisions in India and other countries. (. . .) [It] set a national and international precedent for using constitutions to support maternal health rights and provided advocates with an additional tool for holding governments accountable" (Dunn, Lesyna, and Zaret 2017: 77).

This is, of course, not the only example speaking to the significance of general comments as authoritative interpretations of the international human rights treaties, and this is by far not the only example for violations of human rights. Human rights are contested, are violated, and are denied by governments every day in every part of the world. Yet, human rights law continues to matter for many movements and individuals all over the globe and give hope and voice to those without formal powers (Brysk 2013; Sikkink 2019). What this book highlights and what above example illustrates: through general comments, TLCs can at their best bring change in law and in politics for the life of many.

7.1 TLCS IN HUMAN RIGHTS

TLCs form around independent experts and their mode of operation is determined by the professional relationships among their constituent members mainly outside of the premises of Palais Wilson in Geneva. TLCs are most likely to emerge around those issues where political and social developments challenge the meaning of legal norms (globally and over time), when legal entrepreneurs facilitate the drafting process and provide resources and transnational meetings and conferences provide points of exchange (see Chapter 3). TLCs shed light on the particularities of human rights treaty interpretations and provide an analytical lens to understanding the key role expert bodies and issue professionals play in the development of human rights law.

The linguistic shift from civil society to professionals makes it clear that an actor's ability to provide expertise to the drafting process does not depend on

[2] For summaries of the ruling with regard to ESCR rights, see www.icj.org/escr_litigation/laxmi-mandal-v-deen-dayal-harinagar-hospital-ors-w-p-c-no-8853-of-2008/ and https://www.escr-net.org/caselaw/2010/laxmi-mandal-v-deen-dayal-harinagar-hospital-ors-wpc-nos-8853-2008.

[3] *Laxmi Mandal* v. *Deen Dayal Harinagar Hospital & Ors*: para. 23.

their organizational status and the organization's access to the process, but rather because they are experienced in the process of drafting treaty interpretations or because they provide technical knowledge on the topic of the draft. As legal entrepreneurs, they can initiate the drafting process and actively build a TLC. Next to the usual advocates for human rights politics, TLCs may also include the technical knowledge of issue professionals, for example, medical professionals. What became eminently clear in the empirical chapters is that general comments need more than just knowledge on existing case law for their drafting; multiple perspectives on implementation gaps, blocks, and challengers in different contexts. Within the UN, the treaty body members, the secretariats, specialized agencies, and the Special Procedures mandate holders can be valuable sources of information for a specific general comment. Yet, the expertise within the UN system is often simply not available or sufficient for the draft of a particular general comment because it requires a perspective from external experts to be most suited for implementation in diverse contexts. Here, TLCs of state-empowered experts and issue professionals work together to develop human rights through treaty interpretations.

7.2 TLC EFFECTIVENESS

TLCs are no sufficient explanation for general comments, nor are all general comments the product of a TLC. A TLC's effectiveness is thus understood in its ability to develop a draft that needs to be adopted by the treaty body once the coalition is formed. As a coalition, TLC's are effective because its members provide the technical and legal expertise needed for the draft within an agreed time frame and facilitated by their informal status.

The individual TLC participants who are not themselves members of the state-empowered entity, the treaty body, can therefore influence human rights lawmaking through a mechanism derived from the common explanation of resource exchange – that is, that they can do so by providing resources to the member(s) of the treaty body – but that also highlights the role of their recognition as expert through (previously established) personal and/or professional relationships. One example: The sizeable number of professors serving as independent experts on the treaty bodies facilitates the participation of former students in drafting general comments, who typically are specialized in a particular general comment's topic either as now-academics themselves or because they work on that topic for an NGO, an international institution or even as individual consultant. The important point here is that the TLC's external participants are in on account of their past association with an individual draft member (as prior work colleagues, or as those who crossed paths working within a particular civil society context). To extend these observations into a TLC scope condition: The inner circle of treaty body decision-making thus often coalesces around a common past, its members comprising a select few whose paths crossed at several occasions but not necessarily on the premises in Geneva. This flexibility of the when and where of a TLC members' interactions contributes to their effectiveness, as they can avoid highly formalized deliberation processes.

But that does not explain whether well-acquainted and resource-equipped members in TLCs could go ahead with every draft. The case studies in this book, but also observations beyond them, feature internal discussions and the dual role of the treaty body members as drivers for a TLC's effectiveness. Internal discussions in the TLC often highlight different interests in the draft's content. Remember how ultimately sanitation had to be stripped off the general comment on water, although the members of the TLC were broadly in favor of it – yet the treaty body not at all costs. A treaty body member is elected as an independent expert but needs to be political and diplomatic. While they can, within the TLC, outsource getting the politics around a certain issue to other TLC members, they can only do so to a certain extent. They need to be political in their activities to get the highest degree of clarity of state obligations into the document, but they need to be diplomatic to not do so against the treaty body's will and risk non-adoption.

The role of time, or temporality, has ultimately played a less important role for the effectiveness of TLCs than assumed in Chapter 4. The assumption emerged from the human right to water which was drafted in a short time and because sources pointed to the urgency of a timely adoption at several points in the drafting process. However, other examples in this book have shown that urgency was less relevant and some drafting processes were interrupted for several years before being picked up again. Challenges to human rights can give new or repeated incentives for a drafting process and if a legal entrepreneur is still willing to go ahead with it, and transnational meetings bring the item up again, then a TLC reemerges, but might have a change in membership. The more important driver for the effectiveness of a TLC here is issue salience, which the treaty body often proves by reference to state dialogues. The character of the issue at stake not only drives the question of membership in a TLC, but ultimately the effectiveness for a TLC's mission to shift it from drafting to adoption.

The norm subject to interpretation is a further part of the explanation of why TLCs are successful with their drafting process. TLCs were most likely involved in drafting processes for norms not yet included in the respective covenant, for example, water or racist hate speech. Yet, the treaty body needs to be convinced that this norm is within the treaty's scope.

7.3 TLC LEGITIMACY

TLCs in human rights contribute to the making of human rights law without a formal mandate. Nevertheless, I see a TLC's legitimacy connected to their agency for treaty interpretations which serve to protect human rights from arbitrary interpretation by state parties, to correct historical weaknesses – injustices – in the treaties, and to compensate for unproportionate underfunding of the human rights pillar in the UN. While the first two factors derive a TLC's legitimacy from the illegitimate use of human rights law (Besson 2013), the latter is derived from the IO's inability to provide the resources for the mandated task. In that case, TLCs benefit from the IO's legitimacy deficits, for instance, when other IO entities are not perceived as appropriately exercising their authority, leading to a mismatch between perceptions among different IO bodies to which a TLC might be seen as delegitimizing actors (Tallberg and Zürn 2019). Additionally, their coalition emerges and works for outcomes which the networks and communities of the individuals involved engage with; thus, they believe that the general comment ought to be obeyed.

When leaving this structural and functional consideration of their legitimacy, and taking a perspective of representation, the picture is less favorable though and should provide ample avenues for future research. As a coalition of expert members in state-empowered entities and actors from (mainly) civil society, we can approach their legitimacy in lawmaking from a multiple representation approach (Besson and Martí 2018). However, the representation is not defined in criteria or controlled for by its members. The emphasis of personal relationships among TLC members heightens the risk for privileged access and the reproduction of power structures which could ultimately undermine the perception of expert bodies as impartial. The composition of TLCs is far from democratic and the members' access is not transparent. Sociological institutionalism and social constructivistm have highlighted the normative character of transparency and openness for the legitimacy of international institutions. Here, it is less about the costs and benefits and logics of consequences and more about the logic of appropriateness. International organizations have to be regarded as legitimate institutions to survive. Legitimate global governance from this perspective includes more than only decisions made by governments. Both disciplines, international legal scholarship and international relations, have acknowledged legitimacy as a key dimension for successful legalization (Abbott et al. 2000) or implementation of norms, and in this phase I emphasize the role of TLCs as sources of legitimacy. Including civil society actors in the drafting process can make it more transparent for the public (Black 2009), yet without a formal mandate, TLCs lack human rights accountability mechanisms (Hirschmann 2020; Johansen 2020).[4] A TLC's internal deliberations with professionals from scientific, policy, or legal networks also foster learning processes in the expert committee. This involvement of external actors might be looked at as constituting a turn to more legitimate human rights legislation on the global level, yet it does so without state consent which delegitimizes the principle of state sovereignty for international decision-making.

The work of a TLC is not necessarily public, also because of their informal status. As a counterfactual theoretical exercise, one could ask whether formal regulation of access to the drafting process, as, for example, intended through reform proposals in GA Res. 68/268, would compensate for this lack of transparency and add to a TLC's legitimacy. Formalizing the human rights lawmaking process – that is, erasing the access of non-state actors in consulting and drafting alongside the treaty bodies[5] – would preclude civil society participation in favor of the states (see Chapter 6). Non-regulation also reinforces the legitimacy of the committees as *independent*, leaving the elected experts free to consult with any non-state actor.[6] The treaty body as a collective actor ultimately provides a quality control, not only because they adopt the final decision. If a formalization of the process creates opportunities for all interested actors to formally give input on the process and the scope of the interpretation, then the treaty body members would be confronted with much more diverging input. The treaty bodies would have less control over the process than if they were the ones who asked for input. More participants in the process lead to more complexity, which impedes effective decision-making. Ironically, involvement of civil society actors in international organizations is usually an argument made for more transparent, thus fairer, decision-making. For lawmaking by expert committees, transparency appears to be

[4] Some TLC members might, however, be held accountable by their professional community (Deloffre 2016).

[5] Proposed by the General Assembly resolution on treaty body strengthening A/RES/66/254 2012.

[6] Many interview partners requested to remain anonymous, and some information was strictly confidential. This was justified with the argument that it would not be helpful for either the treaty bodies or civil society if their close collaboration for drafting general comments became public. Governments were described as already very critical toward the close collaboration between treaty bodies and civil society. Many were concerned that information provision and work on the general comments could be hampered by a formalized procedure.

counterproductive for collaboration between committee member and civil society actors.

7.4 TLCS AND THE FUTURE DEVELOPMENT OF HUMAN RIGHTS

As a concept, TLCs help explain the rapidly evolving justiciability of economic, social, and cultural rights, as well as the broader trend of increasing adoptions of general comments (see Chapter 2 2), a trend that occurred despite a reform process that has aimed at slowing down this development (Chapter 6). Economic and social rights have long been neglected or otherwise not been taken seriously by human rights scholars and lawyers as legal norms. For example, in 2013 a treaty body member from another committee was surprised by my interest in the ICESCR and told me that these are not "real" rights.[7] Since then, economic, social, and cultural rights have undergone a rapid normative development, accompanied by strong global mobilization (Hertel 2017; Ratjen and Satija 2014). TLCs are likely found around these human rights because their advocacy depends on clear obligations and a consensus on who needs to do what (Hertel 2006; Jurkovich 2020a). ICESCR leaves interpretative room for governments and their obligations to "progressively realize" the rights using their "maximum available resources."[8] This has consequences for the protection of these rights – and resulted in "an emphasis among both human rights activists and researchers on making ESC rights more justiciable, usually by creating a legal right or through constitutional reforms" (Baer 2015: 355). TLCs provide a lens through which these efforts can be analyzed and give further insights into the advocacy for economic, social, and cultural rights.[9]

While the TLC for a human right to water (Chapter 4) gave a detailed account of how and why this coalition was benefiting from weaknesses in the treaty, the case studies in Chapter 5 gave substance to the book's claim that TLCs are to be found in other treaty bodies, too. Even in treaty bodies monitoring a treaty with rather narrow focus, such as CAT, we find close collaborations between the responsible committee member and outside professionals. TLCs, while most proliferating when initiating drafting processes around a substantial gap in human rights law, are not limited to specific rights

7 Background talk with a treaty body member.

8 United Nations December 16, 1966a: Article 2.1.

9 The business and human rights field has further merits in providing knowledge which is needed for general comments but is not (yet) part of the human rights repertoire knowledge.

or treaty bodies but rather inherent to the entire human rights treaty body system.

This finding, in the end, is connected to the resource scarcity affecting all treaty bodies which proves salient for the need to put the task of drafting general comments into the hands of one or few committee members who, because of their independent expert status, need to carry this one out outside of their committee's work in their main occupancy. Also, as state-elected experts on human rights, they know who could provide valuable input to the process and whose work will likely benefit from a particular general comment.

7.5 TLCS IN GLOBAL GOVERNANCE

TLCs are of relevance to several strands of research and, as a concept, bridge three disparate fields: IO research on their opening up, the influence of transnational actors on international relations, and the role of experts and expertise in international law.

7.5.1 *IOs as Open Systems for Experts*

This book evolved from and is deeply rooted in IR research on IOs, and particularly that which speaks to the ways in which the decision-making processes underlining international law have recently widened to include new actors. As others have argued, formal access is but only one aspect of this increasing openness, with ever more interactions taking place on an informal level (Tallberg, Sommerer, and Squatrito 2013: 57). TLCs are informally built and operative at the boundaries of the UN's human rights system, they highlight the extent to which focus on formal access overlooks how this system skews open. Indeed, expert bodies, through coalitions like TLCs, often construe their practices at the individual level, outside the formal bounds of the system in which they are situated. They do so precisely because of the independent character afforded to them by state empowerment. That is, as a body composed of *independent* experts left with no required state-determined procedure to follow, expert bodies can – and as the TLC concept shows, do – move beyond their core committee to fulfill their tasks with the help of experts from organizations external to their own, transcending their IO boundaries en route. Nevertheless, they still fulfill IO boundary work, often in close cooperation with other bodies of the IO, particularly the IPA (Kranke 2020; Orsini, Louafi, and Morin 2017). As such, TLCs contribute to broader arguments about the informal structures, actors and processes of global governance (Roger 2020; Vabulas and Snidal 2013) by explaining why a potentially influential form of collaboration without any formalized status, without any orchestration through IOs (Abbott et al. 2015; Littoz-Monnet 2020), and without any control mechanisms by states can contribute to the making of treaty interpretations. A TLC's member's access on the grounds of individual evaluation necessarily connects the above-mentioned findings on the facets of TLC legitimacy to research on hierarchies in IOs (Fehl and Freistein 2020; Mattern and Zarakol 2016). The empirical findings of this book also support the notion that parts of an IO can facilitate collective action and seek to achieve common goods, but at the cost of simultaneous "closure" of the system for some (Viola 2020).

The findings of this book show TLCs to be typically found in situations where states do not act (enough) on challenges arising for human rights. Through the instrument of treaty interpretations, these coalitions work on the clarification of state obligations in response to global challenges and crises. TLCs require a focus on agency and on who can act as change makers in international law, broadly informing interdisciplinary scholarship on the politics of international law (Aalberts 2013; Abbott and Snidal 2012). This book also shows how TLCs are facilitated by IO structures, such as inadequate funding and lack of support from governments.

Finally, I see much potential in connecting TLCs to explanations of IO authority in human rights (Heupel, Hirschmann, and Zürn 2018; Heupel and Zürn 2017). The procedures on rule-making appear shallow in expert committees like the UN treaty bodies, but provide key insights into the study of social practices of rule-making (Raymond 2019; Wiener 2018). My concept on TLCs might further add a microsociological perspective to the fragmentation of human rights and regime complexity scholarship (Hafner-Burton 2009; Krisch, Corradini, and Reimers 2020), including facilitating demands for justification of negative spillovers (Faude and Große-Kreul 2020). For example, recent views on human rights as expressed in Geneva stood in sharp contrast to rulings of regional human rights courts, increasing opportunities for forum shopping in human rights. TLCs might arise out of such conflicts, but also could be affected by pathologies arising from new strategic options of IO member states (Hofmann 2019). The role of TLCs in such regime complexes might also be analyzed from the perspective of norm research (Margulis 2013) and in cases where regional organizations overlap in their human rights competencies (Panke and Stapel 2018).

7.5.2 *TLCs as Transnational Actors*

It is hard to pinpoint gaps or introduce novel concepts within the rich literature on transnational actors in IR, and indeed my conceptualization of TLCs

(Chapter 3) does neither. What it does, however, is add to the study of these actors, and IOs in particular, by introducing a new actor type, the TLC, that gives empirical and explanatory insight to the mainly invisible and unpaid labor of transnational actors in collaboration with expert bodies for the development of international law.

That these actors are shown to successfully enact human rights law outside formal treaty-making is actually a novel point, as it transcends current explanations of transnational influence on other phases of the policy cycle, particularly those state-centric, where a focus on multilateral negotiations for treaty-making has led to more cautious assessments of transnational actors' influence without government actors. TLCs directly connect with the scholarship on NGOs and TANs by providing a concept through which successful agenda-setting, but unsuccessful formal treaty-making finds a different form of advocacy – namely within a TLC.

Moreover, that many individual TLC members shown in this book's cases were not affiliated with the "big" – that is, large and well-known – human rights NGOs that usually come across in scholarship on influential advocacy for human rights law has some implication for future NGO research. For one, this empirical point deserves further probing for explanation. Although this book would attribute this lack of affiliation to the personal ties between the experts – a notion borne from the fact that the solicited NGO individuals were drawn from an expert member's or other key drafter's personal network, rather than for their involvement as part of a big NGO – there could be other answers. For instance, this lack may result from the "authority trap" in which these bigger NGOs find themselves in competition for resources (Stroup and Wong 2017).

The book moreover highlighted the role of individuals in fostering change and how, in many cases, their agency did not stem from the features of their organizations. This finding speaks to the rich literature on NGO interactions, and provides us with further opportunities to compare the roles of individuals in and for the formation and operation of different TLCs (Schneiker and Joachim 2020: 2). However, their membership does not aim at interagency cooperation per se. In some cases, such as the right to water, one NGO officer was indeed identified as a gatekeeper to the drafting process by treaty body members and IPA staff as well as other NGO staff. TLCs rather acknowledge a difference between professional and organizational logics, as in scholarship on transnational professionals (Cohen 2010; Harrington and Seabrooke 2020; Henriksen and Seabrooke 2017), especially that on legal professionals (Dezalay and Madsen 2017).

7.5.3 *TLCs and Expertise in International Law*

This book does not claim to bear fruit on the question of general comments' status in human rights law, nor should the "lawmaking" named in the acronym TLC be taken as anything but a reference to self-proclaimed intention – the intention, that is, to use general comments as a popular way "to *influence lawmaking* [italics mine]."[10] Where this book does, however, make a wider contribution potentially relevant to legal scholarship comes in its study of the omnipresent human rights experts and the role of expertise for treaty interpretations, which here comprises both legal and other technical (functional) expertise (Kennedy 2005; Leander and Aalberts 2013). To reiterate key findings: The expert body collectively adopts the interpretation, but it is the individual – *independent* – experts' actions and collaborations which provide this output and which they enact through TLCs. Accordingly, the TLC concept helps to disaggregate which expertise goes into the development of international law. Although many have highlighted the possession of political and policy expertise among treaty body expert members, most have attributed the experts' value to derive from their legal expertise and knowledge on procedures of domestic implementation (Carraro 2019). The findings reveal that the relationship between different types of expertise is not so easily construed, and likely also not separable from the decision at stake. After all, a lawyer with knowledge on procedures of implementation on the right to food within Western democracies with civil law traditions would not equally count as procedural expertise on the implementation of the same right in common law. The human rights treaty bodies feature, and indeed need, more than just legal expertise to interpret the treaties they monitor – contrasting with courts and other judicial bodies, who involve only lawyers in their shaping of law. The focus on treaty bodies as a hybrid lawmaking body has prompted the question as to whether there should be more lawyers, or even only lawyers, serving on the treaty bodies (Rodley 2013: 624). Many treaty body members in interviews and background talks articulated support of such a view, arguing that too many different perspectives from other disciplines led to tunnel vision from their own disciplinary standpoint on the drafting process. Yet, one could equally argue that this tunnel vision is not something exclusive to the nonlegal professions. Plurality in decision-making is still a strong argument for better outcomes. However, if we treat legal expertise as one among many others, it also risks the perception of a decision as being neutral, a feature usually connected with legal expertise (Leander and Aalberts 2013).

[10] Interview with NGO officer as quoted in Chapter 1.

7.6 FUTURE RESEARCH AGENDA ON TLCS

TLCs contribute to several strands of scholarship on IOs, transnational actors, and international law, and I have highlighted a few of such relevant findings and how TLCs might beneficially inform this scholarship. To close this book, I want to propose some further ideas about how to proceed with research on TLCs, that is, to lay out an agenda for future scholarship.

First, and probably most obviously, the concept's generalizability should be tested within the human rights treaty regime. With more than 175 general comments adopted so far, there is ample opportunity to probe this concept further in analyses – say, to identify a more extensive understanding of the patterns and conditions under which TLCs emerge and effectively collaborate. Obviously, we must delve deeper into the question of how TLCs influence the impact of general comments on human rights. In this book, I mainly described general comments as "potentially" impactful. A good starting point to look for causal links between TLCs and impact of general comments here lies in this book's observation that when a TLC is more polarized around a pertinent issue, for example, abortion, it seeks input from diverse sources to aid in its subsequent drafting of a general comment. In some of the book's cases, contestation occurred as a reaction to the progressive normative development of human rights law – not only through states but also through groups equally claiming to present civil society (Goetz 2020; Guns 2013). In the Human Rights Committee's discussions about a general comment on the right to life and state obligations with regard to abortion, there were even more statements by antiabortion groups than by those supporting a progressive general comment on that mater (see Chapter 5).

More research on cases of non-drafting and non-adoption of general comments could also point to causal links between TLCs and the impact of general comments. The only non-developed general comment analyzed in this book occurred in CAT, where treaty body members refrained from an updated definition of torture because civil society actors were afraid such clarification would come at the price of narrowing the scope rather than clarify it (see Chapter 5). TLCs could thus be argued to increase a general comment's impact through their involving of relevant stakeholders in the issue area. TLC research might find a valuable link here with scholarship on compliance as much as other scholars of change in human rights protection do. Experimentalist governance accounts of the effectiveness of human rights law, channeling TLCs as resulting from the significant changes in "the bilateral and formal nature of the interstate monitoring regime" (De Búrca 2017: 310).

Although a TLC's aim becomes accomplished with the adoption of a general comment, the coalition's members' human rights law-shaping activities might not see a paralleling end. Against this backdrop, further areas for investigation might include how a TLC's member relates to TLCs in other treaty bodies. Similarly, it might be interesting to study how the knowledge gained through a TLC's drafting process, in exchange with several professionals, travels to other policy- and treaty-making processes. Cases in this book where members of the TLC did not see their desired goals included in the adopted general comment bear witness to this assumption, often successfully finding new pathways to enact norm change afterward. From this perspective, an extension to TLCs impact on decision-making in regional and international human rights courts as well as in private regimes (Mende 2020) bears fruitful ground for scholarship, also to see how fragmented the regime really is (see also above 7.5.1).

Another research agenda item is to give an analysis of the network that makes up TLCs in the human rights treaty bodies. Connected to the composition of treaty bodies from a professional standpoint, the consideration of gender, race, and class adds not only to a further exploration of the legitimacy of TLCs but also generally connects to research on biased practices and additional burdens of emotional labor in global governance (Bode 2020; Nair 2020) and on elitism and social capital in international law (Dezalay and Madsen 2017; Madsen 2014). In a further step, these internal politics of race, class, and gender could be studied with regard to how they influence directions and characteristics for collective action. While the rules for election as experts often require equal geographical distribution, most treaty body members were educated and trained in the Anglo-American system and gained work experience around the big international hubs. The potential tunnel vision created through such education and experience, particularly as international lawyers (Roberts 2017), bears further analysis.

A further agenda item for scholarship on TLCs is to extend the applicability of the concept beyond the human rights system. Treaty interpretations as a strategic choice to influence preferences of other actors proliferate far beyond the human rights regime (Putnam 2020). Scholarship on sources of IL has recently argued for the role of various judicial and quasi-judicial bodies' interpretations for the development of international law (Azaria 2020; Venzke 2012). The stagnation of formal treaty-making further explains why a turn to interpretations has come to occupy a defining role in this development. Especially entities empowered with the task to speak up on the meaning of a treaty – either explicitly as interpretations or more vaguely as statements – are of interest here to test the generalizability of TLCs. This could be initiated in the institutions of the global political economy where many transnational actor concepts have their empirical home (Djelic and Quack 2010; Seabrooke and Tsingou 2014). For example, the interpretation dynamics in the IMF Board of Directors' in Chapter 3 could provide further points for analysis as well as those in the WTO dispute settlement bodies.

When extending the book's argument to other treaty bodies and expert committees, more transnational actors might be included into the analysis of TLC membership, especially from the private and business sector. Reinsurance companies, for example, show themselves as highly influential for human rights meaning in contexts of private regulation (Scheper and Gördemann 2021). The small circle of professionals found around the independent experts of the UN human rights treaty bodies moreover brings human rights into research on club governance (Tsingou 2015, 2014), further adding substance to the argument that the involvement of civil society actors for standard-setting contributes not necessarily to democratic but rather more to exclusive governance (Schneiker and Joachim 2018).

On a closing note, the value of TLCs and thus more research to be done in this regard lies in their ability to act as change makers in international law in light of political, economic, and social challenges. TLCs can therefore be looked at as agents to push back on the pushback. TLCs, through general comments, make obligations clear(er). This clarification can be used by the members of TANs, epistemic communities, and beyond to inform the public about their rights and advocate for change in front of governments and the judiciary. As such, the development of human rights through TLCs is still progressive rather than reactionary. TLCs are neither the sole cause for the adoption of a general comment, nor does every treaty interpretation require a TLC for its drafting. As it stands, TLCs are actors for progressive normative development and as long as the members elected to the treaty bodies are in the majority on this direction, they will likely proceed to adopt general comments to clarify obligations which state parties might treat indeterminate. TLCs can bring this change to those who need them the most and are not limited do so only in Western democracies. Yet, human rights law has been predominantly generous to those living under already comfortable conditions and all claims to universality in Geneva often feel disconnected from the realities of people whose voices are hardly making it into any constructive dialogue. Many actors within and outside the UN point to this lack of representation repeatedly; every story of treaties for a specific group tells stories about these groups' struggles for recognition – and even more telling are those that lack this status despite years of advocacy and recognition-seeking not to mention those that have neither but whose rights are still not respected. Critical perspectives are necessary wherever few people make decision which impact many. TLCs as informal coalitions among few individuals have privileged access to human rights tools which can contribute to the unmaking of global inequalities. Future research will show to what extent they actually do so.

APPENDIX A

Rules of Procedure

Treaty Body	Rules for General Comments
CESCR	ICESCR Art. 23 *"The States Parties to the present Covenant agree that international action for the achievement of the rights recognized in the present Covenant includes such methods as the conclusion of conventions, the adoption of recommendations, the furnishing of technical assistance and the holding of regional meetings and technical meetings for the purpose of consultation and study organized in conjunction with the Governments concerned."* ECOSOC Res. 1985/17 *"(f) The Committee shall submit to the Council a report on its activities, including a summary of its consideration of the reports submitted by States parties to the Covenant, and shall make suggestions and recommendations of a general nature on the basis of its consideration of those reports and of the reports submitted by the specialized agencies, in order to assist the Council to fulfill, in particular, its responsibilities under articles 21 and 22 of the Covenant."* ECOSOC Res. 1987/5 *"9. Invites the Committee to consider again at its next session the compilation of recommendations in the summary records of the Committee relating to its future work, paying particular regard to practices followed by other treaty bodies, including the preparation of general comments by the Human Rights Committee."* E/C.12/1990/4/Rev.1[1], Rule 65 *"The Committee may prepare general comments based on the various articles and provisions of the Covenant with a view to assisting States parties in fulfilling their reporting obligations."*

[1] Provisional rules of procedure were adopted at session 3 and amended at sessions 4 and 8.

(*continued*)

Treaty Body	Rules for General Comments
CCPR	ICCPR Art. 39 (2) *"The Committee shall establish its own rules of procedure, but these rules shall provide, inter alia, that:* *(a) Twelve members shall constitute a quorum;* *(b) Decisions of the Committee shall be made by a majority vote of the members present."* ICCPR Art. 40(4) *"The Committee shall study the reports submitted by the States Parties to the present Covenant. It shall transmit its reports, and such general comments as it may consider appropriate, to the States Parties. The Committee may also transmit to the Economic and Social Council these comments along with the copies of the reports it has received from States Parties to the present Covenant."* CCPR/C/3/Rev.11 (2019)[2] Rule 76 *"1. The Committee may decide to prepare and adopt general comments on specific topics addressing aspects of the Covenant or its Optional Protocols with a view to assisting States parties in fulfilling their obligations under the Covenant and its Optional Protocols.* *2. Before work on the formulation of a general comment begins, the Chair shall invite members of the Committee to propose suitable topics for a general comment. The Committee shall select from among the proposals a topic and appoint one or more members of the Committee to serve as rapporteur(s) entrusted with facilitating the preparation of the general comment.* *3. The rapporteur(s) will submit an initial proposal for a general comment to the Committee, which will then discuss the proposal and approve it in first reading, in a preliminary manner, with any necessary changes.* *4. The preliminary draft of the general comment will be circulated to the States parties and other relevant stakeholders for comments. The Committee will discuss, in a* second reading, any further changes in the general comment. It shall then consider formally adopting the general comment."

[2] Provisional rules of procedure were adopted at sessions 1 and 2 and amended at sessions 3, 7, and 36. The rules of procedure were adopted at meeting 918 and subsequently amended during sessions 47, 49, 50, 59, 71, 81, 83, 103, and 124.

(continued)

Treaty Body	Rules for General Comments
	CCPR/C/3/Rev. 11 (2019) Rule 77 *"The Committee shall communicate, through the Secretary-General, to States parties the general comments it has adopted under article 40, paragraph 4, of the Covenant."*
CERD	ICERD Art. 9 (2) *"The Committee shall report annually, through the Secretary General, to the General Assembly of the United Nations on its activities and may make suggestions and general recommendations based on the examination of the reports and information received from the States Parties. Such suggestions and general recommendations shall be reported to the General Assembly together with comments, if any, from States Parties."* ICERD Art. 10 (1) *"1. The Committee shall adopt its own rules of procedure."* CERD/C/35/Rev.3 (1989) Rule 67(3) (states parties) *"If, on the basis of its examination of the reports and information supplied by the State party, the Committee determines that some of the obligations of that State under the Convention have not been discharged, it may make suggestions and general recommendations in accordance with article 9, paragraph 2, of the Convention."* CERD/C/35/Rev.3 (1989) Rule 68 (states parties)[3] *"1. Suggestions and general recommendations made by the Committee based on the examination of the reports and information received from States parties under article 9, paragraph 2, of the Convention shall be communicated by the Committee through the Secretary-General to the States parties for their comments.* *2. The Committee may, where necessary, indicate a time-limit within which comments from States parties are to be received.* *3. Suggestions and general recommendations of the Committee, referred to in paragraph 1, shall be reported to the General Assembly, together with comments, if any, from States parties."*
CEDAW	CEDAW 19 (1) *"The Committee shall adopt its own rules of procedure."* CEDAW A/52/38/Rev.1 (1997) at 480 *"The Committee decided that there would be a three-stage process for the preparation of general recommendations, as follows:*

[3] Provisional rules of procedure were adopted at session 1 and amended at sessions 4, 5, 7, 17, 27, 28, and 29.

(*continued*)

Treaty Body	Rules for General Comments
	(*a*) *First, a general discussion and exchange of views on the subject of the proposed general recommendation during an open meeting of the Committee. Specialized agencies and other United Nations bodies, as well as non-governmental organizations, would be encouraged to participate in the discussion and to prepare informal background papers as appropriate;* (*b*) *Second, the result of the general discussion would be compiled by a member of the Committee and the Secretariat into an initial draft general recommendation. That draft would be discussed at the next session by Working Group II, which could invite resource persons and non-governmental organizations to take part in discussions as appropriate. The comments of the Working Group would be incorporated into a revised draft which would be distributed to all experts before the next session;* (*c*) *The revised draft would be submitted by Working Group II at the subsequent session for consideration and adoption by the Committee as a whole.*" CEDAW A/56/38[4] (2001) Rule 52 "1. *In accordance with article 21, paragraph 1, of the Convention, and on the basis of its examination of reports and information received from States parties, the Committee may make general recommendations addressed to States parties.* 2. *The Committee may make suggestions addressed to bodies other than States parties arising out of its consideration of reports of States parties.*" CEDAW A/56/38 (2001) Rule 55 "*In order to enhance understanding of the content and implications of the articles of the Convention or to assist in the elaboration of general recommendations, the Committee may devote one or more meetings of its regular sessions to a general discussion of specific articles of or themes relating to the Convention.*"
CAT	CAT 18 (2) "*The Committee shall establish its own rules of procedure, but these rules shall provide, inter alia, that* 1. *Six members shall constitute a quorum;*

4 Amended by A/62/38 (2007).

(*continued*)

Treaty Body	Rules for General Comments
	2. *Decisions of the Committee shall be made by a majority vote of the members present"*
	CAT/C/3/Rev.6[5] (2014) Rule 74
	"1. The Committee may prepare and adopt general comments on the provisions of the Convention with a view to promoting its further implementation or to assisting States parties in fulfilling their obligations.
	2. The Committee shall include such general comments in its annual report to the General Assembly."
CRC	CRC 43 (8)
	"The Committee shall establish its own rules of procedure."
	CRC/C/4/Rev.5[6] (2019) Rule 77
	"1. The Committee may prepare general comments based on the articles and provisions of the Convention with a view to promoting its further implementation and assisting States parties in fulfilling their reporting obligations.
	2. The Committee shall include such general comments in its reports to the General Assembly."
CMW	ICRMW 75 (1)
	"The Committee shall adopt its own rules of procedure."
	CMW/C/2[7] (2019) Rule 31 (1)
	"In accordance with article 74 (7) of the Convention, the Committee shall submit an annual report on the implementation of the Convention to the General Assembly, containing its considerations and recommendations, based, in particular, on the examination of the reports and any observations presented by States parties."
CED	CPED 26 (6)
	"The Committee shall establish its own rules of procedure."
	CED/C/1[8] (2012) Rule 56
	"1. The Committee may prepare and adopt general comments on the provisions of the Convention with a view to promoting its implementation or to assisting States parties in fulfilling their obligations.

5 Rules of procedure were adopted at sessions 1 and 2 and amended at sessions 13, 15, 28, 45, and 55.

6 Provisional rules of procedure were adopted at session 1 and revised at sessions 33, 55, 62, 67, and 79.

7 Amendments to the provisional rules of procedure were adopted at sessions 2, 15, 16, 24, and 29.

8 Rules of procedure were adopted at sessions 1 and 2.

(continued)

Treaty Body	Rules for General Comments
	2. *Where appropriate, the Committee may circulate the draft general comments for comment among United Nations human rights mechanisms, United Nations Special Procedures, United Nations bodies and specialized agencies, national human rights institutions, non-governmental organizations, as well as individual experts, before their finalization.* 3. *The Committee shall include such general comments in its annual report."*
CRPD	CRPD 34 (10) *"The Committee shall establish its own rules of procedure."* CRPD/C/1/Rev.1 (2016)[9], Rule 47 "1. *The Committee may prepare general comments based on the articles and provisions of the Convention with a view to promoting its further implementation and assisting States Parties in fulfilling their reporting obligations.* 2. *The Committee shall include such general comments in its report to the General Assembly."*

9 Rules of procedure were adopted at session 3 and revised at sessions 10 and 16.

APPENDIX B

Session Overview CESCR and General Comment No. 15

Table B.1 gives an overview of all sessions related to the drafting process of General Comment No. 15.[1] It serves as a guideline for the process described in Chapter 4.

BRIEF CONTENT DESCRIPTION OF THE ADOPTED GC NO. 15

GC No. 15 was adopted by the UN Committee on Economic, Social and Cultural Rights in the 51st meeting of the 29th session, in November 2002 (E/C.12/2002/11 2003). The eighteen-page-long document provides guidelines for states on the interpretation of the right to water. This right to water is deducted from two articles of the ICESCR – Article 11 (the right to an adequate standard of living) and Article 12 (the right to health). GC No. 15's introduction qualifies, and thus affirms, the legal base of the right in its "entitle[ment of] everyone to sufficient, safe, acceptable, physically accessible and affordable water for personal and domestic uses." A right to water is argued not only with regard to the ICESCR, but also with reference to a wide range of international documents.

GC No. 15's second section clarifies the normative content of the right to water. It contains both the right's freedoms and entitlements, as well as the CESCR's acknowledgment that adequacy of the right to water varies under different conditions. Even with this variance, however, "availability," "quality," and "accessibility" – each of which GC No. 15 provides a clear definition for – remain core elements of the right to water under all circumstances. GC No. 15 moreover clarifies the normative content of the

1 Overview is based on summary records and annual reports of CESCR.

TABLE B.1 *CESCR sessions General Comment No. 15*

Session	Date	Meeting	Type	Agenda	Record
27					
	12.11.2001 – 21.11.2001	59–71 (2)	Public/Non-Public	State Party Reports	E/C. 12/2001/SR. 5 9–77
	20.11.2001 – 26.11.2001	72–80	Public	Substantive Issues Concerning the Implementation of ICESCR	E/C. 12/2001/SR.72, 78–80
	30.11.2001	87–89	Public	Closure of the session	E/C. 12/2001/SR. 87–89
28					
	30.04.2002 – 10.05.2002	3–18	Public	State Party Reports	E/C. 12/2002/SR. 3–18
	13.05.2002,	19–20,	Public	Substantive Issues Concerning the	E/C. 12/2002/SR. 19–20,
	14.05.2002	22		Implementation of ICESCR	22
	17.05.2002	27(2)	Public	Closure of the session	E/C. 12/2002/SR.27/ Add. 1
29					
	11.11.2002	28(1)	Public	Opening of the session	E/C. 12/2002/SR.28
	12.11.2002 20.11.2002	30–43	Public	State Party Reports	E/C. 12/2002/SR. 3 0–43
	22.11.2002	46–47	Public	Preliminary discussion of a draft general comment on the right to water	E/C. 12/2002/SR.46–47

TABLE B.1 (*continued*)

Session	Date	Meeting	Type	Agenda	Record
	25.11.2002	49(1)	Public	Substantive Issues Concerning the Implementation of ICESCR	E/C. 12/2002/SR.49
	26.11.2002	50(1)	Public	Introduction of draft general comment No. 15 on the right to water	E/C. 12/2002/SR. 50
	26.11.2002	50 (2)– 51(1)	Non-public	Discussion of draft general comment No. 15 on the right to water	
	26.11.2002	51(2)	Public	Adoption of general comment No. 15	E/C. 12/2002/SR. 51
	29.11.2002	56	Public	Closure of the session	E/C. 12/2002/SR. 56

right to water with regard to different vulnerable groups to guarantee non-discrimination and equality.

The third and longest part of GC No. 15 outlines the obligations of the state parties. Alongside general legal obligations, the ICESCR identifies three types of specific legal obligations for its state parties: (a) an obligation to respect the right to water by refraining from interfering directly or indirectly with the right's enjoyment; (b) an obligation to protect the right to water by preventing third parties from interfering in any way with the right's enjoyment; (c) an obligation to fulfill the right to water by adopting necessary measures for the right's full realization. Beyond these, member states likewise have international obligations connected to the right to water, with GC No. 15 specifying further core obligations for every state regardless of the economic situation.

The fourth section of GC No. 15 considers possible violations of the right but emphasizes that a state party cannot justify its own noncompliance with the core obligations, which are nonnegotiable. The CESCR, however, distinguishes between the inability of a state to comply with these obligations and its unwillingness. If a state is unwilling to use the maximum of its available resources for the realization of the right to water, this constitutes a violation.

The GC's fifth part gives an overview of those measures that are needed for the implementation of the right to water at the national level.[2] Here, the CESCR also encourages the state parties to employ indicators and benchmarks for their national water strategies and to ensure universal access to legal remedies in case of violation.

The GC's final section briefly remarks on the obligations of non-state actors, giving foremost attention to international organizations and UN agencies. It encourages cooperation of these actors with state parties and demands the consideration of water as a human right when planning policies and programs.

[2] "Existing legislation, strategies and policies should be reviewed to ensure that they are compatible with obligations arising from the right to water, and should be repealed, amended or changed if inconsistent with Covenant requirements."

APPENDIX C

Analytical Framework Process Analysis (Chapter 4)

DATA COLLECTION

Data for the analysis in Chapter 4 was collected in different settings over a time span of almost seven years (see also Appendix D). The data for the case studies in Chapter 5 was collected between 2018 and 2021. Methods for data collection included desk studies in my office; archival studies in Geneva; semi-structured and narrative interviews personally or via video, phone, or email; and participatory observations in events inside and outside UN. The material was constantly evaluated throughout the process and used to gather new ideas for data collection. Software-based data interpretation was used to detect common categories in the process over time.

There is no general rule which documents are available for the public: some committees publish drafts of the general comment; some publish the statements that react to these drafts by state and non-state actors; and some only present the adopted general comment online. As this refers to the present practices, it has to be noted that for the time of the process in 2002 digitalization of the documents was even less common.

PROCESS-TRACING ANALYSIS

To highlight the usefulness of the novel TLC concept, I apply the framework from Chapter 3 to the CESCR's GC No. 15 on the human right to water. In the following, I give an overview of the analytical framework for the process analysis of how TLCs facilitated the drafting of GC15.[1] It is based on an

[1] On the method of process-tracing as applied for this study, please see Beach and Pedersen 2013. The case study on the right to water originates from my doctoral thesis in which I followed an inductive approach to process-tracing and developed a causal mechanism for non-state

exploratory case study to interpret the broader meaning (Klotz and Prakash 2008) of TLCs' role in the drafting process of general comments of the human rights treaty bodies for scholarship on transnational actors in international relations.

The first step of my analysis was to create a "prototypical" drafting process around which I could structure my analysis. While individual processes vary, all treaty bodies' drafting processes include the following steps: A starting point, that is, the time at which a treaty body decides to draft a general comment; the preparation phase of the first draft; a discussion of this first draft; a revision of this draft; a discussion of the revised draft; and the outcome of the process as adopted by the treaty body.

Starting Point

Treaty bodies are authorized by states to adopt general comments (see Appendix A). Yet, the various particularities of their adoption processes – the "when" of publishing, the "how" of drafting, the input used to base a comment's final content – are not clearly regulated. To wit, while the rules of procedure adopted by the various treaty bodies are abundantly clear at the level of purpose – their interpretations are intended as a substantive advisory tool for state parties' domestic implementation of treaty obligations – there exists no explicit directive on how they should be initiated in practice (see Chapter 2). Empirical observation leads to conclude that drafting of a general comment generally follows statements that "clarify and confirm its position with respect to major international developments and issues that bear upon the implementation of the Covenant"[2] – in other words, statements that respond to a topical need to further flesh the legal sense of a treaty provision.

Yet entirely unclear here are the causal processes that connect this A to B: that is, when exactly the need for treaty interpretation appears evident and who takes the first step to suggest its drafting. Usually, general comments start with

influence on human rights treaty interpretation. TLCs were thus an explanation for the actor constellation observed in the case. For this book, I started with the introduction of the concept and use the water case study to discuss its validity and usefulness in-depth. Chapter 5 is devoted to the discussion of generalizability and further refinement of this concept. In short: I think this is the most logical and readable structure for this book, yet I want to make it fully transparent that the original research design was different.

2 See Appendix A for a comparative overview of the rules of procedure. Most of the treaty bodies (CAT, CRC, CED, CRPD) include the following phrase in their rules of procedure: "The Committee may prepare and adopt general comments on the provisions of the Convention with a view to promoting its further implementation or to assisting States parties in fulfilling their obligations."

an article on the committee's experience in monitoring reports, thus connecting the decision on drafting a general comment to an overall need for interpretation of one or more of the treaty's provisions. However, it remains unclear when exactly this need is evident and who takes the first step to suggest such a draft. Here, empirical observation again offers further procedural insight, finding a certain standard, albeit informal, course of action within expert committee sessions. During dialogue on state parties' reports, for instance, committee members often tie their questions to a single article or provision, a notably narrow emphasis, given the diversity of implementation issues among state parties. In the concluding remarks published at the end of these sessions, this singular provision often provides – and motivates – the subject framing for a subsequent general comment. With respect to the who and what that then decisively steer the committee toward the preparation of a draft, it appears incentive generally spawns via two factors: stimulating intra-committee consultations regarding general discussions or topical side events, and the make-up of work experience that define the careers of the respective treaty body members.[3]

Preparing a First Draft

In general, once the decision to initiate preparation of a general comment draft is made by a committee, one treaty body member becomes the rapporteur, whose role is to prepare a first draft of the prospective general comment. The decision of who will be that rapporteur is made among the committee members in a closed meeting. Usually, one committee member who considers the aim of the general comment in his or her field of expertise volunteers for the position.[4] In some cases, other committee members are appointed to assist the rapporteur, thereby establishing a working group for a draft.[5] To this aim, the rapporteur primarily examines state reports, concluding observations, statements, and other documents. Often,

[3] Composed of independent experts who all pursue a profession outside their committee membership, it is likely the case that individual treaty body members act with some level of a personal agenda: that is, with an interest in strengthening those norms that lie within their field of expertise.

[4] One former rapporteur reported in an interview from his experience that the rapporteur has to have a legal education background for the draft. That the rapporteur needs to be a lawyer is neither known from official documents, nor did anyone in the secretariats or the treaty body themselves confirm this. Cases are known where the rapporteur of a general comment did not have a legal education background.

[5] E.g. for the general comment on equal recognition before the law, CRPD General Comment No. 1: Arstein-Kerslake and Flynn 2016 or CAT GC2 in Chapter 5.

documents from other treaty bodies are considered as well, given that many of the debates sparkling the draft of a general comment also appear in the discourse of other committees.

At this stage, there exists the possibility to consult with "experts"[6] in private meetings, who could be anyone internal or external to the UN system. If a rapporteur, for example, wants to prepare a first draft of a specific general comment connected to, but in some points exceeding his personal expertise, he or she may contact an expert for consultancy. Often, the experts contacted at this early stage are those who have previously collaborated with the rapporteur, either in their capacity as treaty body members or within their primary profession. OHCHR and the treaty body secretariats are officially mandated to provide support to the treaty body, and further, for preparing and drafting a general comment. Once a draft is prepared, practice for consultancy on the first draft differs among the respective treaty bodies, from rapporteur to rapporteur. Some send the first draft to other actors inside and outside the UN system, either for proofreading of formal aspects or for substantial remarks regarding the content, while others pen the draft before sending it directly to the secretariat of the treaty body for inclusion in the planning of the next session.

Discussing a Draft

The first reading of a draft general comment usually takes place in a formal meeting within a treaty body session. A paragraph-by-paragraph discussion enables every treaty body member to ask questions on the wording and make suggestions for modifications. This can take substantial time, depending on the general comment's length and quality (for the CCPR see: Keller and Grover 2012). Proceedings of the first reading are usually included in the summary records of the session. One observation from the field is that the openness of the first readings differs sharply from treaty body to treaty body. The procedure ranges from very closed meetings during which only the treaty body is present[7] to public meetings that include other actors'[8] opinions on the draft and thus more take the form of a day of general discussion. The participants in the

6 E.g. https://academy.ishr.ch/learn/treaty-bodies/general-comments–what-do-the-treaty-bodies-do? There are no official guidelines defining who might be considered an expert.

7 Like CESCR at that time Riedel 2005: 314.

8 CEDAW refers to these actors as "resource persons:" "A Committee member is then asked to draft the general recommendation, which is discussed at the next or a subsequent session of the Committee. *Resource persons* [italics mine] may be invited to participate in the discussion" CEDAW/C/2004/I/4/Add. 1 2004.

discussion of the first draft remain generally unspecified and off record, and likewise unavailable are the criteria used for their selection. How the discussion is organized has implications for its quality: public stakeholder meetings, for instance, are subject to time constraints and rather resemble a sequence of oral statements than a substantial discussion of the draft.

Revising the Draft

The next stage of a drafting process of a general comment is the revision of the draft. After the first reading, the rapporteur or the working group holds responsibility for revising the draft. Based on the discussion of the first draft, they have to decide which formulations ought to be changed or omitted. Depending on the subject of the general comment, this is a tricky task: when a first draft receives a lot of criticism and views differ sharply among the stakeholders, the rapporteur must either be diplomatic, and then risk that the final draft is less substantial, or opt for a more substantial version of the draft, and then risk that the general comment will not be fully considered by the state parties. That is why, sometimes, the rapporteur decides to put the draft general comment on hold and wait for its revision at a better time. However, nothing is known about the evaluative specifics of the input received in the discussion by the rapporteur – that is, nothing regarding which comments make it into a future draft, or the reasoning used for their inclusion. For the revision, the procedures range from a dark black box, where nothing is known about the revision until the final draft is discussed and adopted, to a grey box. These greyer procedures include publishing the first draft on the treaty body's (e.g., CEDAW and CRPD) website alongside an explicit appeal for commentary, or distributing it to specialized agencies and other actors concerned with the issue at stake. Moreover of note: even if some treaty bodies have a general publication policy, that does not mean that they follow it in every case. Sometimes, timely action is required, and the broadly defined mandate of the treaty bodies to draft general comments imposes no further rules on the process. The rapporteur may thus consult with other actors on the revisions to get their opinion on the applicability of the provisions.

Final Reading and Adoption

The final reading of a GC draft takes place during the sessions of the treaty body. As in the first reading, this is conducted by way of a paragraph-by-paragraph discussion. Observations of treaty body practice generally show discussions of a final draft to lead only to general remarks, with no substantial changes demanded. But this is no rule. Indeed it is possible that critique arises that had gone unconsidered before, or that many reservations are put forward regarding certain substantial paragraphs. As this phase presents the last discussion before adoption, the treaty body members must be confident that the draft will serve as an authoritative interpretation of the pertinent right and ultimately be accepted by states and made use of by human rights practitioners and even courts

Immediately after the final reading, and given that no substantial critique or reservation has been made on one of the paragraphs, the general comment is adopted by the members of the treaty body and therefore directly enters into force. Usually, it is sent to the state parties and published on the website of the treaty body afterward. The general comment is then made public, and states parties are expected to consider it in every report afterward. In general, this last step "remains in the hands of the Committee alone" (Riedel 2005: 314).

PROCESS ANALYSIS IN CHAPTER 4

Figure C.1 gives an overview of the analysis as structured around the prototypical drafting process. I used this prototype to structure my analysis of how, when, and why TLCs emerged and then codified water as a human right. Based on public information and my knowledge from observations of treaty bodies' drafting procedures on the different phases, questions emerged with regard to uncover the agents behind the drafting process.

Development Stages of General Comment No. 15 on the Right to Water

Phase zero: Starting point	Phase one: Preparation of a first draft	Phase two: Discussion of the first draft	Phase three: Revision of the draft	Phase four: Discussion of the revised draft	Phase five: Adoption of the draft
Introduction of the issue through external means	Completion of a first draft on 29 July 2002	Absence of any official, formal or public discussion of the first draft	Absence of information on revision process in official data sources	Formal discussion of the revised draft with a number of stakeholders during the CESCR's 29th session	Adoption of General Comment No. 15 during the 51st meeting on 26 November 2002
Information unavailable on the draft's formal starting point		Informal consultation in October 2002 in Washington		Draft confirmed to have circulated to selected participants in advance of this discussion	

Questions for the collection of empirical evidence

Phase zero: Starting point	Phase one: Preparation of a first draft	Phase two: Discussion of the first draft	Phase three: Revision of the draft	Phase four: Discussion of the revised draft	Phase five: Adoption of the draft
Who raised the issue?	How did Eibe Riedel come to serve as the draft's Rapporteur?	Who initiated this meeting in Washington and why?	What was the Rapporteur's position regarding the scope of the right to water, and how did this affect the draft and its revision?	How many actors wanted to participate in the discussion of the draft?	Why was the general comment not adopted immediately after a final public reading?
Why was the drafting of a general comment not announced in a statement at the end of the previous session?	Where do we find the comment's first draft to surface within official records, if anywhere?	Who were the participants of this meeting?	Which information/input inspired the Rapporteur's changes to the 29 July draft?	Who selected, based on which criteria, those allowed to participate?	How does the outcome of the final comment reflect the discussion of its content in the drafting stages?
Did other events related to the issue take place outside of the CESCR's sessions that included treaty body members as participants?	Why is the draft dated to 29 July, when there was no session that day to present or discuss it?	Who were the actors that provided feedback on the 29 July draft?	How did the AAAS meeting affect the revisions?	What contributory role, if any, did the individual experts mentioned in the session report play in the comment's drafting and adoption?	How does the outcome reflect the positions of the various actors involved?
	How long did it take to draft the 29 July version?	How was this feedback delivered to the rapporteur?	How did the Rapporteur evaluate the feedback received on the draft?	How do these experts evaluate the impact of their contribution against the backdrop of the final comment (the outcome)?	
	Who was involved in drafting the 29 July version?	How much feedback did the rapporteur receive and by whom?	Who was/were the Rapporteur's main consultant(s) for addressing further questions?	Why were the final changes discussed in a closed session and not in a paragraph-by-paragraph reading?	
	Who brought it to the attention of other actors and how, if not via public call for statements?		Who assisted the Rapporteur in revising the draft?	Was this closed meeting only with members of the committee?	
	Who selected, based on which criteria, the recipients of the first draft?			Which topics framed the decision on the final draft?	

FIGURE C.1 Analytical framework

APPENDIX D

Interviews and Background Talks

The following list identifies the affiliated occupations of my interview subjects who are referenced as such in this book. I conducted the majority of *interviews* during several research stays in Geneva, Switzerland between 2013 and 2019. I conducted interviews via online conference tools and telephone, with some preferring to reply to my questions in written form via e-mail. All interviews referenced in this book were semi-structured and averaged approximately half an hour in length. In the case that individuals agreed to their name and position being used, such is identified within the text unless it would expose other resource persons who requested anonymity. Some interview subjects requested personal anonymity but allowed for identification of their affiliated organizations. As the circle of people around the UN human rights treaty bodies is relatively small, I opted for more generous application of anonymity rules when in doubt.

Type of Organization	Position	Interview
Treaty Bodies		
CESCR	Member	Phone
CESCR	Member	Phone
CCPR	Member	Online
CAT	Member	Online
CESCR	Member	Personal
CCPR	Member	Personal
IOs		
WHO	Representative	E-Mail
Civil Society		
ICJ	Officer	Personal
AAAS	Director	E-Mail
FIAN	Officer	Personal

(*continued*)

Academia	Professor	E-Mail
WaterAid	Officer	Personal
CESCR	Officer	Personal

I refer in the text to *background talks*, whenever individuals were willing to talk to me and share information but requested either for this information to not be revealed or allowed for its reveal but wanted our conversation off-record. I mainly used these background talks as leads for further research, and they are not included as proof of evidence in the list above. I also explicitly refer to them in the analysis as such background talks, so that it is transparent when I cannot provide records for my evidence. Most of these background talks were with individuals who are or have been members of the UN treaty bodies, working for OHCHR, government actors, people working for other international organizations in Geneva, members of civil society, academia, and advocacy networks. Some took place spontaneously in the cafeterias or the archives of the UN or at events or social life in Geneva; others were scheduled ahead and took place in a more formal setting.

Type of Organization
Treaty Bodies (15+)
OHCHR (10+)
IOs (5)
State Delegates (10+)
NGOs (15+)

Bibliography

A/55/18 Annex V, Committee on the Elimination of Racial Discrimination. 2000. CERD General Recommendation XXVII on Discrimination against Roma. In *A/55/18, annex V*, edited by UN Office for the High Commissioner for Human Rights: CERD.

A/59/2005, UN Secretary-General. 2005. In Larger Freedom: Towards Development, Security and Human Rights for All. Report of the Secretary-General. New York: United Nations.

A/61/18, Committee on the Elimination of Racial Discrimination. 2006. Report of the Committee on the Elimination of Racial Discrimination, 68th session (February 20–March 10, 2006), 69th session (July 31–August 8, 2006). New York: United Nations.

A/66/18, Committee on the Elimination of Racial Discrimination. 2011. Report of the Committee on the Elimination of Racial Discrimination, 78th session (February 14–March 11, 2011), 79th session (August 8–September 2, 2011). New York: United Nations.

A/67/18, Committee on the Elimination of Racial Discrimination. 2012. Report of the Committee on the Elimination of Racial Discrimination, 80th session (February 13–March 9, 2012). New York: United Nations.

A/68/18, Committee on the Elimination of Racial Discrimination. 2013. Report of the Committee on the Elimination of Racial Discrimination, 81st session (August 6–31, 2012), 82nd session (February 11–March 1, 2013). New York: United Nations.

A/73/10, UN General Assembly. 2018. Report of the International Law Commission, 70th session (April 30–June 1 and July 2–August 10, 2018).

A/HRC/22/17/Add.4, UN High Commissioner for Human Rights. 2013. Report of the United Nations High Commissioner for Human Rights on the Expert Workshops on the Prohibition of Incitement to National, Racial or Religious Hatred. Geneva: United Nations.

A/RES/60/251, UN General Assembly. 2006. Resolution adopted by the General Assembly on March 15, 2006, edited by United Nations. New York / Geneva: United Nations.

A/RES/66/254, UN General Assembly. 2012. Resolution adopted by the General Assembly on February 23, 2012, edited by United Nations. New York / Geneva: United Nations.

A/RES/68/268, UN General Assembly. 2014. Resolution adopted by the General Assembly on April 9, 2014, edited by United Nations. New York/Geneva: United Nations.

A/RES/73/165, UN General Assembly. 2019. United Nations Declaration on the Rights of Peasants and Other People Working in Rural Areas: Resolution adopted by the General Assembly on December 17, 2018. New York: United Nations.

A/RES/174(II), UN General Assembly. 1947. Establishment of an International Law Commission. New York: United Nations.

Aalberts, Tanja E. 2013. "The Politics of International Law and the Perils and Promises of Interdisciplinarity." *Leiden Journal of International Law* 26 (3): 503–508.

Aalberts, Tanja and Thomas Gammeltoft-Hansen. 2018. "Conclusion: The Dark Side of Legalization." In *The Changing Practices of International Law*, 208–219. Cambridge: Cambridge University Press.

Abbott, Kenneth W, Philipp Genschel, Duncan Snidal, and Bernhard Zangl. 2015. *International Organizations as Orchestrators*. Cambridge: Cambridge University Press.

Abbott, Kenneth O, Robert O Keohane, Andrew Moravcsik, Anne-Marie Slaughter, and Duncan Snidal. 2000. "The Concept of Legalization." *International Organization* 54 (3): 401–419. https://doi.org/10.1162/002081800551271.

Abbott, Kenneth W, David Levi-Faur, and Duncan Snidal. 2017. "Theorizing Regulatory Intermediaries: The RIT Model." *The ANNALS of the American Academy of Political and Social Science* 670 (1): 14–35.

Abbott, Kenneth W and Duncan Snidal. 2012. "Law, Legalization, and Politics." In *Interdisciplinary Perspectives on International Law and International Relations: The State of the Art*, edited by Jeffrey L Dunoff and Mark A Pollack, 33–56. Cambridge: Cambridge University Press.

Ackerly, Brooke A. 2011. "Human Rights Enjoyment in Theory and Activism." *Human Rights Review* 12 (2): 221–239.

Ackerly, Brooke A. 2008. *Universal Human Rights in a World of Difference*. Cambridge: Cambridge University Press.

Aberbach, Joel D and Tom Christensen. 2018. "Academic Autonomy and Freedom Under Pressure: Severely Limited, or Alive and Kicking?" *Public Organization Review* 18 (4): 487–506. https://doi.org/10.1007/s11115-017-0394-2.

Adler, Emanuel. 2008. "The Spread of Security Communities: Communities of Practice, Self-Restraint, and NATO's Post – Cold War Transformation." *European Journal of International Relations* 14 (2): 195–230. https://doi.org/10.1177/1354066108089241.

Adler, Emanuel and Peter M Haas. 1992. "Conclusion: Epistemic Communities, World Order, and the Creation of a Reflective Research Program." *International Organization* 46 (1): 367–390. https://doi.org/10.1017/S0020818300001533.

Adler, Emanuel and Vincent Pouliot. 2011. "International Practices." *International Theory* 3 (1): 1–36. https://doi.org/10.1017/S175297191000031X.

Adler-Nissen, Rebecca. 2015. "Conclusion: Relationalism or Why Diplomats Find International Relations Theory Strange." In *Diplomacy and the Making of World Politics*, edited by Ole Jacob Sending, Vincent Pouliot, and Iver B Neumann, 284–308. Cambridge: Cambridge University Press.

Alkarama et al. 2014. *Joint NGO Statement on the Draft Resolution of the UN General Assembly on "Strengthening and Enhancing the Effective Functioning of the Human Rights Treaty Body System."* www.ishr.ch/sites/default/files/article/files/2014-02-20-ngo_statement_on_tbsp_final.pdf.

Allison, Graham and Philip Zelikow. 1999. *Essence of Decision: Explaining the Cuban Missile Crisis*. Vol. 2. New York: Longman.

Alston, Philip. 1987. "Out of the Abyss – the Challenges Confronting the New UN Committee on Economic, Social and Cultural Rights." *Human Rights Quarterly* 9 (3): 332–381. https://doi.org/10.2307/761879.

Alston, Philip. 2001. "The Historical Origins of the Concept of 'General Comments' in Human Rights Law." In *The International Legal System in Quest of Equity and Universality / L'Ordre Juridique International, un Système en Quête D'Equité et D'Universalité: Liber Amicorum Georges Abi-Saab*, edited by Laurence Boisson de Chazournes and Vera Gowlland-Debbas, 763–776. The Hague: Martinus Nijhoff.

Alston, Philip and Frédéric Mégret. 2020. *The United Nations and Human Rights: A Critical Appraisal*. 2nd ed. Oxford: Oxford University Press.

Alter, Karen J. 2014. *The New Terrain of International Law: Courts, Politics, Rights*. Princeton: Princeton University Press.

Alter, Karen J and Laurence R Helfer. 2010. "Nature or Nurture? Judicial Lawmaking in the European Court of Justice and the Andean Tribunal of Justice." *International Organization* 64 (4): 563–592. https://doi.org/10.1017/S0020818310000238.

Alves, JA Lindgren. 2003. "The Durban Conference against Racism and Everyone's Responsibilities." *Netherlands Quarterly of Human Rights* 21 (3): 361–384. https://doi.org/10.1177/016934410302100302.

Anderl, Felix, Priska Daphi, and Nicole Deitelhoff. 2021. "Keeping Your Enemies Close? The Variety of Social Movements' Reactions to International Organizations' Opening Up." *International Studies Review*. https://doi.org/10.1093/isr/viaa103.

Anderson, Kenneth. 2000. "The Ottawa Convention Banning Landmines, the Role of International Non-governmental Organizations and the Idea of International Civil Society." *European Journal of International Law* 11 (1): 91–120. https://doi.org/10.1093/ejil/11.1.91.

Ando, Nisuke. 2010. "General Comments / Recommendations." In *Max Planck Encyclopedia of Public International Law*, edited by Rüdiger Wolfrum, 334–344. Heidelberg: Max Planck Institute for Comparative Public Law and International Law.

Andonova, Liliana and Manfred Elsig. 2012. "Informal International Law-Making: A Conceptual View from International Relations." In *Informal International Law-Making*, edited by Joost Pauwelyn, Ramses Wessel, and Jan Wouters, 63–80. Oxford: Oxford University Press.

Anthes, Carolin. 2019. *Institutional Roadblocks to Human Rights Mainstreaming in the FAO: A Tale of Silo Culture in the United Nations System*. Wiesbaden: VS Verlag für Sozialwissenschaften.

Arstein-Kerslake, Anna and Eilionóir Flynn. 2016. "The General Comment on Article 12 of the Convention on the Rights of Persons with Disabilities: A Roadmap for

Equality before the Law." *International Journal of Human Rights* 20 (4): 471–490. https://doi.org/10.1080/13642987.2015.1107052.

Avant, Deborah D, Martha Finnemore, and Susan K Sell. 2010. *Who Governs the Globe?* Vol. 114. Cambridge: Cambridge University Press.

Azaria, Danae. 2020. "'Codification by Interpretation': The International Law Commission as an Interpreter of International Law." *European Journal of International Law* 31 (1): 171–200. https://doi.org/10.1093/ejil/chaa016.

Baer, Madeline. 2015. "From Water Wars to Water Rights: Implementing the Human Right to Water in Bolivia." *Journal of Human Rights* 14 (3): 353–376. https://doi.org/10.1080/14754835.2014.988782.

Baer, Madeline. 2017a. "The Human Right to Water and Sanitation: Champions and Challengers in the Fight for New Rights Acceptance." In *Expanding Human Rights*, edited by Alison Brysk and Michael Stohl, 94–114. Cheltenham: Edward Elgar.

Baer, Madeline. 2017b. *Stemming the Tide: Human Rights and Water Policy in a Neoliberal World*. New York: Oxford University Press.

Baker, Andrew. 2017. "Esteem as Professional Currency and Consolidation: The Rise of the Macroprudential Cognoscenti." In *Professional Networks in Transnational Governance*, edited by Lasse Folke Henriksen and Leonard Seabrooke, 149–164. Cambridge: Cambridge University Press.

Bakker, Karen. 2007. "The 'Commons' versus the 'Commodity': Alter-Globalization, Anti-Privatization and the Human Right to Water in the Global South." *Antipode* 39 (3): 430–455. https://doi.org/10.1111/j.1467-8330.2007.00534.x.

Barnett, Michael N and Martha Finnemore. 1999. "The Politics, Power, and Pathologies of International Organizations." *International Organization* 53 (4): 699–732. https://doi.org/10.1162/002081899551048.

Barnett, Michael N and Martha Finnemore. 2004. *Rules for the World: International Organizations in Global Politics*. Ithaca: Cornell University Press.

Bayefsky, Anne F. 2001. *United Nations Human Rights Treaty System: Universality at the Crossroads*. Ardsley: Transnational.

Beach, Derek and Rasmus B Pedersen. 2013. *Process-Tracing Methods: Foundations and Guidelines*. Ann Arbor: University of Michigan Press.

Beisheim, Marianne and Andrea Liese, eds. 2014. *Transnational Partnerships: Effectively Providing for Sustainable Development?* Basingstoke: Palgrave Macmillan.

Benvenisti, Eyal. 2007. "'Coalitions of the Willing' and the Evolution of Informal International Law." In *Coalitions of the Willing: Avantgarde or Threat?*, edited by Christian Calliess, Georg Nolte, and Peter-Tobias Stoll, 1–23. Cologne: Heymanns.

Besson, Samantha. 2013. "The Legitimate Authority of International Human Rights: On the Reciprocal Legitimation of Domestic and International Human Rights." In *The Legitimacy of International Human Rights Regimes: Legal, Political and Philosophical Perspectives*, edited by Andreas Føllesdal, Geir Ulfstein, and Johan Karlsson Schaffer, In Studies on Human Rights Conventions, 32–83. Cambridge: Cambridge University Press.

Besson, Samantha and José Luis Martí. 2018. "Legitimate Actors of International Law-Making: Towards a Theory of International Democratic Representation." *Jurisprudence* 9 (3): 504–540. https://doi.org/10.1080/20403313.2018.1442256.

Betsill, Michele M and Elisabeth Corell. 2001. "NGO Influence in International Environmental Negotiations: A Framework for Analysis." *Global Environmental Politics* 1 (4): 65–85. https://doi.org/10.1162/152638001317146372.

Betsill, Michele M and Elisabeth Corell. 2008. *NGO Diplomacy: The Influence of Nongovernmental Organizations in International Environmental Negotiations*. Cambridge, MA: The MIT Press.

Biermann, Rafael and Joachim A Koops. 2017. "Studying Relations among International Organizations in World Politics: Core Concepts and Challenges." In *Palgrave Handbook of Inter-Organizational Relations in World Politics*, edited by Rafael Biermann and Joachim A Koops, 1–46. London: Palgrave Macmillan.

Birkenkötter, Hannah. 2015. "Menschenrechte in (fast) allen Rechtsgebieten." *Vereinte Nationen* 2015 (2): 90–91.

Birkenkötter, Hannah. 2020. "International Law as a Common Language across Spheres of Authority?" *Global Constitutionalism* 9 (2): 318–342. https://doi.org/10.1017/S2045381720000155.

Biswas, Asit K. 2004. "From Mar del Plata to Kyoto: An Analysis of Global Water Policy Dialogue." *Global Environmental Change* 14 (Supplement): 81–88. https://doi.org/10.1016/j.gloenvcha.2003.11.003.

Black, Julia. 2009. "Legitimacy, Accountability and Polycentric Regulation: Dilemmas, Trilemmas and Organisational Response." In *Non-state Actors As Standard Setters*, edited by Anne Peters, Lucy Koechlin, and Till Förster, 241–269. Cambridge: Cambridge University Press.

Blake, Conway. 2008. "Normative Instruments in International Human Rights Law: Locating the General Comment." NYU Center for Human Rights and Global Justice Working Paper (17): 2–38.

Bloodgood, Elizabeth A. 2011. "The Interest Group Analogy: International Non-Governmental Advocacy Organisations in International Politics." *Review of International Studies* 37 (1): 93–120. https://doi.org/10.1017/S0260210510001051.

Bode, Ingvild. 2015. *Individual Agency and Policy Change at the United Nations: The People of the United Nations*. London: Routledge.

Bode, Ingvild. 2020. "Women or Leaders? Practices of Narrating the United Nations as a Gendered Institution." *International Studies Review* 22 (3): 347–369. https://doi.org/10.1093/isr/viz004.

Bodig, Matyas. 2016. "Soft Law, Doctrinal Development, and the General Comments of the UN Committee on Economic, Social and Cultural Rights." In *Tracing the Roles of Soft Law in Human Rights*, edited by Stéphanie Lagoutte, Thomas Gammeltoft-Hansen, and John Cerone, 69–88. Oxford: Oxford University Press.

Böhling, Kathrin. 2014. "Sidelined Member States: Commission-Learning from Experts in the Face of Comitology." *Journal of European Integration* 36 (2): 117–134. https://doi.org/10.1080/07036337.2013.818992.

Börzel, Tanja A and Thomas Risse. 2016. "Dysfunctional State Institutions, Trust, and Governance in Areas of Limited Statehood." *Regulation & Governance* 10 (2): 149–160. https://doi.org/10.1111/rego.12100.

Börzel, Tanja A and Thomas Risse. 2010. "Governance without a State: Can It Work?" *Regulation & Governance* 4 (2): 113–134. https://doi.org/10.1111/j.1748-5991.2010.01076.x.

Boyle, Alan and Christine Chinkin. 2007. *The Making of International Law*. Oxford: Oxford University Press.

Braithwaite, John and Peter Drahos. 2000. *Global Business Regulation*. Cambridge: Cambridge University Press.

Brem, Stefan and Ken Rutherford. 2001. "Walking Together or Divided Agenda? Comparing Landmines and Small-arms Campaigns." *Security Dialogue* 32 (2): 169–186. https://doi.org/10.1177/0967010601032002004.

Brès, Luc, Sébastien Mena, and Marie-Laure Salles-Djelic. 2019. "Exploring the Formal and Informal Roles of Regulatory Intermediaries in Transnational Multistakeholder Regulation." *Regulation & Governance* 13 (2): 127–140. https://doi.org/10.1111/rego.12249.

Brett, Rachel. 1995. "The Role and Limits of Human Rights NGOs at the United Nations." *Political Studies* 43 (1): 96–110. https://doi.org/10.1111/j.1467-9248.1995.tb01738.x.

Brölmann, Catherine and Yannick Radi, eds. 2016. *Research Handbook on Theory and Practice of International Lawmaking*. Cheltenham and Northampton: Edward Elgar.

Broude, Tomer and Yuval Shany. 2008. *The Shifting Allocation of Authority in International Law*. Oxford: Hart.

Brühl, Tanja. 2003. *Nichtregierungsorganisationen als Akteure internationaler Umweltverhandlungen. Ein Erklärungsmodell auf der Basis der situationsspezifischen Ressourcennachfrage*. Frankfurt am Main: Campus Verlag.

Brunnée, Jutta and Stephen J Toope. 2010. *Legitimacy and Legality in International Law: An Interactional Account*. Vol. 67. Cambridge: Cambridge University Press.

Brunner, Norbert, Vijay Mishra, Ponnusamy Sakthivel, Markus Starkl, and Christof Tschohl. 2015. "The Human Right to Water in Law and Implementation." *Laws* 4 (3): 413–471. https://doi.org/doi.org/10.3390/laws4030413.

Brysk, Alison. 1993. "From Above and Below. Social Movements, the International System, and Human Rights in Argentina." *Comparative Political Studies* 26 (3): 259–285. https://doi.org/10.1177/0010414093026003001.

Brysk, Alison. 2013. *Speaking Rights to Power: Constructing Political Will*. Oxford: Oxford University Press.

Brysk, Alison. 2020. "Introduction to a Research Agenda for Human Rights: Generations of Human Rights Scholarship." In *A Research Agenda for Human Rights*, edited by Michael Stohl and Alison Brysk, 1–8. Cheltenham: Edward Elgar.

Bulto, Takele S. 2011. "The Emergence of the Human Right to Water in International Human Rights Law: Invention or Discovery?" *Melbourne Journal of International Law* 12 (2): 1–25.

Busch, Per-Olof, Mirko Heinzel, Mathies Kempken, and Andrea Liese. 2020. "Mind the Gap? Comparing De Facto and De Jure Expert Authority of International Public Administrations in Financial and Agricultural Policy." *Journal of Comparative Policy Analysis: Research and Practice*: 1–24. https://doi.org/10.1080/13876988.2020.1820866.

Byrnes, Andrew C. 1989. "The Other Human Rights Treaty Body: The Work of the Committee on the Elimination of Discrimination Against Women." *Yale Journal of International Law* 14 (1): 1–67.

C-Fam, Center for Family and Human Rights. 2020. "Recommendations for Treaty Body Review." Accessed February 9, 2021. www.ohchr.org/Documents/HRBodies/TB/HRTD/CoFacilitationProcess/OtherStakeholders/CFAM.pdf.

Cahill, Amanda. 2005. "'The Human Right to Water – A Right of Unique Status': The Legal Status and Normative Content of the Right to Water." *International Journal of Human Rights* 9 (3): 389–410. https://doi.org/10.1080/13642980500170840.

Cali, Basak and Stewart Cunningham. 2018. "Part 2: A Few Steps Forward, a Few Steps Sideways and a Few Steps Backwards: The CAT's Revised and Updated GC on Non-refoulement." *EJIL: Talk!* (blog). www.ejiltalk.org/part-2-a-few-steps-forward-a-few-steps-sideways-and-a-few-steps-backwards-the-cats-revised-and-updated-gc-on-non-refoulement/.

Camponovo, Christopher N. 2002. "Disaster in Durban: The United Nations World Conference against Racism, Racial Discrimination, Xenophobia, and Related Intolerance." *The George Washington International Law Review* 34: 659.

Carayannis, Tatiana, and Thomas G Weiss. 2021. *The' Third' United Nations: How a Knowledge Ecology Helps the UN Think*. Oxford: Oxford University Press.

Carpenter, Charlie R. 2007. "Setting the Advocacy Agenda: Theorizing Issue Emergence and Nonemergence in Transnational Advocacy Networks." *International Studies Quarterly* 51 (1): 99–120. https://doi.org/10.1111/j.1468-2478.2007.00441.x.

Carpenter, Charlie R, Sirin Duygulu, Alexander H Montgomery, and Anna Rapp. 2014. "Explaining the Advocacy Agenda: Insights from the Human Security Network." *International Organization* 68 (2): 449–470. https://doi.org/10.1017/S0020818313000453.

Carraro, Valentina. 2017. "The United Nations Treaty Bodies and Universal Periodic Review: Advancing Human Rights by Preventing Politicization?" *Human Rights Quarterly* 39 (4): 943–970. https://doi.org/10.1353/hrq.2017.0055.

Carraro, Valentina. 2019. "Electing the Experts: Expertise and Independence in the UN Human Rights Treaty Bodies." *European Journal of International Relations* 25 (3): 1–26. https://doi.org/1354066118819138.

Carraro, Valentina, Thomas Conzelmann, and Hortense Jongen. 2019. "Fears of Peers? Explaining Peer and Public Shaming in Global Governance." *Cooperation and Conflict* 54 (3): 335–355. https://doi.org/10.1177/0010836718816729.

Cassidy, Julie. 2008. "Watchdog or Paper Tiger: The Enforcement of Human Rights in International Forums." *University of Notre Dame Australia Law Review* 10: 37–59.

CAT/C/3/Rev.6, Committee against Torture. 2014. *Rules of Procedure: Committee against Torture*. Geneva: United Nations.

CAT/C/SR.435, Committee against Torture. 2000. Summary Record of the 435th Meeting, Held at the Palais des Nations, Geneva, on Wednesday, May 17, 2000: Committee against Torture, 24th session. Geneva: United Nations.

CAT/C/SR.439, Committee against Torture. 2000. Summary Record of the 1st Part (Public) of the 439th Meeting, Held at the Palais Wilson, Geneva, on Monday, November 13, 2000: Committee against Torture, 25th session. Geneva: United Nations.

CAT/C/SR.532, Committee against Torture. 2002. Summary Record of the 532nd Meeting, Held at the Palais des Nations, Geneva, on Wednesday, November 13, 2002: Committee against Torture, 29th session. Geneva: United Nations.

CAT/C/SR.560, Committee against Torture. 2003. Compte rendu analytique de la 1re partie (publique) de la 560e séance tenue au Palais Wilson, à Genève, le mercredi mai 7, 2003: Comité contre la torture, 30e session. Geneva: United Nations.

CAT/C/SR.638, Committee against Torture. 2004. Summary Record of the 1st Part (Public) of the 638th Meeting, Held at the Palais des Nations, Geneva, on Friday,

November 26, 2004: Committee against Torture, 33rd session. Geneva: United Nations.

CAT/C/SR.717, Committee against Torture. 2006. Summary Record of the 717th Meeting, Held at the Palais des Nations, Geneva, on Tuesday, May 16, 2006: Committee against Torture, 36th session. Geneva: United Nations.

CAT/C/SR.752, Committee against Torture. 2006. Compte rendu analytique de la 752e séance tenue au Palais Wilson, à Genève, le vendredi novembre 24, 2006: Comité contre la torture, 37e session. Geneva: United Nations.

CAT/C/SR.775, Committee against Torture. 2007. Summary Record of the 775th Meeting, Held at the Palais Wilson, Geneva, on Tuesday, May 15, 2007: Committee against Torture, 38th session. Geneva: United Nations.

CAT/C/3/Rev.5, Committee against Torture. 2011. *Rules of Procedure: Committee against Torture*. Geneva: United Nations.

CCPR/C/IRL/CO/4, Human Rights Committee. 2014. Concluding Observations on the Fourth Periodic Report of Ireland.

CCPR/C/GC/36, Human Rights Committee. 2018. General Comment No. 36 on Article 6 of the International Covenant on Civil and Political Rights, on the Right to Life.

CCPR/C/GC/R.36/Rev.2, Human Rights Committee. 2015. Draft General Comment No. 36: Article 6, Right to Life: International Covenant on Civil and Political Rights: Draft / Prepared by Yuval Shany and Nigel Rodley, Rapporteurs.

CEDAW/C/2004/I/4/Add. 1, Committee on the Elimination of All Forms of Discrimination against Women. 2004. *Overview of the Current Working Methods of the Committee on the Elimination of Discrimination against Women*, edited by United Nations. New York: United Nations.

CEDAW/C/GC/35, Committee on the Elimination of Discrimination against Women. 2017. General Recommendation No. 35 on Gender-Based Violence against Women, Updating General Recommendation No. 19. New York: United Nations.

CERD/C/GC/35, Committee on the Elimination of Racial Discrimination. 2013. *General Recommendation No. 35, Combating Racist Hate Speech*. Geneva: United Nations.

CERD/C/SR.2126, Committee on the Elimination of Racial Discrimination. 2012. Summary Record (Partial) of the 2126th Meeting, Held at the Palais Wilson, Geneva, on Monday, February 13, 2012 : Human Rights Committee, 80th session. Geneva: United Nations.

CERD/C/SR.2197, Committee on the Elimination of Racial Discrimination. 2013. Summary Record of the 2197th Meeting, Held at the Palais des Nations, Geneva, on Tuesday, August 28, 2012: Committee on the Elimination of Racial Discrimination, 81st session. Geneva: United Nations.

Charnovitz, Steve. 2006. "Nongovernmental Organizations and International Law." *American Journal of International Law* 100 (2): 348–372. https://doi.org/10.1017/S0002930000016699.

Chayes, Abram and Antonia Handler Chayes. 1993. "On Compliance." *International Organization* 47 (2): 175–205. https://doi.org/10.1017/S0020818300027910.

Checkel, Jeffrey T. 1998. "The Constructive Turn in International Relations Theory." *World Politics* 50 (2): 324–348. https://doi.org/10.1017/S0043887100008133.

Clark, Ann M. 2001. *Diplomacy of Conscience: Amnesty International and Changing Human Rights Norms*. Princeton: Princeton University Press.

Clark, Ann M, Elisabeth Friedman, and Kathryn Hochstetler. 1998. "The Sovereign Limits of Global Civil Society – A Comparison of NGO Participation in UN World Conferences on the Environment, Human Rights, and Women." *World Politics* 51 (1): 1–35. https://doi.org/10.1017/S0043887100007772.

Clark, Cristy. 2017. "Of What Use Is a Deradicalized Human Right to Water?" *Human Rights Law Review* 17 (2): 231–260. https://doi.org/10.1093/hrlr/ngx006.

Claude, Richard Pierre. 2002. *Science in the Service of Human Rights*. Philadelphia: University of Pennsylvania Press.

Cohen, Antonin. 2010. "Legal Professionals or Political Entrepreneurs? Constitution Making as a Process of Social Construction and Political Mobilization." *International Political Sociology* 4 (2): 107–123. https://doi.org/10.1111/j.1749-5687.2010.00095.x.

COHRE, AAAS, SDC, and UN-HABITAT. 2008. *Manual on the Right to Water and Sanitation. A Tool to Assist Policy Makers and Practitioners Develop Strategies for Implementing the Human Right to Water and Sanitation*. Geneva: Centre on Housing Rights and Evictions.

Collier, David. 2011. "Understanding Process Tracing." *PS: Political Science & Politics* 44 (4): 823–830. https://doi.org/10.1017/S1049096511001429.

Comstock, Audrey L. 2021. *Committed to Rights: UN Human Rights Treaties and Legal Paths for Commitment and Compliance*. Cambridge: Cambridge University Press.

Copelon, Rhonda. 1993. "Recognizing the Egregious in the Everyday: Domestic Violence as Torture." *Columbia Human Rights Law Review* 25 (2): 291–368.

Copelon, Rhonda. 2000. "Gender Crimes as War Crimes: Integrating Crimes against Women into International Criminal Law." *McGill Law Journal* 46 (1): 217–240.

Copelon, Rhonda. 2008. "Gender Violence as Torture: The Contribution of CAT General Comment No. 2." *City University of New York Law Review* 11 (2): 229–264.

Cox, Robert W and Harold K Jacobson. 1973a. *The Anatomy of Influence: Decision Making in International Organization*. Cambridge: Cambridge University Press.

Cox, Robert W and Harold K Jacobson. 1973b. "The Framework for Inquiry." In *The Anatomy of Influence: Decision Making in International Organizations*, edited by Harold K Jacobson and Robert W Cox, 1–36. New Haven: Yale University Press.

Craven, Matthew. 2006. "Some Thoughts on the Emergent Right to Water." In *The Human Right to Water*, edited by Eibe Riedel and Peter Rothen, 37–47. Berlin: BWV.

Crawford, James. 2000. "The UN Human Rights Treaty System: A System in Crisis?" In *The Future of UN Human Rights Treaty Monitoring*, edited by Philip Alston and James Crawford, 1–12. Cambridge: Cambridge University Press.

Creamer, Cosette D and Beth A Simmons. 2015. "Ratification, Reporting, and Rights: Quality of Participation in the Convention against Torture." *Human Rights Quarterly* 37 (3): 579–608. https://doi.org/10.1353/hrq.2015.0041.

Creamer, Cosette D and Beth A Simmons. 2020. "The Proof Is in the Process: Self-Reporting under International Human Rights Treaties." *American Journal of International Law* 114 (1): 1–50. https://doi.org/10.1017/ajil.2019.70.

d'Aspremont, Jean. 2016. "Subjects and Actors in International Lawmaking: The Paradigmatic Divides in the Cognition of International Norm-Generating

Processes." In *Research Handbook on the Theory and Practice of International Lawmaking*, edited by Catherine Brölmann and Yannick Radi, 32–55. Cheltenham: Edward Elgar.

da Conceição-Heldt, Eugénia. 2013. "Do Agents 'Run Amok'? A Comparison of Agency Slack in the EU and US Trade Policy in the Doha Round." *Journal of Comparative Policy Analysis: Research and Practice* 15 (1): 21–36. https://doi.org/10.1080/13876988.2012.754152.

Daku, Mark and Krzysztof J Pelc. 2017. "Who Holds Influence over WTO Jurisprudence?" *Journal of International Economic Law* 20 (2): 233–255.

Dany, Charlotte. 2012. *Global Governance and NGO Participation: Shaping the Information Society in the United Nations*. New York: Routledge.

Davis, Lisa. 2007. "Preventing Torture: An Introduction to the Symposium Issue." *City University of New York Law Review* 11 (2): 179–186. https://doi.org/10.31641/clr110201.

Davis Cross, Mai'a K. 2013a. "The Military Dimension of European Security: An Epistemic Community Approach." *Millennium-Journal of International Studies* 42 (1): 45–64. https://doi.org/10.1177/0305829813497821.

Davis Cross, Mai'a K. 2013b. "Rethinking Epistemic Communities Twenty Years Later." *Review of International Studies* 39 (1): 137–160. https://doi.org/10.1017/S0260210512000034.

De Búrca, Gráinne. 2017. "Human Rights Experimentalism." *American Journal of International Law* 111 (2): 277–316. https://doi.org/10.1017/ajil.2016.16.

De Búrca, Gráinne, Robert O Keohane, and Charles Sabel. 2014. "Global Experimentalist Governance." *British Journal of Political Science* 44 (3): 477–486. https://doi.org/10.1017/S0007123414000076.

De Londras, Fiona and Mairead Enright. 2018. *Repealing the 8th*. Bristol: Bristol University Press.

Deitelhoff, Nicole. 2009. "The Discursive Process of Legalization: Charting Islands of Persuasion in the ICC Case." *International Organization* 63 (1): 33–65. https://doi.org/10.1017/S002081830909002X.

Della Porta, Donatella and Sidney G Tarrow, eds. 2005. *Transnational Protest and Global Activism*. Lanham: Rowman & Littlefield.

Dellapenna, Joseph and Joyeeta Gupta. 2008. "Toward Global Law on Water." *Global Governance* 14 (4): 437–453.

Dellmuth, Lisa M and Elizabeth A Bloodgood. 2019. "Advocacy Group Effects in Global Governance: Populations, Strategies, and Political Opportunity Structures." *Interest Groups & Advocacy* 8 (3): 255–269. https://doi.org/10.1057/s41309-019-00068-7.

Dellmuth, Lisa Maria and Jonas Tallberg. 2017. "Advocacy Strategies in Global Governance: Inside versus Outside Lobbying." *Political Studies* 65 (3): 705–723. https://doi.org/10.1177/0032321716684356.

Deloffre, Maryam Zarnegar. 2016. "Global Accountability Communities: NGO Self-regulation in the Humanitarian Sector." *Review of International Studies* 42 (4): 724–747.

Desierto, Diane. 2017. "The ICESCR as a Legal Constraint on State Regulation of Business, Trade, and Investment: Notes from CESCR General Comment No. 24 (August 2017)." *EJIL: Talk!* (blog). www.ejiltalk.org/the-icescr-as-a-legal-constraint-on-state-regulation-of-business-trade-and-investment-notes-from-cescr-general-comment-no-24-august-2017/.

Desierto, Diane A. 2015. *Public Policy in International Economic Law: The ICESCR in Trade, Finance, and Investment*. Oxford: Oxford University Press.

Dezalay, Yves and Mikael Rask Madsen. 2017. "In the 'Field' of Transnational Professionals: A Post-Bourdieusian Approach to Transnational Legal Entrepreneurs." In *Professional Networks in Transnational Governance*, edited by Lasse Folke Henriksen and Leonard Seabrooke, 25–38. Cambridge: Cambridge University Press.

Dingwerth, Klaus. 2007. *The New Transnationalism: Transnational Governance and Democratic Legitimacy*. London: Springer.

Dingwerth, Klaus, Henning Schmidtke, and Tobias Weise. 2020. "The Rise of Democratic Legitimation: Why International Organizations Speak the Language of Democracy." *European Journal of International Relations* 26 (3): 714–741.

Dingwerth, Klaus, Antonia Witt, Ina Lehmann, Ellen Reichel, and Tobias Weise. 2019. *International Organizations under Pressure: Legitimating Global Governance in Challenging Times*. Oxford: Oxford University Press.

Displacement Solutions. 2016. "About Scott Leckie, Director of Displacement Solutions." Accessed March 13. http://displacementsolutions.org/about-ds/scott-leckie/.

Djelic, Marie-Laure and Sigrid Quack. 2010. "Transnational Communities and Governance." In *Transnational Communities: Shaping Global Economic Governance*, edited by Marie-Laure Djelic and Sigrid Quack, 3–36. Cambridge: Cambridge University Press.

Domínguez-Redondo, Elvira. 2020. *Defense of Politicization of Human Rights: The UN Special Procedures*. New York: Oxford University Press.

Donnelly, Jack. 2007. "The Relative Universality of Human Rights." *Human Rights Quarterly* 29 (2): 281–306. https://doi.org/10.1353/hrq.2007.0016.

Dörfler, Thomas. 2019. *Security Council Sanctions Governance: The Power and Limits of Rules*. Abingdon: Routledge.

Dunn, Jennifer Templeton, Katherine Lesyna, and Anna Zaret. 2017. "The Role of Human Rights Litigation in Improving Access to Reproductive Health Care and Achieving Reductions in Maternal Mortality." *BMC Pregnancy and Childbirth* 17 (2): 367. https://doi.org/10.1186/s12884-017-1496-0.

E/C.12/2002/11, Committee on Economic, Social and Cultural Rights. 2003. General Comment No. 15: The Right to Water (Art. 11 and 12 of the Covenant). Accessed March 20. www.refworld.org/docid/4538838d11.html.

E/C.12/2002/13, ECOSOC, Committee on Economic, Social and Cultural Rights. 2003. *Report on the Twenty-Eighth and Twenty-Ninth Session*, edited by United Nations. New York / Geneva.

E/C.12/2002/SR.28, ECOSOC, Committee on Economic, Social and Cultural Rights. 2002. *Summary Record of the First Part (Public) of the 28th Meeting*, edited by United Nations. New York / Geneva.

E/C.12/2002/SR.46, ECOSOC, Committee on Economic, Social and Cultural Rights. 2002. *Summary Record of the 46th Meeting*, edited by United Nations. New York / Geneva.

E/C.12/2002/SR.50, ECOSOC, Committee on Economic, Social and Cultural Rights. 2002. *Summary Record of the First Part of the 50th Meeting*, edited by United Nations. New York / Geneva.

E/C.12/GC/23, Committee on Economic, Social and Cultural Rights. 2016. General Comment No. 23 (2016) on the Right to Just and Favourable Conditions of Work (Article 7 of the International Covenant on Economic, Social and Cultural Rights).

E/CN.4/2006/18, Commission on Human Rights. 2006. Report of the Intergovernmental Working Group on the Effective Implementation of the Durban Declaration and Programme of Action on Its 4th Session. Geneva: United Nations.

Ecker-Ehrhardt, Matthias. 2018. "Self-legitimation in the Face of Politicization: Why International Organizations Centralized Public Communication." *The Review of International Organizations* 13 (4): 519–546.

Eckhard, Steffen and Jörn Ege. 2016. "International Bureaucracies and Their Influence on Policy-Making: A Review of Empirical Evidence." *Journal of European Public Policy* 23 (7): 960–978.

Egan, Suzanne. 2020. "Transforming the UN Human Rights Treaty System: A Realistic Appraisal." *Human Rights Quarterly* 42 (4): 762–789.

Eiken, Jan. 2020. "Breaking New Ground? The CERD Committee's Decision on Jurisdiction in the Inter-State Communications Procedure between Palestine and Israel." *EJIL: Talk! – Blog of the European Journal of International Law* (blog). January 29, 2020. www.ejiltalk.org/breaking-new-ground-the-cerd-committees-decision-on-jurisdiction-in-the-inter-state-communications-procedure-between-palestine-and-israel/.

Eilstrup-Sangiovanni, Mette and Teale N Phelps Bondaroff. 2014. "From Advocacy to Confrontation: Direct Enforcement of Environmental NGOs." *International Studies* 58 (2): 348–361.

Elizalde, Pilar. 2019. "A Horizontal Pathway to Impact? An Assessment of the Universal Periodic Review at 10." In *Contesting Human Rights*, edited by Alison Brysk and Michael Stohl, 83–106. Cheltenham: Edward Elgar.

Elsig, Manfred and Mark A Pollack. 2014. "Agents, Trustees, and International Courts: The Politics of Judicial Appointment at the World Trade Organization." *European Journal of International Relations* 20 (2): 391–415.

Evans, Malcolm D. 2002. "Getting to Grips with Torture." *International & Comparative Law Quarterly* 51 (2): 365–383. https://doi.org/10.1093/iclq/51.2.365.

FAO. 2004. *Implications of the Voluntary Guidelines for Parties and Non-parties to the International Covenant on Economic, Social and Cultural Rights*, edited by Intergovernmental Working Group for the Elaboration of a Set of Voluntary Guidelines to Support the Progressive Realization of the Right to Adequate Food in the Context of National Food Security. Rome: FAO.

Faude, Benjamin and Felix Große-Kreul. 2020. "Let's Justify! How Regime Complexes Enhance the Normative Legitimacy of Global Governance." *International Studies Quarterly* 64 (2): 431–439.

FDFA, Swiss Federal Department of Foreign Affairs. 2015. The Human Rights Council: A Practical Guide. www.eda.admin.ch/eda/de/home/dienstleistungenundpublikationen/publikationen/alle-publikationen.html/content/publikationen/de/eda/internationale-organisationen/uno/human-rights-council-practical-guide.

Fehl, Caroline and Katja Freistein. 2020. "(Un)making Global Inequalities: International Institutions in a Stratified International Society." *Journal of International Relations and Development* 24 (2): 251–278. https://doi.org/10.1057/s41268-020-00190-z.

Finnemore, Martha and Kathryn Sikkink. 1998. "International Norm Dynamics and Political Change." *International Organization* 52 (4): 887–917. https://doi.org/10.1162/002081898550789.

Finnemore, Martha and Stephen J Toope. 2001. "Alternatives to 'Legalization': Richer Views of Law and Politics." *International Organization* 55 (3): 743–758. https://doi.org/10.2307/3078663.

Fitzmaurice, Malgosia. 2013. "Interpretation of Human Rights Treaties." In *The Oxford Handbook of International Human Rights Law*, edited by Dinah Shelton.

Fleischer, Julia and Nina Reiners. 2021. "Connecting International Relations and Public Administration: Toward a Joint Research Agenda for the Study of International Bureaucracy." *International Studies Review*: 1–18. https://doi.org/10.1093/isr/viaa097.

Forsythe, David P. 2012. *Human Rights in International Relations*. Cambridge: Cambridge University Press.

Fraser, Nancy, ed. 2014. *Transnationalizing the Public Sphere*. Cambridge: Polity Press.

Freedman, Rosa. 2015. *Failing to Protect: The UN and the Politicization of Human Rights*. Oxford: Oxford University Press.

Fröhlich, Manuel. 2014. "The John Holmes Memorial Lecture: Representing the United Nations – Individual Actors, International Agency, and Leadership." *Global Governance: A Review of Multilateralism and International Organizations* 20 (2): 169–193.

Gaer, Felice. 2020. "The Committee against Torture: Implementing the Prohibition against Torture." In *Research Handbook on Torture*, edited by Malcom D Evans and Jens Modvig, 128–153. Cheltenham: Edward Elgar.

Gaer, Felice D. 2011. "Rape as a Form of Torture: The Experience of the Committee against Torture." *City University of New York Law Review* 15 (2): 293–308.

Gaer, Felice D. 2003. "Implementing International Human Rights Norms: UN Human Rights Treaty Bodies and NGOs." *Journal of Human Rights* 2 (3): 339–357. https://doi.org/10.1080/1475483032000133024.

Gehring, Thomas and Thomas Dörfler. 2013. "Division of Labor and Rule-Based Decisionmaking within the UN Security Council: The Al-Qaeda/Taliban Sanctions Regime." *Global Governance* 19 (4): 567–587.

Geneva Academy. 2018. *Optimizing the UN Treaty Body System. Academic Platform Report on the 2020 Review*. www.geneva-academy.ch/joomlatools-files/docman-files/Optimizing%20UN%20Treaty%20Bodies.pdf.

GI-ESCR, Global Initiative for Economic, Social and Cultural Rights. 2020. "States Urged to Truly Strengthen the International Human Rights Monitoring Bodies, through Adequate Funding and Support for Concrete Reforms." Accessed February 11, 2021. www.gi-escr.org/latest-news/ensuring-human-rights-accountability-in-the-context-of-the-covid-19-pandemic-opportunities-and-challenges-of-online-work-for-the-un-human-rights-treaty-bodies-kwly3.

Gilpin, Robert G. 1984. "The Richness of the Tradition of Political Realism." *International Organization* 38 (2): 287–304.

Glasius, Marlies. 2002. "Expertise in the Cause of Justice: Global Civil Society Influence on the Statute for an International Criminal Court." *Global Civil Society* 2002: 137–168.

Gleick, Peter H. 1998. "The Human Right to Water." *Water Policy* 1 (5): 487–503. https://doi.org/10.1016/S1366-7017(99)00008-2.

Gleick, Peter H and Jon Lane. 2005. "Large International Water Meetings: Time for a Reappraisal: A Water Forum Contribution." *Water International* 30 (3): 410–414. https://doi.org/10.1080/02508060508691883.

Goetz, Anne Marie. 2020. "The New Competition in Multilateral Norm-setting: Transnational Feminists & the Illiberal Backlash." *Daedalus* 149 (1): 160–179.

Golay, Christophe, Claire Mahon, and Ioana Cismas. 2011. "The Impact of the UN Special Procedures on the Development and Implementation of Economic, Social and Cultural Rights." *The International Journal of Human Rights* 15 (2): 299–318.

Gold, Joseph. 1967. "Interpretation by the International Monetary Fund of Its Articles of Agreement II." *The International and Comparative Law Quarterly* 16 (2): 289–329.

Goldman, Michael. 2005. *Imperial Nature: The World Bank and Struggles for Social Justice in the Age of Globalization*. New Haven: Yale University Press.

Goodhart, Michael. 2003. "Origins and Universality in the Human Rights Debates: Cultural Essentialism and the Challenge of Globalization." *Human Rights Quarterly* 25 (4): 935–964. https://doi.org/10.1353/hrq.2003.0043.

Goodman, Ryan. 2002. "Human Rights Treaties, Invalid Reservations, and State Consent." *American Journal of International Law* 96 (3): 531–560.

Gordenker, Leon and Thomas G Weiss. 1995. "Pluralising Global Governance: Analytical Approaches and Dimensions." *Third World Quarterly* 16 (3): 357–388.

Grillot, Suzette R, Craig S Stapley, and Molly E Hanna. 2006. "Assessing the Small Arms Movement: The Trials and Tribulations of a Transnational Network." *Contemporary Security Policy* 27 (1): 60–84. https://doi.org/10.1080/13523260600602354.

Grimm, Jannis and Ilyas Saliba. 2017. "Free Research in Fearful Times: Conceptualizing an Index to Monitor Academic Freedom." *Interdisciplinary Political Studies* 3 (1): 41–75.

Grossmann, Claudio, Evans Malcom, Alexey Avtonomov, Zdzislaw Kedzia, Nicole Ameline, Maria Reyes, Emmanuel Decaux, and Benyam D Mezmur. 2014. "Chairpersons' Statement on the Intergovernmental Process on Treaty Body Strengthening." Accessed June 19. www.ohchr.org/EN/NewsEvents/Pages/DisplayNews.aspx?NewsID=14506&.

Guns, Wendy. 2013. "The Influence of the Feminist Anti-Abortion NGOs as Norm Setters at the Level of the UN: Contesting UN Norms on Reproductive Autonomy, 1995–2005." *Human Rights Quarterly* 35 (3): 673–700.

Haas, Ernst B. 2008a. *Beyond the Nation State: Functionalism and International Organization*. reprint (1964) ed. Colchester: ECPR Press. 1964.

Haas, Peter. 2008b. "Epistemic Communities." In *The Oxford Handbook of International Environmental Law*, edited by Daniel Bodansky, Jutta Brunnee, and Ellen Hey, 791–806. Oxford: Oxford University Press.

Haas, Peter M. 1992. "Introduction: Epistemic Communities and International Policy Coordination." *International Organization* 46 (1): 1–35. https://doi.org/10.1017/S0020818300001442.

Haas, Peter M. 2004. "When Does Power Listen to Truth? A Constructivist Approach to the Policy Process." *Journal of European Public Policy* 11 (4): 569–592. https://doi.org/10.1080/1350176042000248034.

Haddad, Heidi Nichols. 2013. "After the Norm Cascade: NGO Mission Expansion and the Coalition for the International Criminal Court." *Global Governance: A Review of*

Multilateralism and International Organizations 19 (2): 187–206. https://doi.org/10.5555/1075-2846-19.2.187.

Haddad, Heidi Nichols. 2018. *The Hidden Hands of Justice: NGOs, Human Rights, and International Courts*. Cambridge: Cambridge University Press.

Hafner-Burton, Emilie M. 2008. "Sticks and Stones: Naming and Shaming the Human Rights Enforcement Problem." *International Organization* 62 (4): 689–716. https://doi.org/10.2307/40071894.

Hafner-Burton, Emilie M. 2009. "The Power Politics of Regime Complexity: Human Rights Trade Conditionality in Europe." *Perspectives on Politics* 7 (1): 33–37. https://doi.org/Doi10.1017/S1537592709090057.

Hafner-Burton, Emilie M. and Kiyoteru Tsutsui. 2005. "Human Rights in a Globalizing World: The Paradox of Empty Promises." *American Journal of Sociology* 110 (5): 1373–1411. https://doi.org/10.1086/428442.

Hakimi, Monica. 2009. "Secondary Human Rights Law." *Yale Journal of International Law* 34 (2): 596–604.

Hale, Thomas and David Held. 2017. *Beyond Gridlock*. Cambridge: Polity Press.

Hale, Thomas, David Held, and Kevin Young. 2013. *Gridlock: Why Global Cooperation Is Failing When We Need It Most*. Cambridge: Polity Press.

Hall, Nina. 2016. *Displacement, Development, and Climate Change: International Organizations Moving Beyond Their Mandates*. Abingdon: Routledge.

Hall, Nina, Hans Peter Schmitz, and J Michael Dedmon. 2020. "Transnational Advocacy and NGOs in the Digital Era: New Forms of Networked Power." *International Studies Quarterly* 64 (1): 159–167.

Hall, Rodney Bruce and Thomas J Biersteker. 2002. *The Emergence of Private Authority in Global Governance*. Vol. 85. Cambridge: Cambridge University Press.

Halliday, Terence C and G Shaffer. 2015. "Transnational Legal Orders." In *Transnational Legal Orders*, edited by Terence C Halliday and Gregory Shaffer, 3–72. New York: Cambridge University Press.

Halme-Tuomisaari, Miia. 2018. "Methodologically Blonde at the UN in a Tactical Quest for Inclusion." *Social Anthropology* 26 (4): 456–470.

Hanegraaff, Marcel, Jan AN Beyers, and Iskander De Bruycker. 2016. "Balancing Inside and Outside Lobbying: The Political Strategies of Lobbyists at Global Diplomatic Conferences." *European Journal of Political Research* 55 (3): 568–588.

Hanrieder, Tine. 2014. "Local Orders in International Organisations: The World Health Organization's Global Programme on AIDS." *Journal of International Relations and Development* 17 (2): 220–241. https://doi.org/10.1057/jird.2013.7.

Hanrieder, Tine. 2015. *International Organization in Time: Fragmentation and Reform*. Oxford: Oxford University Press.

Hanschel, Dirk, Sebastian Graf Kielmansegg, Uwe Kischel, Christian Koenig, and Ralph Alexander Lorz. 2013. *Mensch und Recht: Festschrift für Eibe Riedel zum 70. Geburtstag*. Berlin: Duncker & Humblot.

Harrington, Brooke and Leonard Seabrooke. 2020. "Transnational Professionals." *Annual Review of Sociology* 46: 399–417.

Hawkins, Darren and Wade Jacoby. 2008. "Agent Permeability, Principal Delegation and the European Court of Human Rights." *The Review of International Organizations* 3 (1): 1–28. https://doi.org/10.1007/s11558-007-9014-1.

Hawkins, Darren G, David A Lake, Daniel L Nielson, and Michael J Tierney. 2006a. *Delegation and Agency in International Organizations*. Cambridge: Cambridge University Press.

Hawkins, Darren G, David A Lake, Daniel L Nielson, and Michael J Tierney. 2006b. "Delegation under Anarchy: States, International Organizations, and Principal-Agent Theory." In *Delegation and Agency in International Organizations*, edited by Darren G Hawkins, David A Lake, Daniel L Nielson, and Michael J Tierney, 3–38. Cambridge: Cambridge University Press.

Heldt, Eugénia. 2017. "Regaining Control of Errant Agents? Agency Slack at the European Commission and the World Health Organization." *Cooperation and Conflict* 52 (4): 469–484. https://doi.org/10.1177/0010836717703673.

Helfer, Laurence R. 2015. "Pharmaceutical Patents and the Human Right to Health." In *Transnational Legal Orders*, edited by Terence C Halliday and G Shaffer, 311–339. New York: Cambridge University Press.

Henriksen, Lasse Folke and Leonard Seabrooke. 2016. "Transnational Organizing: Issue Professionals in Environmental Sustainability Networks." *Organization* 23 (5): 722–741.

Henriksen, Lasse Folke and Leonard Seabrooke. 2017. "Issue Professionals and Transnational Organizing." In *Professional Networks in Transnational Governance*, edited by Lasse Folke Henriksen and Leonard Seabrooke, 286–299. Cambridge: Cambridge University Press.

Hertel, Shareen. 2006. *Unexpected Power: Conflict and Change among Transnational Activists*. Ithaca: Cornell University Press.

Hertel, Shareen. 2017. "Re-framing Human Rights Advocacy: The Rise of Economic Rights." In *Human Rights Futures*, edited by Stephen Hopgood, Richard C Snyder, and Leslie Vinjamuri, 237–260. Cambridge: Cambridge University Press.

Heupel, Monika, Gisela Hirschmann, and Michael Zürn. 2018. "International Organisations and Human Rights: What Direct Authority Needs for Its Legitimation." *Review of International Studies* 44 (2): 343–366.

Heupel, Monika and Michael Zürn, eds. 2017. *Protecting the Individual from International Authority: Human Rights in International Organizations*. Cambridge: Cambridge University Press.

Heyse, Liesbet. 2011. "From Agenda Setting to Decision Making: Opening the Black Box of Non-governmental Organizations." In *Ashgate Research Companion to Non State Actors*, edited by Bob Reinalda, 277–290. Abingdon: Ashgate.

Hickmann, Thomas. 2015. *Rethinking Authority in Global Climate Governance: How Transnational Climate Initiatives Relate to the International Climate Regime*. Abingdon: Routledge.

Hickmann, Thomas. 2017. "The Reconfiguration of Authority in Global Climate Governance." *International Studies Review* 19 (3): 430–451.

Higgins, Rosalyn. 1995. *Problems and Process: International Law and How We Use It*. Oxford: Oxford University Press.

Hillebrecht, Courtney. 2014. *Domestic Politics and International Human Rights Tribunals: The Problem of Compliance*. Vol. 104. New York: Cambridge University Press.

Hirschmann, Gisela. 2020. *Accountability in Global Governance: Pluralist Accountability in Global Governance*. Oxford: Oxford University Press.

Hoffman, Aaron M. 2002. "A Conceptualization of Trust in International Relations." *European Journal of International Relations* 8 (3): 375–401. https://doi.org/10.1177/1354066102008003003.

Hofmann, Stephanie C. 2019. "The Politics of Overlapping Organizations: Hostage-Taking, Forum-Shopping and Brokering." *Journal of European Public Policy* 26 (6): 883–905.

Hooghe, Liesbet and Gary Marks. 2015. "Delegation and Pooling in International Organizations." *The Review of International Organizations* 10 (3): 305–328. https://doi.org/10.1007/s11558-014-9194-4.

Hopgood, Stephen. 2006. *Keepers of the Flame: Understanding Amnesty International*. Ithaca: Cornell University Press.

Hopgood, Stephen. 2013. *The Endtimes of Human Rights*. Ithaca: Cornell University Press.

Hosli, Madeleine O and Thomas Dörfler. 2019. "Why Is Change so Slow? Assessing Prospects for United Nations Security Council Reform." *Journal of Economic Policy Reform* 22 (1): 35–50. https://doi.org/10.1080/17487870.2017.1305903.

Hurd, Ian. 1999. "Legitimacy and Authority in International Politics." *International Organization* 53 (2): 379–408. https://doi.org/10.1162/002081899550913.

ICJ, International Commission of Jurists. 2017. "The ICJ Mourns Its President Professor Sir Nigel Rodley." Last Modified January 25, 2017. Accessed February 11, 2021. www.icj.org/the-icj-mourns-its-president-professor-sir-nigel-rodley/.

ILA, International Law Association. 2004. *Final Report on the Impact of Findings of the United Nations Human Rights Treaty Bodies*. (Berlin Conference).

IMF, International Monetary Fund. 2020. Articles of Agreement of the International Monetary Fund: Adopted at the United Nations Monetary and Financial Conference, Bretton Woods, New Hampshire, July 22, 1944 . . . amended effective January 26, 2016 by the modifications approved by the Board of Governors in Resolution No. 66–2, adopted December 15, 2010. Washington, DC: International Monetary Fund.

Jetschke, Anja and Andrea Liese. 2013. "The Power of Human Rights a Decade after: From Euphoria to Contestation." In *The Persistent Power of Human Rights. From Commitment to Compliance*, edited by Thomas Risse, Stephen C. Ropp, and Kathryn Sikkink, 26–42. Cambridge: Cambridge University Press.

Joachim, Jutta M. 2003. "Framing Issues and Seizing Opportunities: The UN, NGOs, and Women's Rights." *International Studies Quarterly* 47 (2): 247–274. https://doi.org/10.1111/1468-2478.4702005.

Joachim, Jutta M. 2007. *Agenda Setting, the UN, and NGOs: Gender Violence and Reproductive Rights*. Washington, DC: Georgetown University Press.

Johansen, Stian Øby. 2020. *The Human Rights Accountability Mechanisms of International Organizations*. Cambridge: Cambridge University Press.

Johnson, Tana. 2014. *Organizational Progeny: Why Governments are Losing Control Over the Proliferating Structures of Global Governance. Transformations in Governance*. Oxford: Oxford University Press.

Johnstone, Ian. 1990. "Treaty Interpretation: The Authority of Interpretive Communities." *Michigan Journal of International Law* 12 (2): 371–419.

Jönsson, Christer and Jonas Tallberg, eds. 2010. *Transnational Actors in Global Governance: Patterns, Explanations and Implications*. Basingstoke: Palgrave Macmillan.

Joseph, Sarah. 2019. "Extending the Right to Life under the International Covenant on Civil and Political Rights: General Comment 36." *Human Rights Law Review* 19 (2): 347–368. https://doi.org/10.1093/hrlr/ngz003.

Josselin, Daphné and William Wallace. 2001. "Non-state Actors in World Politics. A Framework." In *Non-state Actors in World Politics*, edited by Daphné Josselin and William Wallace, 1–15. London: Palgrave.

Jung, Courtney, Ran Hirschl, and Evan Rosevear. 2014. "Economic and Social Rights in National Constitutions." *The American Journal of Comparative Law* 62 (4): 1043–1094.

Jurkovich, Michelle. 2020a. *Feeding the Hungry: Advocacy and Blame in the Global Fight against Hunger*. Ithaca: Cornell University Press.

Jurkovich, Michelle. 2020b. "What Isn't a Norm? Redefining the Conceptual Boundaries of 'Norms' in the Human Rights Literature." *International Studies Review* 22 (3): 693–711. https://doi.org/10.1093/isr/viz040.

Kahler, Miles. 1998. "Rationality in International Relations." *International Organization* 52 (4): 919–941. https://doi.org/10.1162/002081898550680.

Kanetake, Machiko. 2018. "UN Human Rights Treaty Monitoring Bodies before Domestic Courts." *International & Comparative Law Quarterly* 67 (1): 201–232.

Karpik, Lucien and Terence C Halliday. 2011. "The Legal Complex." *Annual Review of Law and Social Science* 7: 217–236.

Keane, David. 2020. "Mapping the International Convention on the Elimination of All Forms of Racial Discrimination as a Living Instrument." *Human Rights Law Review* 20 (2): 236–268.

Keane, David and Annapurna Waughray. 2017. *Fifty Years of the International Convention on the Elimination of All Forms of Racial Discrimination: A Living Instrument*. Manchester: Manchester University Press.

Keck, Margaret E and Kathryn Sikkink. 1998. *Activists Beyond Borders: Advocacy Networks in International Politics*. 1. print. ed. Ithaca: Cornell University Press.

Keller, Helen and Leena Grover. 2012. "General Comments of the Human Rights Committee and their Legitimacy." In *UN Human Rights Treaty Bodies: Law and Legitimacy*. Studies on Human Rights Conventions, edited by Helen Keller and Geir Ulfstein, 116–198. Cambridge: Cambridge University Press.

Keller, Helen and Geir Ulfstein, eds. 2012. *UN Human Rights Treaty Bodies. Law and Legitimacy*. Studies on Human Rights Conventions. Cambridge: Cambridge University Press.

Kennedy, David. 2005. "Challenging Expert Rule: The Politics of Global Governance." *Sydney Law Review* 27 (1): 5.

Klein, Eckart. 2005. "Impact of Treaty Bodies on the International Legal Order." In *Developments of International Law in Treaty Making*, edited by Rüdiger Wolfrum and Volker Röben, 571–579. Heidelberg: Springer.

Klotz, A and D Prakash. 2008. *Qualitative Methods in International Relations : A Pluralist Guide*. London: Palgrave Macmillan.

Koch, Martin. 2015. "World Organizations–(Re-)Conceptualizing International Organizations." *World Political Science* 11 (1): 97–131.

Koliev, Faradj, Thomas Sommerer, and Jonas Tallberg. 2020. "Compliance without Coercion: Effects of Reporting on International Labor Rights." *Journal of Peace Research* 58 (3), 1–16. https://doi.org/10.1177/0022343320910254.

Koremenos, Barbara. 2001. "Loosening the Ties that Bind: A Learning Model of Agreement Flexibility." *International Organization* 55 (2): 289–325.

Koremenos, Barbara. 2016. *The Continent of International Law: Explaining Agreement Design*. Cambridge: Cambridge University Press.

Koremenos, Barbara, Charles Lipson, and Duncan Snidal. 2001. "The Rational Design of International Institutions." *International Organization* 55 (4): 761–799.

Koskenniemi, Martti. 2007. "The Fate of Public International Law: Between Technique and Politics." *Modern Law Review* 70 (1): 1–30.

Kranke, Matthias. 2020. "Exclusive Expertise: The Boundary Work of International Organizations." *Review of International Political Economy*: 1–24.

Krasner, Stephen D and Thomas Risse. 2014. "External Actors, State-Building, and Service Provision in Areas of Limited Statehood: Introduction." *Governance* 27 (4): 545–567.

Krieger, Heike. 2019. "Populist Governments and International Law." *European Journal of International Law* 30 (3): 971–996. https://doi.org/10.1093/ejil/chz046.

Krieger, Heike, Georg Nolte, and Andreas Zimmermann. 2019. *The International Rule of Law: Rise or Decline?* Oxford: Oxford University Press.

Krisch, Nico. 2014. "The Decay of Consent: International Law in an Age of Global Public Goods." *American Journal of International Law* 108 (1): 1–40.

Krisch, Nico. 2017. "Liquid Authority in Global Governance." *International Theory* 9 (2): 237–260. https://doi.org/10.1017/S1752971916000269.

Krisch, Nico, Francesco Corradini, and Lucy Lu Reimers. 2020. "Order at the Margins: The Legal Construction of Interface Conflicts over Time." *Global Constitutionalism* 9 (2): 343–363.

Krommendijk, Jasper. 2015. "The Domestic Effectiveness of International Human Rights Monitoring in Established Democracies. The Case of the UN Human Rights Treaty Bodies." *The Review of International Organizations* 10 (4): 489–512. https://doi.org/10.1007/s11558-015-9213-0.

Kumar, Raj C. 2006. "National Human Rights Institutions and Economic, Social, and Cultural Rights: Toward the Institutionalization and Developmentalization of Human Rights." *Human Rights Quarterly* 28 (3): 755–779. https://doi.org/DOI10.1353/hrq.2006.0035.

Lagoutte, Stéphanie, Thomas Gammeltoft-Hansen, and John Cerone, eds. 2016. *Tracing the Roles of Soft Law in Human Rights*. Oxford: Oxford University Press.

Lake, David A. 2010. "Rightful Rules: Authority, Order, and the Foundations of Global Governance." *International Studies Quarterly* 54 (3): 587–613. https://doi.org/10.1111/j.1468-2478.2010.00601.x.

Lake, David A and Mathew D McCubbins. 2006. "The Logic of Delegation to International Organizations." In *Delegation and Agency in International Organizations*, edited by Darren G Hawkins, David A Lake, Daniel L Nielson, and Michael J Tierney, 341–368. Cambridge: Cambridge University Press.

Land, Molly K. 2018. "The Marrakesh Treaty as Bottom Up Lawmaking: Supporting Local Human Rights Action on IP Policies." *UC Irvine Law Review* 8 (3): 513–554.

Langford, Malcolm. 2005. "The United Nations Concept of Water as a Human Right: A New Paradigm for Old Problems?" *International Journal of Water Resources Development* 21 (2): 273–282. https://doi.org/10.1080/07900620500035887.

Langford, Malcolm. 2006. "Ambition That Overleaps Itself? A Response to Stephan Tully's Critique of the General Comment on the Right to Water." *Netherlands Quarterly of Human Rights* 24 (3): 433–459. https://doi.org/10.1177%2F016934410602400304.

Langford, Malcolm, Jamie Bartram, and Virginia Roaf. 2017. "The Human Right to Sanitation." In *The Human Right to Water: Theory, Practice and Prospects*, edited by Malcolm Langford and Anna Russell, 345–395. Cambridge: Cambridge University Press.

Langford, Malcolm and Anna FS Russell. 2017. *The Human Right to Water: Theory, Practice and Prospects*. Cambridge: Cambridge University Press.

Lantos, Tom. 2002. "The Durban Debacle: An Insider's View of the UN World Conference against Racism." *Fletcher Forum of World Affairs* 26: 31.

Leander, Anna. 2017. "From Cookbooks to Encyclopaedias in the Making: Methodological Perspectives for Research of Non-state Actors and Processes." In *Researching Non-state Actors in International Security*, edited by Andreas Kruck and Andrea Schneiker, 233–244. Abingdon and New York: Routledge.

Leander, Anna and Tanja Aalberts. 2013. "Introduction: The Co-constitution of Legal Expertise and International Security." *Leiden Journal of International Law* 26 (4): 783–792.

Leao Soares Pereira, L and N Ridi. 2020. "Mapping the 'Invisible College of International Lawyers' through Obituaries." *Leiden Journal of International Law* 34 (1): 67–91. https://doi.org/10.1017/S0922156520000667.

Lesch, Max. 2020. "Dynamics of Deviance: Torture and Its Prohibition in World Politics." PhD, Johann-Wolfgang-Goethe-Universität.

Levit, Janet Koven. 2007. "Bottom-Up International Lawmaking: Reflections on the New Haven School of International Law." *Yale Journal of International Law* 32 (2): 393–420.

Liese, Andrea. 2009. "Exceptional Necessity-How Liberal Democracies Contest the Prohibition of Torture and Ill-Treatment When Countering Terrorism." *Journal of International Law & International Relations* 5 (1): 17–47.

Liese, Andrea. 2010. "Explaining Varying Degress of Openness in the Food and Agriculture Organization of the United Nations (FAO)." In *Transnational Actors in Global Governance. Patterns, Explanations and Implications*, edited by Christer Jönsson and Jonas Tallberg, 88–108. Basingstoke: Palgrave Macmillan.

Liese, Andrea, Jana Herold, Hauke Feil, and Per-Olof Busch. 2021. "The Heart of Bureaucratic Power: Explaining International Bureaucracies' Expert Authority." *Review of International Studies* 47 (3): 353–376. https://doi.org/10.1017/S026021052100005X.

Littoz-Monnet, Annabelle. 2017. *The Politics of Expertise in International Organizations: How International Bureaucracies Produce and Mobilize Knowledge*. New York: Taylor & Francis.

Littoz-Monnet, Annabelle. 2020. *Governing through Expertise: The Politics of Bioethics*. Cambridge: Cambridge University Press.

Lopez, Julia Costa. 2020. "Political Authority in International Relations: Revisiting the Medieval Debate." *International Organization* 74 (2): 1–31. https://doi.org/10.1017/S0020818319000390.

Lupu, Yonatan. 2013. "Best Evidence: The Role of Information in Domestic Judicial Enforcement of International Human Rights Agreements." *International Organization* 67 (3): 469–503.

Lynch, Colum. 2018. "At the U.N., China and Russia Score Win in War on Human Rights." *Foreign Policy*, March 26, 2018. https://foreignpolicy.com/2018/03/26/at-the-u-n-china-and-russia-score-win-in-war-on-human-rights/.

Madsen, Mikael R. 2014. "The International Judiciary as Transnational Power Elite." *International Political Sociology* 8 (3): 332–334. https://doi.org/10.1111/ips.12063.

Mantilla, Giovanni. 2020. *Lawmaking under Pressure: International Humanitarian Law and Internal Armed Conflict*. Ithaca oder London: Cornell University Press.

Margulis, Matias E. 2013. "The Regime Complex for Food Security: Implications for the Global Hunger Challenge." *Global Governance: A Review of Multilateralism and International Organizations* 19 (1): 53–67.

Marsh, Elizabeth. 2001. Overseeing the Refugee Convention: General Comments (December 2001). ICVA Working Paper No. 3. https://ssrn.com/abstract=294184 or http://dx.doi.org/10.2139/ssrn.294184.

Martens, Kerstin. 2004. "An Appraisal of Amnesty International's Work at the United Nations: Shifting Priorities since the 1990s." *Human Rights Quarterly* 26 (4): 1050–1070. https://doi.org/10.1353/hrq.2004.0052.

Martens, Kerstin. 2006. "Professionalised Representation of Human Rights NGOs to the United Nations." *The International Journal of Human Rights* 10 (1): 19–30.

Martin, Lisa L and Beth A Simmons. 2013. "International Organizations and Institutions." In *Handbook of International Relations*, edited by Walter Carlsnaes, Thomas Risse, and Beth A Simmons, 326–351. Los Angeles: SAGE.

Mattern, Janice Bially and Ayşe Zarakol. 2016. "Hierarchies in World Politics." *International Organization* 70 (3): 623–654.

Mattli, Walter and Tim Büthe. 2005. "Accountability in Accounting? The Politics of Private Rule-Making in the Public Interest." *Governance* 18 (3): 399–429.

Mayntz, Renate. 2010. "Global Structures: Markets, Organizations, Networks – and Communities?" In *Transnational Communities: Shaping Global Economic Governance*, edited by Marie-Laure Djelic and Sigrid Quack, 37–54. Cambridge: Cambridge University Press.

McCall-Smith, Kasey L. 2016. "Interpreting International Human Rights Standards. Treaty Body General Comments as a Chisel or a Hammer." In *Tracing the Roles of Soft Law in Human Rights*, edited by Stéphanie Lagoutte, Thomas Gammeltoft-Hansen, and John Cerone, 27–46. Oxford: Oxford University Press.

McGonagle, Tarlach. 2017. "General Recommendation 35 on Combating Racist Hate Speech." In *Fifty Years of the International Convention on the Elimination of All Forms of Racial Discrimination*, edited by David Keane, 246–268. Manchester: Manchester University Press.

Mechlem, Kerstin. 2009. "Treaty Bodies and Their Interpretation of Human Rights." *Vanderbilt Journal of Transnational Law* 42: 905–7.

Mende, Janne. 2020. *Global Governance und Menschenrechte: Konstellationen zwischen Privatheit und Öffentlichkeit. 1 ed. Vol. 8. Internationale Politische Theorie*. Baden-Baden: Nomos Verlagsgesellschaft mbH & Co. KG.

Menéndez, Fernando M Mariño. 2014. "El Comité contra la Tortura de Naciones Unidas. Balance de su actual situación." *LEX-REVISTA DE LA FACULTAD DE DERECHO Y CIENCIAS POLÍTICAS* 12 (13): 15–34.

Meron, Theodor. 1985. "The Meaning and Reach of the International Convention on the Elimination of All Forms of Racial Discrimination." *The American Journal of International Law* 79 (2): 283–318. https://doi.org/10.2307/2201704.

Merry, Sally Engle. 2009. *Human Rights and Gender Violence: Translating International Law into Local Justice*. Chicago oder London: University of Chicago Press.

Mert, Ayşem. 2019. "Participation (s) in Transnational Environmental Governance: Green Values versus Instrumental Use." *Environmental Values* 28 (1): 101–121.

Michel, Torsten. 2013. "Time to Get Emotional: Phronetic Reflections on the Concept of Trust in International Relations." *European Journal of International Relations* 19 (4): 869–890. https://doi.org/10.1177/1354066111428972.

Mitchell, George E and Hans P Schmitz. 2014. "Principled Instrumentalism: A Theory of Transnational NGO Behavior." *Review of International Studies* 40 (3): 487–504. https://doi.org/10.1017/S0260210513000387.

Mitchell, George E, Hans Peter Schmitz, and Tosca Bruno-van Vijfeijken. 2020. *Between Power and Irrelevance: The Future of Transnational NGOs*. Oxford: Oxford University Press.

Moeckli, Daniel and Nigel D White. 2016. "Treaties as 'Living Instruments'." In *Conceptual and Contextual Perspectives on the Modern Law of Treaties*, edited by Dino Kritsiotis and Michael Bowman, 136–171. Cambridge: Cambridge University Press.

Moyn, Samuel. 2012. *The Last Utopia*. Cambridge: Harvard University Press.

Moyn, Samuel. 2018. *Not Enough: Human Rights in an Unequal World*. Cambridge: Harvard University Press.

Müller, Harald. 2004. "Arguing, Bargaining and All That: Communicative Action, Rationalist Theory and the Logic of Appropriateness in International Relations." *European Journal of International Relations* 10 (3): 395–435. https://doi.org/10.1177/1354066104045542.

Murdie, Amanda M and David R Davis. 2012. "Shaming and Blaming: Using Events Data to Assess the Impact of Human Rights INGOs." *International Studies Quarterly* 56 (1): 1–16.

Mutua, Makau. 2007. "Standard Setting in Human Rights: Critique and Prognosis." *Human Rights Quarterly* 29 (3): 547–630.

Nair, Deepak. 2020. "Emotional Labor and the Power of International Bureaucrats." *International Studies Quarterly* 64 (3): 573–587.

Nasiritousi, Naghmeh, Mattias Hjerpe, and Karin Bäckstrand. 2016. "Normative Arguments for Non-state Actor Participation in International Policymaking Processes: Functionalism, Neocorporatism or Democratic Pluralism?" *European Journal of International Relations* 22 (4): 920–943.

Nelson, Paul. 2015. "The Human Right to Water and Advocacy for Urban Water Supply: After the Privatization Struggles." In *The Social Practice of Human Rights*, edited by Joel R Pruce, 81–99. New York: Palgrave Macmillan.

Nelson, Paul and Ellen Dorsey. 2007. "New Rights Advocacy in a Global Public Domain." *European Journal of International Relations* 13 (2): 187–216.

Nelson, Paul J and Ellen Dorsey. 2008. *New Rights Advocacy: Changing Strategies of Development and Human Rights NGOs. Advancing Human Rights*. Washington, DC: Georgetown University Press.

Neumayer, Eric. 2007. "Qualified Ratification: Explaining Reservations to International Human Rights Treaties." *The Journal of Legal Studies* 36 (2): 397–429.

Niederberger, Aurel. 2020. "Independent Experts with Political Mandates: 'Role Distance' in the Production of Political Knowledge." *European Journal of International Security*. 5(3): 350–371. https://doi.org/10.1017/eis.2019.13.

Nielson, Daniel L and Michael J Tierney. 2003. "Delegation to International Organizations: Agency Theory and World Bank Environmental Reform." *International Organization* 57 (2): 241–276. https://doi.org/10.1017/S0020818303572010.

Nolan, Aoife. 2014. *Economic and Social Rights after the Global Financial Crisis*. Cambridge: Cambridge University Press.

Noortmann, Math, August Reinisch, and Cedric Ryngaert. 2015. *Non-state Actors in International Law. Studies in International Law*. London: Bloomsbury.

Odello, Marco and Francesco Seatzu. 2012. *The UN Committee on Economic, Social and Cultural Rights: The Law, Process and Practice*. New York: Routledge.

Oette, Lutz. 2018. "The UN Human Rights Treaty Bodies: Impact and Future." In *International Human Rights Institutions, Tribunals, and Courts*, edited by Gerd Oberleitner, 1–21. Singapore: Springer Singapore.

OHCHR, Office of the High Commissioner for Human Rights. 2009. "Anti-Racism Durban Review Conference Adopts Final Outcome Document." Last Modified April 2009. Accessed February 11, 2021. www.ohchr.org/EN/NewsEvents/Pages/DRCAdoptsFinalOutcomeDocument.aspx.

OHCHR, United Nations Human Rights – Office of the High Commissioner for Human Rights. 2012. *Report on Austerity Measures and Economic and Social Rights*.

OHCHR, United Nations Human Rights – Office of the High Commissioner for Human Rights. 2014. "Human Rights Bodies." Accessed March 6. www.ohchr.org/EN/HRBodies/Pages/HumanRightsBodies.aspx.

OHCHR, United Nations Human Rights – Office of the High Commissioner for Human Rights. 2020. *United Nations Human Rights Appeal 2020*. www.ohchr.org/Documents/Publications/AnnualAppeal2020.pdf.

OHCHR, United Nations Human Rights – Office of the High Commissioner for Human Rights. n.d. "Treaty Body Strengthening." Accessed October 3, 2019. www.ohchr.org/EN/HRBodies/HRTD/Pages/TBStrengthening.aspx.

OHCHR, United Nations Human Rights Office of the High Commissioner. 2017. "Elections of the Treaty Body Members." Accessed March 15. www.ohchr.org/EN/HRBodies/Pages/ElectionsofTreatyBodiesMembers.aspx.

Onuf, Nicholas. 2016. "Constructivism at the Crossroads; or, the Problem of Moderate-Sized Dry Goods." *International Political Sociology* 10 (2): 115–132. https://doi.org/10.1093/ips/olw001.

Orsini, Amandine. 2011. "Thinking Transnationally, Acting Individually: Business Lobby Coalitions in International Environmental Negotiations." *Global Society* 25 (3): 311–329.

Orsini, Amandine, Sélim Louafi, and Jean-Frédéric Morin. 2017. "Boundary Concepts for Boundary Work between Science and Technology Studies and International Relations: Special Issue Introduction." *Review of Policy Research* 34 (6): 734–743. https://doi.org/10.1111/ropr.12273.

Panjabi, Ranee KL. 1995. "Human Rights in the 1990's: Promise or Peril." *Cornell International Law Journal* 28 (1): 229–240.

Panke, Diana and Ulrich Petersohn. 2012. "Why International Norms Disappear Sometimes." *European Journal of International Relations* 18 (4): 719–742.

Panke, Diana and Sören Stapel. 2018. "Exploring Overlapping Regionalism." *Journal of International Relations and Development* 21 (3): 635–662. https://doi.org/10.1057/s41268-016-0081-x.

Pantzerhielm, Laura, Anna Holzscheiter, and Thurid Bahr. 2019. "Governing Effectively in a Complex World? How Metagovernance Norms and Changing Repertoires of Knowledge Shape International Organization Discourses on Institutional Order in Global Health." *Cambridge Review of International Affairs* 32: 1–26. https://doi.org/10.1080/09557571.2019.1678112.

Parízek, Michal. 2017. "Control, Soft Information, and the Politics of International Organizations Staffing." *The Review of International Organizations* 12 (4): 559–583. https://doi.org/10.1007/s11558-016-9252-1.

Partzsch, Lena. 2017. "Powerful Individuals in a Globalized World." *Global Policy* 8 (1): 5–13.

Pattberg, Philipp. 2005. "The Institutionalization of Private Governance: How Business and Nonprofit Organizations Agree on Transnational Rules." *Governance* 18 (4): 589–610. https://doi.org/10.1111/j.1468-0491.2005.00293.x.

Patz, Ronny and Klaus H Goetz. 2019. *Managing Money and Discord in the UN: Budgeting and Bureaucracy*. Oxford: Oxford University Press.

Pauwelyn, Joost, Ramses Wessel, and Jan Wouters. 2012. *Informal International Lawmaking*. Oxford: Oxford University Press.

Pauwelyn, Joost, Ramses A Wessel, and Jan Wouters. 2014. "When Structures Become Shackles: Stagnation and Dynamics in International Lawmaking." *European Journal of International Law* 25 (3): 733–763.

Payne, Rodger A. 2001. "Persuasion, Frames and Norm Construction." *European Journal of International Relations* 7 (1): 37–61. https://doi.org/10.1177/1354066101007001002.

Pegram, Tom. 2017. "Regulatory Stewardship and Intermediation: Lessons from Human Rights Governance." *The ANNALS of the American Academy of Political and Social Science* 670 (1): 225–244. https://doi.org/10.1177/0002716217693986.

Peterson, Timothy M, Amanda Murdie, and Victor Asal. 2018. "Human Rights, NGO Shaming and the Exports of Abusive States." *British Journal of Political Science* 48 (3): 767–786.

Pillay, Navanethem. 2012. *Strengthening the United Nations Human Rights Treaty Body System*. New York: UN Office of the High Commissioner for Human Rights.

Posner, Eric. 2014. *The Twilight of Human Rights Law*. New York: Oxford University Press.

Price Cohen, Cynthia. 1990. "The Role of NGOs in the Drafting of the Convention on the Rights of the Child." *Human Rights Quarterly* 12 (1): 137–147.

Pruce, Joel R. 2015. "The Practice Turn in Human Rights Research." In *The Social Practice of Human Rights*, 1–17. New York: Palgrave Macmillan.

Putnam, Tonya L. 2020. "Mingling and Strategic Augmentation of International Legal Obligations." *International Organization* 74 (1): 31–64. https://doi.org/10.1017/S0020818319000377.

Quack, Sigrid. 2007. "Legal Professionals and Transnational Law-Making: A Case of Distributed Agency." *Organization* 14(5): 643–666. https://doi.org/10.1177/1350508407080313.

Ranganathan, Surabhi. 2016. *Strategically Created Treaty Conflicts and the Politics of International Law*. Cambridge: Cambridge University Press.

Ratjen, Sandra and Manav Satija. 2014. "Realizing Economic, Social, and Cultural Rights for All." In *Economic, Social, and Cultural Rights in International Law. Contemporary Issues and Challenges*, edited by Eibe Riedel et al., 111–133. Oxford: Oxford University Press.

Raustiala, Kal. 1997. "States, NGOs, and International Environmental Institutions." *International Studies Quarterly* 41 (4): 719–740. https://doi.org/10.1111/1468-2478.00064.

Raymond, Mark. 2019. *Social Practices of Rule-Making in World Politics*. New York: Oxford University Press.

Reinalda, Bob and Bertjan Verbeek. 2004. "The Issue of Decision Making within International Organizations." *ECPR Studies In European Political Science* 31: 9–42.

Reiners, Nina. 2018. "Kontroversen um die Reform der UN-Menschenrecht svertragsorgane." *Vereinte Nationen* 66 (6): 266–271.

Reiners, Nina. 2019. "Undermining Authority from Within." *The Global* (blog). January 3, 2019. https://theglobal.blog/2019/01/03/undermining-authority-from-within/.

Reiners, Nina. 2021. "Despite or Because of Contestation? How Water Became a Human Right." *Human Rights Quarterly* 43 (2): 329–343.

Reisman, W Michael. 2005. "The Democratization of Contemporary International Law-Making Processes and the Differentiation of Their Application." In *Developments of International Law in Treaty Making*, edited by Rüdiger Wolfrum and Volker Röben, 15–30. Heidelberg: Springer.

Ricks, Jacob I and Amy H Liu. 2018. "Process-Tracing Research Designs: A Practical Guide." *PS: Political Science & Politics* 51 (4): 842–846. https://doi.org/10.1017/S1049096518000975.

Riedel, Eibe. 2005. "The Development of International Law: Alternatives to Treaty-Making? International Organizations and Non-state Actors." In *Developments of International Law in Treaty Making*, edited by Rüdiger Wolfrum and Volker Röben, 301–318. Heidelberg: Springer.

Riedel, Eibe. 2006. "The Human Right to Water and General Comment No. 15 of the CESCR." In *The Human Right to Water*, edited by Eibe Riedel and Peter Rothen, 19–36. Berlin: BWV.

Riedel, Eibe, Gilles Giacca, and Christophe Golay. 2014. *Economic, Social, and Cultural Rights in International Law: Contemporary Issues and Challenges*. Oxford: Oxford University Press.

Rietig, Katharina. 2016. "The Power of Strategy: Environmental NGO Influence in International Climate Negotiations." *Global Governance* 22 (2): 269–288. https://doi.org/10.1163/19426720-02202006.

Risse, Thomas. 2013. "Transnational Actors and World Politics." In *Handbook of International Relations*, edited by Walter Carlsnaes, Thomas Risse, and Beth A Simmons, 426–452. Los Angeles: SAGE.

Risse, Thomas, Stephen C Ropp, and Kathryn Sikkink, eds. 1999. *The Power of Human Rights. International Norms and Domestic Change*. Cambridge: Cambridge University Press.

Risse, Thomas, Stephen C Ropp, and Kathryn Sikkink, eds. 2013. *The Persistent Power of Human Rights: From Commitment to Compliance*. Cambridge: Cambridge University Press.

Roaf, Virginia, Ashfaq Khalfan, and Malcom Langford. 2005. "Monitoring Implementation of the Right to Water. A Framework for Developing Indicators." *Global Issue Papers* 14.

Roberts, Anthea. 2017. *Is International Law International?* New York: Oxford University Press.

Roberts, Anthea and Sandesh Sivakumaran. 2012. "Lawmaking by Nonstate Actors: Engaging Armed Groups in the Creation of International Humanitarian Law." *Yale Journal of International Law* 37: 107.

Rodiles, Alejandro. 2018. *Coalitions of the Willing and International Law: The Interplay between Formality and Informality*. Vol. 135. Cambridge: Cambridge University Press.

Rodley, Nigel S. 2013. "The Role and Impact of Treaty Bodies." In *The Oxford Handbook of International Human Rights Law*, edited by Dinah Shelton, 621–648. New York.

Roger, Charles B. 2020. *The Origins of Informality: Why the Legal Foundations of Global Governance Are Shifting, and Why It Matters*. New York: Oxford University Press.

Roger, Charles B and Peter Dauvergne. 2016. "The Rise of Transnational Governance as a Field of Study." *International Studies Review* 18 (3): 415–437.

Rosenau, James N and Ernst O Czempiel. 1992. *Governance without Government: Order and Change in World Politics*. Vol. 20. Cambridge: Cambridge University Press.

Rosert, Elvira. 2019. "Norm Emergence as Agenda Diffusion: Failure and Success in the Regulation of Cluster Munitions." *European Journal of International Relations* 25 (4): 1354066119842644.

Ross, Stephen A. 1973. "The Economic Theory of Agency: The Principal's Problem." *The American Economic Review* 63 (2): 134–139.

Roth-Isigkeit, David. 2012. "Die General Comments des Menschenrechtsausschusses der Vereinten Nationen: ein Beitrag zur Rechtsentwicklung im Völkerrecht." *MenschenRechtsMagazin* 2012 (2): 196–210.

Ruzicka, Jan and Vincent Charles Keating. 2015. "Going Global: Trust Research and International Relations." *Journal of Trust Research* 5 (1): 8–26. https://doi.org/10.1080/21515581.2015.1009082.

Salman, Salman MA and Siobhán McInerney-Lankford. 2004. *The Human Right to Water: Legal and Policy Dimensions*. Washington, DC: World Bank.

Sandholtz, Wayne. 2007. *Prohibiting Plunder: How Norms Change*. New York: Oxford University Press.

Sandholtz, Wayne. 2008. "Dynamics of International Norm Change: Rules against Wartime Plunder." *European Journal of International Relations* 14 (1): 101–131.

Satterthwaite, David, Diana Mitlin, and Sheridan Bartlett. 2015. "Is It Possible to Reach Low-Income Urban Dwellers with Good-Quality Sanitation?" *Environment and Urbanization* 27 (1): 3–18. https://doi.org/10.1177/0956247815576286.

Schachter, Oscar. 1977. "Invisible College of International Lawyers." *Northwestern University Law Review* 72: 217–226.

Schapper, Andrea. 2021. "The 'Super-Network': Fostering Interaction between Human Rights and Climate Change Institutions." *Complexity, Governance & Networks* 6 (1): 32–45.

Scheper, Christian and Johanna Gördemann. 2021. "Human Rights and Corporate Reinsurance: From Ensuring Rights to Insuring Risks." *New Political Economy*: 1–15. https://doi.org/10.1080/13563467.2021.1881470.

Schlemmer-Schulte, Sabine. 2014. "International Monetary Fund (IMF)." *Max Planck Encyclopedia of Public International Law* 5: 1037–1062.

Schlütter, Birgit. 2012. "Aspects of Human Rights Interpretation by the UN Treaty Bodies." In *UN Human Rights Treaty Bodies: Law and Legitimacy*, edited by Leena Grover, Helen Keller, and Geir Ulfstein, 261–319. Cambridge: Cambridge University Press.

Schmitz, Hans Peter and Kathryn Sikkink. 2013. "International Human Rights." In *Handbook of International Relations*, edited by Walter Carlsnaes, Thomas Risse, and Beth A Simmons, 827–852. London: SAGE.

Schneiker, Andrea and Jutta Joachim. 2018. "Revisiting Global Governance in Multistakeholder Initiatives: Club Governance Based on Ideational Prealignments." *Global Society* 32 (1): 2–22.

Schneiker, Andrea and Jutta Joachim. 2020. "Linking Pins as Drivers of Interagency Cooperation: Humanitarian NGOs and Security Networks." *Globalizations*: 1–17.

Scholte, Jan Aart, ed. 2011. *Building Global Democracy?: Civil Society and Accountable Global Governance*. Cambridge: Cambridge University Press.

Seabrooke, Leonard and Lasse Folke Henriksen. 2017a. "Issue Control in Transnational Professional and Organizational Networks." In *Professional Networks in Transnational Governance*, edited by Lasse Folke Henriksen and Leonard Seabrooke, 3–24. Cambridge: Cambridge University Press.

Seabrooke, Leonard and Lasse Folke Henriksen. 2017b. *Professional Networks in Transnational Governance*. New York: Cambridge University Press.

Seabrooke, Leonard and Eleni Tsingou. 2014. "Distinctions, Affiliations, and Professional Knowledge in Financial Reform Expert Groups." *Journal of European Public Policy* 21 (3): 389–407. https://doi.org/10.1080/13501763.2014.882967.

Sending, Ole Jacob. 2015. *The Politics of Expertise. Competing for Authority in Global Governance*. Michigan: University of Michigan Press.

Shaffer, G. 2012. "International Law and Global Public Goods in a Legal Pluralist World." *European Journal of International Law* 23 (3): 669–693. https://doi.org/Doi10.1093/Ejil/Chs036.

Sievers, Loraine and Sam Daws. 2014. *The Procedure of the UN Security Council*. Oxford: Oxford University Press.

Sikkink, Kathryn. 2005. "Patterns of Dynamic Multilevel Governance and the Insider-Outsider Coalition." In *Transnational Protest and Global Activism*, edited by Donatella Della Porta and Sidney Tarrow, 151–173. Oxford: Rowman & Littlefield.

Sikkink, Kathryn. 2011. *The Justice Cascade: How Human Rights Prosecutions Are Changing World Politics*. The Norton Series in World Politics. New York: WW Norton.

Sikkink, Kathryn. 2019. *Evidence for Hope: Making Human Rights Work in the 21st Century*. Vol. 28. Princeton: Princeton University Press.

Sikkink, Kathryn and Carrie Booth Walling. 2007. "The Impact of Human Rights Trials in Latin America." *Journal of Peace Research* 44 (4): 427–445. https://doi.org/10.1177/0022343307078953.

Simma, Bruno. 2005. "Commissions and Treaty Bodies of the UN System." In *Development of International Law in Treaty Making*, edited by Rüdiger Wolfrum and Volker Röben, 581–586. Heidelberg: Springer.

Simmons, Beth A. 2009. *Mobilizing for Human Rights. International Law in Domestic Politics*. Cambridge: Cambridge University Press.

Simonson, Karin. 2003. *The Global Water Crisis: NGO and Civil Society Perspectives*. Geneva: CASIN.

Sinclair, Guy Fiti. 2017. *To Reform the World: International Organizations and the Making of Modern States*. New York: Oxford University Press.

Sivakumaran, Sandesh. 2016. "Beyond States and Non-state Actors: The Role of State-Empowered Entities in the Making and Shaping of International Law." *Columbia Journal of Transnational Law* 55: 343–393.

Sommerer, Thomas, Jonas Tallberg, and Theresa Squatrito. 2015. "Transnational Access to International Organizations 1950–2010." *Harvard Dataverse*.

Squatrito, Theresa. 2012. "Opening the Doors to the WTO Dispute Settlement: State Preferences on NGO Access as Amici." *Swiss Political Science Review* 18 (2): 175–198.

Stappert, Nora. 2020. "Practice Theory and Change in International Law: Theorizing the Development of Legal Meaning through the Interpretive Practices of International Criminal Courts." *International Theory* 12 (1): 33–58.

Steffek, Jens. 2013. "Explaining Cooperation between IGOs and NGOs – Push Factors, Pull Factors, and the Policy Cycle." *Review of International Studies* 39 (4): 993–1013.

Stevens, Andrea. 2018. "Pushing a Right to Abortion through the Back Door: The Need for Integrity in the UN Treaty Monitoring System, and Perhaps a Treaty Amendment." *Pennsylvania State Journal of Law and International Affairs* 6: 70.

Stroup, Sarah S and Wendy H Wong. 2017. *The Authority Trap: Strategic Choices of International NGOs*. Ithaca: Cornell University Press.

Swarns, Rachel L. 2001. The Racism Walkout: The Overview; U.S. And Israelis Quit Racism Talks Over Denunciation. Accessed February 11, 2021.

Tallberg, Jonas, Lisa M Dellmuth, Hans Agné, and Andreas Duit. 2015. "NGO Influence in International Organizations: Information, Access and Exchange." *British Journal of Political Science* 48 (1): 1–26.

Tallberg, Jonas, Thomas Sommerer, and Theresa Squatrito. 2013. *The Opening Up of International Organizations: Transnational Access in Global Governance*. Cambridge: Cambridge University Press.

Tallberg, Jonas, Thomas Sommerer, and Theresa Squatrito. 2016. "Democratic Memberships in International Organizations: Sources of Institutional Design." *The Review of International Organizations* 11 (1): 59–87.

Tallberg, Jonas, Thomas Sommerer, Theresa Squatrito, and Christer Jönsson. 2014. "Explaining the Transnational Design of International Organizations." *International Organization* 68 (4): 741–774.

Tallberg, Jonas and Michael Zürn. 2019. *The Legitimacy and Legitimation of International Organizations: Introduction and Framework*. Berlin: Springer.

Tarrow, Sidney G. 1994. *Power in Movement: Social Movements, Collective Action and Politics*. Cambridge: Cambridge University Press.

Tarrow, Sidney G. 2011. *Power in Movement: Social Movements and Contentious Politics*. Cambridge: Cambridge University Press.

Terman, Rochelle and Erik Voeten. 2018. "The Relational Politics of Shame: Evidence from the Universal Periodic Review." *The Review of International Organizations* 13 (1): 1–23.

Thielbörger, Pierre. 2013. *The Right (S) to Water: The Multi-level Governance of a Unique Human Right*. Springer Science & Business Media.

Thornberry, Patrick. 2015. "International Convention on the Elimination of All Forms of Racial Discrimination: The Prohibition of 'Racist Hate Speech'." In *The United Nations and Freedom of Expression and Information: Critical Perspectives*, edited by Tarlach McGonagle and Yvonne Donders, 121–144. Cambridge: Cambridge University Press.

Tiboris, Michael. 2019. "Against the Human Right to Water?" *Human Rights Quarterly* 41 (4): 916–938. https://doi.org/10.1353/hrq.2019.0067.

Tistounet, Eric. 2020. *The UN Human Rights Council. A Practical Anatomy*. Cheltenham: Edward Elgar.

Truscan, Ivona. 2018. *Diversity in Membership of the UN Human Rights Treaty Bodies*. Geneva: Geneva Academy.

Tsingou, Eleni. 2014. "Power Elites and Club-Model Governance in Global Finance." *International Political Sociology* 8 (3): 340–342.

Tsingou, Eleni. 2015. "Club Governance and the Making of Global Financial Rules." *Review of International Political Economy* 22 (2): 225–256.

Tully, Stephen. 2005. "A Human Right to Access Water–A Critique of General Comment No. 15." *Netherlands Quarterly of Human Rights* 23 (1): 35–63. https://doi.org/10.1177%2F016934410502300103.

Türkelli, Gamze E, Wouter Vandenhole, and Arne Vandenbogaerde. 2013. "NGO Impact on Law-Making: The Case of a Complaints Procedure under the International Covenant on Economic, Social and Cultural Rights and the Convention on the Rights of the Child." *Journal of Human Rights Practice* 5 (1): 1–45.

United Nations. 1977. *Report of the UN Water Conference*. New York: United Nations. www.internationalwaterlaw.org/bibliography/UN/Mar_del_Plata_Report.pdf.

United Nations, Treaty Series, vol. 993, p. 3, General Assembly. December 16, 1966a. International Covenant on Economic, Social and Cultural Rights (ICESCR).

United Nations, Treaty Series, vol. 999, p. 171, UN General Assembly. December 16, 1966b. International Covenant on Civil and Political Rights (ICCPR).

Urpelainen, Johannes and Thijs Van de Graaf. 2015. "The International Renewable Energy Agency: A Success Story in Institutional Innovation?" *International Environmental Agreements: Politics, Law and Economics* 15 (2): 159–177.

Vabulas, Felicity A and Duncan Snidal. 2013. "Organization without Delegation: Informal Intergovernmental Organizations (IIGOs) and the Spectrum of

Intergovernmental Arrangements." *The Review of International Organizations* 8 (2): 193–220.

Van Alebeek, Rosanne and PA Nollkaemper. 2012. "The Legal Status of Decisions by Human Rights Treaty Bodies in National Law." In *UN Human Rights Treaty Bodies. Law and Legitimacy*, edited by Helen Keller and Geir Ulfstein, 356–413. Cambridge: Cambridge University Press.

van Boven, Theodore. 2007. "Remarks on the Convention against Torture's General Comment No. 2." *City University of New York Law Review* 11 (2): 217.

Van de Graaf, Thijs. 2013. "Fragmentation in Global Energy Governance: Explaining the Creation of IRENA." *Global Environmental Politics* 13 (3): 14–33.

Vaubel, Roland. 2006. "Principal-Agent Problems in International Organizations." *The Review of International Organizations* 1 (2): 125–138. https://doi.org/10.1007/s11558-006-8340-z.

Venzke, Ingo. 2012. *How Interpretation Makes International Law: On Semantic Change and Normative Twists*. Oxford: Oxford University Press.

Viola, Lora Anne. 2020. *The Closure of the International System: How Institutions Create Political Equalities and Hierarchies. Cambridge Studies in International Relations*. Cambridge: Cambridge University Press.

Voeten, Erik. 2007. "The Politics of International Judicial Appointments: Evidence from the European Court of Human Rights." *International Organization* 61 (4): 669–701. https://doi.org/10.1017/S0020818307070233.

Voeten, Erik. 2019. "Making Sense of the Design of International Institutions." *Annual Review of Political Science* 22: 147–163.

Voss, M Joel. 2018. "Contesting Sexual Orientation and Gender Identity at the UN Human Rights Council." *Human Rights Review* 19 (1): 1–22. https://doi.org/10.1007/s12142-017-0483-1.

Walling, Carrie Booth. 2015. "Human Rights Norms, State Sovereignty and Humanitarian Intervention." *Human Rights Quarterly* 37 (2): 383. https://doi.org/10.1353/hrq.2015.0034.

Walling, Carrie Booth. 2020. "The United Nations Security Council and Human Rights." *Global Governance: A Review of Multilateralism and International Organizations* 26 (2): 291–306. https://doi.org/10.1163/19426720-02602011.

Weinhardt, Clara. 2015. "Relational Trust in International Cooperation: The Case of North–South Trade Negotiations." *Journal of Trust Research* 5 (1): 27–54.

Weinlich, Silke. 2014. *The UN Secretariat's Influence on the Evolution of Peacekeeping*. Hampshire: Palgrave.

Weiss, Thomas George. 2011. *Thinking about Global Governance: Why People and Ideas Matter*. Abingdon: Routledge.

Wheatley, Steven. 2013. "On the Legitimate Authority of International Human Rights Bodies." In *The Legitimacy of International Human Rights Regimes: Legal, Political and Philosophical Perspectives*, edited by Andreas Føllesdal, Johan K Schaffer, and Geir Ulfstein, 84–116. Cambridge: Cambridge University Press.

Wheeler, Nicholas J. 2018. *Trusting Enemies: Interpersonal Relationships in International Conflict*. New York: Oxford University Press.

WHO, World Health Organization. 2003. *The Right to Water*. Geneva: World Health Organization. www.who.int/water_sanitation_health/en/righttowater.pdf.

Wiener, Antje. 2008. *The Invisible Constitution of Politics*. Cambridge: Cambridge University Press.

Wiener, Antje. 2009. "Enacting Meaning-in-Use: Qualitative Research on Norms and International Relations." *Review of International Studies* 35 (1): 175–193. https://doi.org/10.1017/S0260210509008377.

Wiener, Antje. 2018. *Contestation and Constitution of Norms in Global International Relations*. New York: Cambridge University Press.

Winkler, Inga T. 2012. *The Human Right to Water: Significance, Legal Status and Implications for Water Allocation*. 1st ed. Oxford: Hart.

Winston, Carla. 2018. "Norm Structure, Diffusion, and Evolution: A Conceptual Approach." *European Journal of International Relations* 24 (3): 638–661.

Wong, Wendy H. 2012. *Internal Affairs: How the Structure of NGOs Transforms Human Rights*. Ithaca: Cornell University Press.

World Trade Organization. n.d. "Misunderstandings and Scare Stories: The WTO Is Not after Your Water." Accessed April 28. www.wto.org/english/tratop_e/serv_e/gats_factfiction8_e.htm.

World Water Forum. 2003. *Analysis of the 3rd World Water Forum*. Marseille: World Water Council.

Yildiz, Ezgi. 2020. "A Court with Many Faces: Judicial Characters and Modes of Norm Development in the European Court of Human Rights." *European Journal of International Law* 31 (1): 73–99. https://doi.org/10.1093/ejil/chaa014.

Zarbiyev, Fuad. 2018. "Saying Credibly What the Law Is: On Marks of Authority in International Law." *Journal of International Dispute Settlement* 9: 291–314.

Zilli, Livio. 2019. "The UN Human Rights Committee's General Comment 36 on the Right to Life and the Right to Abortion." *Opinio Juris* (blog). February 11, 2021. http://opiniojuris.org/2019/03/06/the-un-human-rights-committees-general-comment-36-on-the-right-to-life-and-the-right-to-abortion/.

Zimmermann, Lisbeth. 2017. *Global Norms with a Local Face: Rule-of-Law Promotion and Norm Translation*. Vol. 143. Cambridge: Cambridge University Press.

Zürn, Michael. 2004. "Global Governance and Legitimacy Problems." *Government and Opposition* 39 (2): 260–287.

Zürn, Michael. 2018. *A Theory of Global Governance: Authority, Legitimacy, and Contestation*. New York: Oxford University Press.

Zürn, Michael, Martin Binder, and Matthias Ecker-Ehrhardt. 2012. "International Authority and Its Politicization." *International Theory* 4 (1): 69–106.

Zvobgo, Kelebogile and Benjamin Graham. 2020. "The World Bank as an Enforcer of Human Rights." *Journal of Human Rights* 19 (4): 425–448. https://doi.org/10.1080/14754835.2020.1786358.

Zvobgo, Kelebogile, Wayne Sandholtz, and Suzie Mulesky. 2020. "Reserving Rights: Explaining Human Rights Treaty Reservations." *International Studies Quarterly* 64 (4): 785–797. https://doi.org/10.1093/isq/sqaa070.

Index